The Complete Guide to

LABYRINTHS

The Complete Guide to

LABYRINTHS

Using the Sacred Spiral
for Power, Protection,
Transformation,
and Healing

Cassandra Eason

THE CROSSING PRESS
Berkeley | Toronto

The Crossing Press
A Division of Ten Speed Press
PO Box 7123
Berkeley, California 94707
www.tenspeed.com

Distributed in Australia by Simon and Schuster Australia, in Canada by Ten Speed Press
Canada, in New Zealand by Southern Publishers Group, in South Africa by Real Books,
and in the United Kingdom and Europe by Airlift Book Company.

Cover design and text production by Lisa Buckley Design
Cover photograph by Bilderberg/Photonica
Illustrations by Richard Sheppard
Text design by Toni Tajima

Library of Congress Cataloging-in-Publication Data

Eason, Cassandra.
  The complete guide to labyrinths : using the sacred spiral for
power, protection, transformation, and healing / Cassandra Eason.
      p. cm.
  Includes bibliographical references and index.
  ISBN 1-58091-126-9
  1. Labyrinths. I. Title.
  BL325.L3E25 2004
  203'.7--dc22
                                          2004012647

Printed in the United States of America
First printing, 2004

1 2 3 4 5 6 7 8 9 10 — 08 07 06 05 04

contents

PROLOGUE: ENTERING THE LABYRINTH

THE YOUNG COUPLE stood at the entrance to the labyrinth. She was clothed in the tight-waisted finery befitting a woman who was not only a princess of Crete but also a high priestess of the goddess Ariadne, whose name she bore. He, short and lithe, was nearly naked, as he was when he faced the bulls in the sacred arena for the ritual of the bull dance. In his right hand he held a *labrys*, a double-bladed axe, the symbol of the Minoan Empire, now poised to bring about the Minotaur's downfall.

He was Theseus, acknowledged son of the king of Athens (although his true father was Poseidon, god of the sea). Theseus had traveled willingly to Crete as a sacrifice to the Minoans, but he had survived and thrived thanks to his skill in the arena where men and women faced the sacred bulls, not to kill them but to dance with them, grasping their horns and leaping over their backs. Through his prowess he had won the heart of Ariadne, daughter of the king, and now with her help he was setting about to fulfill the real purpose of his mission— to kill the Minotaur, who dwelt in the sacred labyrinth of Knossos. In doing so he would bring to an end almost two thousand years of goddess worship centered within the sacred labyrinth. Here in the labyrinth, the bull had served as the goddess's sacred symbol.

Each year Minos forced Athens to offer seven young men and women as sacrifice to the Minotaur. By killing the Minotaur, Theseus

would end this practice and spearhead a campaign against the king of
Minos by killing this monstrous symbol of Minoan power. On a deeper
level, the bull and bull worship was a symbol of the older Mother
Goddess religions, and by killing the Minotaur, Theseus would bring
an end to this worship, favoring instead the patriarchal sky gods.

A roar came from deep within the labyrinth. Was it really a monster within, half-bull and half-human? Or was it a priest or warrior
wearing the bull mask? Theseus would soon find out. However, before
entering the twisting, turning maze constructed by the master crafts-
man Daedalus, he handed Ariadne a ball of twine and instructed her
to hold the twine and play out the thread. However complex the
labyrinth, he would find his way back to her.

Ariadne did as he asked despite the unanswered questions in her
mind. Surely Theseus knew the layout of the labyrinth, she wondered.
It was printed plainly on every Minoan coin. Moreover, anyone could
see that, despite its twists and turns, it was but a single pathway that
led inexorably to the center. To find his way back, he simply had to
retrace his steps. So why did he need the ball of twine?

INTRODUCTION

WE HAVE ALL heard the legend of Theseus and the Minotaur so many times that we have forgotten the significance that labyrinths had for ancient peoples. Indeed, the labyrinth design was well known during that era.

What Is a Labyrinth?

Labyrinths, in contrast to mazes (which set out to *amaze* you), are unicursal, meaning they have but a single pathway leading to the center. Apart from the underground Minoan labyrinth in Crete, which was built to keep a rather nasty being under wraps, most labyrinths are etched onto a flat surface on the ground so you can always keep the center in view during your journey. The key to experiencing a labyrinth is to keep walking even if it seems like you are being led astray or moving in the wrong direction at times. If you put one foot in front of the other, then suddenly, inexplicably, just as you were losing faith, you will step into the center.

If you've only experienced mazes like Alice's Wonderland Maze at Disney World, where mock pirates soak you with water and children dash by dripping ice cream and yelling that they know the way (they instinctively do), then the idea of walking the paths of a labyrinth may seem more like a third-grade cross-country trek than an otherworldly experience. But labyrinths are a cosmos or more away from mazes. You cannot get lost in a true labyrinth as it has a purpose, leading you

on a meaningful journey to its center. Theseus had ulterior motives
in wanting to hold onto Ariadne's thread, but more on that appears
in chapter 2. You can't get lost in a labyrinth because the path always
leads to the center and you don't have choices. In contrast, a maze
has many alternative paths and false ways that lead nowhere. Following
a maze requires logic, the very opposite of the spiritual process of
surrendering yourself to the only path in the labyrinth.

Take, for example, the labyrinth at Chartres Cathedral in southwest France, shown here. It looks complicated, but if you trace the
pattern with your fingertip you will see that one cannot get lost and
that the pathway eventually, inevitably, leads you to the center.

It is interesting to see how the labyrinth can fool you. Note how,
after seemingly leading you to the center, the spiraling path spins away.
The shaded area in the diagram here shows how far you still have
to walk.

The first stage of the Chartres labyrinth

Labyrinths need not be circular. This beautiful example from France's Amiens Cathedral is octagonal. But if you study the loops carefully you will see that it is actually a squared-off version of the Chartres labyrinth and so one would follow or trace the same sort of path.

The Amiens labyrinth

Compare the classic labyrinth of Crete and a labyrinth of the North American Hopi tribe.

The classic labyrinth, left, and the Hopi labyrinth, right

Trace with your finger the Minoan labyrinth shown below. Although the twists and turns you take before you reach the center can certainly throw you off, you will reach the center if you persist—and trust. If you trust the labyrinth, whether you walk it with your finger or your feet, it will always take you to the center. This trust is very hard for modern humans who are used to logic and decision making at every turn. In a labyrinth, you surrender.

The classic labyrinth

The Minoan labyrinth is perhaps the most familiar to us, despite the fact that its ancient remains, and those of the royal palace at Knossos, have yet to be unearthed. However, labyrinths do not belong only to ancient Greek legends.

Labyrinths are sacred forms that have been etched or otherwise created on the ground; when their pathways are walked, these forms renew our connection with the power and sanctity of the earth. Labyrinths are also to be found carved or hung high on walls or gateways, radiating protection to all who pass beneath. When drawn in miniature on paper, stone, fabric, or clay, labyrinths form a gateway in the mind to a meditative state.

Labyrinths have been part of the world's traditions since the Bronze Age and have featured in pre-Christian, Christian, and modern societies in both religious and secular settings. They bring sanctity to cities and suburban parks, and they attract people of many faiths (or no particular faith) to churches and cathedrals. Within the labyrinth's sacred spirals, people meditate and pray to many gods and goddesses, to a single god or goddess form, to an abstract power of light and love, or to the divine core within us and all forms of existence.

Learning about Labyrinths

In the course of researching and writing this book, I have visited and experienced a number of labyrinths. Each labyrinth is unique, whether created at home or set in a medieval cathedral, but all represent a journey of personal transformation—or at least the first stages of it.

In the United States, labyrinths have enjoyed a great revival in recent years, due in large part to individuals such as the Reverend Dr. Lauren Artress, canon of Grace Cathedral in San Francisco, California (see chapter 2), who has overseen the creation of walkable indoor and outdoor labyrinths modeled on the eleven-coil labyrinth at Chartres Cathedral, located about an hour southwest of Paris.

The Grace Cathedral labyrinth, based upon that at Chartres

But instead it was to the modern, planned English city of Milton Keynes, site of a recently constructed labyrinth, that I made a pilgrimage. In so doing, I followed the traditions of our ancestors, some of whom, as a substitute for the impossible pilgrimage to the Holy Land, traveled long, lonely miles to walk the labyrinth's spiraling pathways in prayer or in the hope for enlightenment. And as I trekked along two miles to the center of the seventeen-coil Milton Keynes labyrinth (modeled on the ancient Saffron Walden Turf labyrinth about fifty miles to the east), I recalled tales of monks who crawled the paths as penance.

Willens Park, where the Milton Keynes labyrinth is located, is a fairy-tale world of shady paths and rolling green hillsides that lead down to a lake where wildlife flourishes. A gold and white peace pagoda created by Buddhist monks and nuns as a prayer against nuclear war stands in the center of the park, and in its shadow is the fabulous labyrinth, with its path carved into the grass and bastions at each corner.

In the center is an oak, now felled, a symbol of the world tree that connects the earth to the heavens. Although the tree no longer stands tall, acorns still grow on the oak's dying branches, offering a symbol of renewal and rebirth—the promise to all who walk the labyrinth.

Although I was less than two miles from the town's center, there was no litter surrounding the labyrinth, only a mother and child happily playing around the pathways, which I took as a reminder that we should take neither labyrinths nor ourselves too seriously. If we approach them as would-be spiritual gurus, demanding enlightenment, or as experts in sacred geometry, we cannot re-enter the magical world of childhood, where enlightenment ultimately resides. This magic is what the poet T. S. Eliot called "a condition of complete simplicity, costing not less than everything," which leads the way back to the earth womb. From this womb, after death, our spirits can soar free as beings of light or return in a new more perfected form. As we walk the pathways of a labyrinth, the mind is temporarily released from its worries and so can float and become stilled, allowing us to leave the world behind and return to the mother, represented by the tree at the center of the labyrinth.

Picture a small child spiraling along a beach, turning circles along a street, or standing in a supermarket tracing patterns in the tiles while her mother pays for her groceries. Watch young animals running in circles for pure joy, or adults kicking off their shoes and dancing in the grass on the first sunny day of spring. The May Day dances of northern and western Europe take place even today around Maypoles that have stood on the same site for hundreds or even thousands of years, symbolizing the World Tree or the Midsummer Tree (in Scandinavia). Around them, dancers weave intricate designs with their ribbons, the dances taking place at times when the energies of the earth and sky come together in glorious union. When the dance reaches its midpoint, the ribbons form a complex weblike shape and the dancers retrace their labyrinthine dance until all the ribbons are untangled. In effect, the dancers have worked their way to the center of a labyrinth and then out again. The significance is clear. Labyrinths transmit the fertility of the earth mother, not just in physical reproduction, but also in growth and abundance in every aspect of life. As you lie, sit, or stand in the center, you receive the power of the earth through your roots and, like a tree, you extend your arms and allow sunlight from the sky father to filter down. Thus, the maypole ceremony takes place at the time of rebirth and fertility.

Labyrinths can be walked alone or with someone with whom you are spiritually and emotionally in tune. Find a deserted one early in the morning or late in the evening, or better yet, create your own on a remote beach or forest clearing and make cosmically orgasmic love in the center, recreating the union of earth and sky. Notice that children, too, instinctively know how to connect with the labyrinth energies; you'll see that even the most hyperactive infant will become focused or will dance with spontaneous joy.

My mission to fully understand the labyrinth also took me to Bayeux Cathedral in northern France. I arrived late on a dark Sunday afternoon, having gotten lost while driving there. I was nearly out of gas and was worried that I would not find an open gas station in what seemed to be a forbidding old Norman town. Tired and stressed, I rushed around the almost deserted cathedral and was deeply disappointed not to find the labyrinth. I was about to give up when I was approached by the caretaker of the cathedral. Upon hearing that I was searching for the labyrinth, he took me to the chapter house, unlocked it, and showed me the small, circular labyrinth by the light of his torch (due to a power outage). After I walked the labyrinth, he showed me around the cathedral, illuminating paintings, statues, and smiling angels playing drums, trumpets, and bagpipes.

The Bayeux labyrinth

The people I have met around labyrinths have invariably been kind and helpful. They have shared their lives, their hopes, and their dreams in a space where there is no separation of souls. At the labyrinth in Chartres Cathedral, I met Marie-Louise and her husband, Alain, who traced for me the ancient pilgrimage route signified in the labyrinth itself, translated the crypt tour narration into perfect English, and taught me about the ancient, secret earth powers beneath the cathedral. As I left they pressed a precious gift into my hand, a picture of the labyrinth that they had purchased without my knowledge. A helpful warden at Bayeux was quite exceptional, and at Ely, too, one of the custodians gave up her coffee break to talk to me about the labyrinth, showing the same love and respect she held for all of the cathedral's treasures.

In my pilgrimage I have experienced both frustration and joy in exploring labyrinths. On the summer and winter solstices, a shaft of light illuminates the center of the Amiens Cathedral labyrinth, celebrating the light and promising its rebirth, respectively. One solstice, I clambered over chairs, set over part of the Amiens labyrinth for services, and was rewarded by seeing a glorious rainbow-colored pillar of light. In Cornwall, I crossed a river and scrambled down the aptly named Rocky Valley to trace Bronze Age labyrinths set in rocks where river and sea meet in glorious cascade. I have created my own wobbly spirals on beaches, aided by curious children who then danced with me or made infinitely superior sand labyrinths of their own. And in the tiny stone labyrinth I built in my narrow garden next to the wash line, I have created a refuge from the world, where I have laughed, cried, triumphed, and despaired in sunshine, showers, and even a hailstorm.

How to Use This Book

In the following pages I will share with you what I have learned about labyrinths, their history and mythology, their rituals and empowerments. If you already have some knowledge about labyrinths and want to skip ahead to the labyrinth work that will be directly and individually effective to you, then go ahead. Although I've structured the book in three parts, I don't mind if you read out of order.

In part 1, "Mythology and History," I will introduce some of the labyrinth's basic tools and methods as well as the central concepts associated with labyrinth work so that you can begin exploration at once. Chapter 1 provides basic information about labyrinths and their origins, chapter 2 discusses labyrinths and their connection to the mother goddess, and chapter 3 considers how labyrinths figure in the Christian tradition.

In part 2, "Labyrinth Work," I consider the various methods of labyrinth work for power, protection, transformation, and healing. Chapters 4 and 5 discuss how to create labyrinths and the various pathways to divinity. Chapter 6 explains how to use the power of the labyrinth to tap into your own psychic development, and chapter 7 discusses the planets and archangels associated with labyrinth work. Chapters 8, 9, and 10 focus on healing, past lives, and chakras.

In part 3, "Deities, Locations, and Rituals," I give practical information that you can use when you embark on your labyrinth work. Chapter 11 suggests gods and goddesses that will be most relevant to focus on in your labyrinth work. Chapter 12 explains how to find labyrinths in your own city or town and around the world. And Chapter 13 presents a collection of rituals that you can either use as they are or tailor to suit your own needs.

Most important, throughout the book I suggest ways that you can easily create temporary or permanent labyrinths of your own, whether on your computer screen at work, on a deserted shore at sunrise, or in your own backyard.

Whether or not you have worked with labyrinths before, I can promise you an exciting journey as you explore the hidden world not only of your own psyche but also of the mythology of the labyrinth. Within it you will meet gods, goddesses, angels, and planetary energies. And whether you work alone or with a lover, a friend, a child, or a group, you will learn much about the interconnections between people and nature. You will learn to pray, to dance, to chant, to heal yourself and others, and to meditate within the labyrinth in ways that are more profound than those experienced in the everyday world. The secret lies in the energies within the sacred labyrinth form. I hope you enjoy our walk.

Part One

MYTHOLOGY aND HISTOrY

Chapter 1

Labyrinth Basics

IN CREATING our own sacred forms, whether they are large labyrinths to walk or miniature ones to wear as amulets, we become part of a long river of folk tradition. Native North Americans created medicine wheels—circular areas dedicated to meditation and healing—from stones and in the earth outside tepees. The Druids had stones on which they created small labyrinths for meditation in sun or moonlight (see chapter 6); Hindu midwives still use labyrinthine forms to assist women in childbirth; and women in southern India draw labyrinths at the entrances to their homes during the winter solstice, the rebirth of light.

But countless people throughout the millennia must have created labyrinths in sand, earth, or chalk for rituals, much as Hindus and Buddhists—especially Tibetan Buddhists—create *mandalas*, sacred circle patterns, and then destroyed them after their ceremonies. Prehistoric people may have drawn the triple spiral, the original mother goddess symbol from Paleolithic times, and the original seed or basic form of labyrinth (see chapter 2) in front of their shelters for protection or in unsown fields to raise the energies needed for cultivation and the germination of seeds.

Today, researchers and workshop leaders throughout the world are demonstrating how to create labyrinths in sand, earth, and chalk from sticks, stones, natural fabrics, and clay—materials our ancestors possessed. So, in creating modern-day labyrinths, we are tapping into the folk memory of our ancestors, connecting with their wisdom and passing their art on to future generations.

The Labyrinth as a Symbol of the Mother

Labyrinths are a nearly universal phenomenon. Since the Bronze Age they have appeared concurrently in many cultures between which there was no geographical or trade connection. Like the magic circle that is common to every culture, the spiraling labyrinth is embedded in human consciousness.

The spiral shell and the coiled snake symbolized the mother goddess and earth mother in some ancient civilizations. The coil symbol, representing the mother goddess, dates back to Paleolithic hunter-gatherer societies in which the earth mother was worshipped as the giver of all life and fertility. The Venus of Willendorf, the earliest fertility figurine, dates from around 24,000 to 22,000 B.C.E.; as with similar fertility figures, her rows of plaited hair are wrapped around her head in coils. The first labyrinths, which had three coils (see chapter 2), may have been drawn to invoke the power of the mother.

Entering the coils of the labyrinth can be like returning to the womb. The art of several ancient cultures depicts birth as a difficult process in which an infant travels down a series of spirals toward light. As we walk the pathways of the labyrinth toward the center, we are returning to the sense of security and contentment that we may recall feeling while being cradled in our mother's arms or perhaps while float-ing in the warm waters of the womb. Once we have reached the center, we emerge, restored and renewed, like an infant who is eager to be out exploring again. Entering a labyrinth, walking the path to the center, and then reemerging make up the three stages of labyrinth work.

Labryinths and Spiritual Rebirth

Unlike the settings of Druidic spiritual rebirth ceremonies, which take place in the darkness beneath huge dolmens or in long barrows, the center of the labyrinth is not like a dark cave. Rather it is filled with light. Though you may only see the light in your mind, after extended labyrinth work, you may also see it externally. It can be described as the light of understanding and healing. It makes you feel peaceful and connected with the universe and other people. The labyrinth is built on the principle that darkness and death exist outside it, and that the center is a place of healing and rebirth for the spirit, mind, and body.

Although labyrinths are not solely, or even primarily, Celtic, the concept of the Celtic otherworld expresses the essence of the center of the labyrinth as a place of joy and light, where the mother waits with her cauldron of renewal in the land of apples. Souls are said to shuttle on the cosmic loom between worlds—when they die on earth they go to the otherworld to be healed and restored. When their allotted life span ends in the otherworld, they return to the earthly plane in an evolved state, until, eventually, they need to return no more.

However sad or anxious you are when you enter the labyrinth, upon reaching the center you feel that all sorrows have been taken away. Of course, this is neither a permanent nor instantaneous transformation; each labyrinth experience brings incremental spiritual and personal growth, so you will need to return many, many times in order to fulfill your spiritual destiny.

Even the simplest labyrinth provides a space of power and protection. Our ancestors believed that a labyrinth, etched at the front of a building, prevented the forces of evil from entering that building. At Ely Cathedral, for example, a paved labyrinth stands just inside the west door beneath the west tower, whose height is the same as the length of the labyrinth paths. This paved labyrinth was created, or so the guides say, to fool the devil, who would enter the coils of the semi-octagonal tiled paths and follow the paths straight out the door again.

In Scandinavia and Germany, labyrinths were sometimes called "spirit traps," for it was believed that spirits traveled only in straight lines (along "leys") and, if caught in the spiral, could not escape. Just as our predecessors sought to ward off their devils, we modern people can lose our destructive habits, dead relationships, and fears along the labyrinth's pathways and then return, feeling renewed by the cauldron of regeneration in the center.

THE DOOR IN THE LABYRINTH

But the center is also a doorway into another world, like the wardrobe in C. S. Lewis's *The Chronicles of Narnia,* or like the rabbit hole in *Alice in Wonderland.* These realms, sometimes called "astral planes," can also be accessed through prayer, meditation, or dreams. In the labyrinth, you can walk your way out of your body, travel through time and space into the past and future, tap into the universal memory bank, or channel the wisdom of angels or spirit guides (see chapter 7). You can open yourself up to healing from the divine source.

THE LABYRINTH AND THE LIFE FORCE

Labyrinths can, by their shape, concentrate the life force, or *ch'I,* or in Gallic, the *wouivre*—the underground psycho-physical forces that are most easily felt at a sacred site that has survived changes of religion. The center, or heart, of the labyrinth has been described as a vortex of energy. I have found that lying in the center of a grass labyrinth and closing my eyes is like being on a golden red carousel. I can feel the outline of my body melting and spiraling around in a warm pool of liquid energy. The nearest physical sensation I can think of is the feeling of being in a hot tub, where you can feel the pressure beneath you, but you never fear that you will be sucked in. People talk about *surrendering* to the labyrinth, but that seems too forceful a word—*merging* is perhaps closer.

One example of a site where the surge of the sacred earth energy is easily felt is the eleven-coil labyrinth at Chartres Cathedral, which was a Celtic Druidic center in pre-Christian times.

Newer sites like San Francisco's Grace Cathedral are built on places of pure earth power because of the energy-sensing instincts of the original creators. What is more, in a relatively recent sacred building where there is a labyrinth, the power increases as more people worship and walk the sacred spirals. Your own backyard labyrinth will similarly amplify the life force.

Sites like Chartres Cathedral have enduring connections to the earth mother. Even before Christianity, Celtic Druids at Chartres created an underground shrine and wooden statue of the Black Madonna and her child (a pre-Christian version of the virgin, made from dark wood, sometimes associated with the Egyptian mother goddess, Isis, and her son Horus). The Chartres Black Madonna statue, which remained in the crypt of the cathedral until it was destroyed in 1793 during the French Revolution, was called the *Virgini Pariturae,* the virgin who, according the Druidic tradition, would give birth to a divine child. In the original Druidic grotto, there was an ancient healing well, which, along with a replica of the Black Madonna statue, is now within the present crypt.

Within the cathedral itself are more than 175 representations of the virgin, including another beautiful Black Madonna, Our Lady of the Pillar. Significantly, the earth force rises from the well in the crypt, through the floor, and into the pillar above it in the main cathedral. On this pillar, where stands the Black Madonna, the energies from the well rise through her, continuing upward to the Blue Madonna in the sky with whose energies she merges. This life force flows into the nearby labyrinth and is mutually energized by the labyrinth's powers.

Forgotten Labyrinths

Many labyrinths inside churches and cathedrals were destroyed in the eighteenth century because children used to play in them, and this was seen as unseemly behavior in a house of God (despite stories of medieval priests dancing the labyrinths as a way of celebrating the resurrection and tossing a ball to represent the path the sun takes through the skies). Today, directors of some cathedrals and churches in Europe seem almost ashamed, or at least oblivious, of their labyrinths, including only scant references to them on guided tours. The Chartres labyrinth near Paris is only walkable between March and the end of October, and then only on Fridays; the rest of the time it is covered with chairs. Many tour guides, even those who love their cathedrals, will lead parties straight across labyrinths or stand gazing up at a window, unaware that they are blocking the way of the labyrinth walkers.

The Power of the Labyrinth

Labyrinths of concentrated power do seem to subtly alter the patterns of brain waves, inducing the deep, slow alpha and theta waves that are associated with meditation and psychic experiences. Labyrinths also inspire peak or mystical experiences (see chapter 6), in which there is sudden illumination, joy, and a sense of oneness with the universe.

HEIDI IN THE LABYRINTH

I met Heidi when I visited Ely Cathedral. She approached me in the cathedral coffee shop after I had walked the labyrinth several times in succession and become truly amazed (and was in need of a grounding latte and slice of cake). She told me she was a Dutch student traveling around the United Kingdom but had a temporary holiday job in Ely to restore her diminishing funds. This is how she described her experiences.

> I started coming into the cathedral after work, because the Saxon women saints who founded the original abbey fascinated me. I identified with their strength and independence, and I was feeling lonely, missing my family. Then one day I saw a woman walking round what I thought was just a floor design and I could see light round her, as though she was connecting to a power supply. I did not like to talk to her, because she looked like the saints in the pictures with their halos and I felt I might be intruding on her special moment that I longed to share.
>
> So next day, a Saturday, I tried walking, putting one foot in front of the other, so slowly, not at all like my normal rushing-about self. I did feel people might look at me, but then I became aware only of my feet and the path. I stood in the center, and I felt very safe, very happy, and suddenly connected with my own mother who since her remarriage I do not see that often even when I am in Holland. I decided to telephone her that night and experienced a sudden rush of love and remembered running along by the canal with her, picking bright red flowers, both putting them in our hair and laughing.

As I walked out of the labyrinth I felt as though I belonged again to my family and to the world. The next week I walked the labyrinth again, this time in the evening; the sun was lighting up the pathway; it was like walking on gold. When I reached the center, it was like bathing in a thousand golden jets of warm water and I felt total and utter joy, peace, and purpose all mixed up, and I laughed and cried at the same time. Now I felt as though my mother was all mothers and a great all-embracing goddess who caressed and comforted me and reminded me of my dreams. Then the sun went behind a cloud and the moment passed, but I have carried it with me, in my heart. I wrote to my mother, saying all the things I had locked inside, the hurt, the loneliness, and the longing, and she wrote back and we ended up crying and laughing at the same time on the phone. Once again for a moment I recalled the golden center.

I am going home next week, but I have decided that the course I am doing, Art History, that I took to please my mother, is not for me. I am transferring to study nursing so I can heal people, my childhood dream.

The Labyrinth and the Seasons

Labyrinth energies are subtly affected by the weather and the seasons. In turn, these energies amplify the ebbing and flowing energies of the earth as she continues her annually repeating dance with the sun god. The ancients likewise believed that labyrinths could affect the weather; Viking sailors created boulder labyrinths on islands and near the mainland shore to raise the winds when they were becalmed.

You can walk a labyrinth at any time of the year, but if you do so at one of the seasonal high or low points, such as the equinoxes or solstices, you can tap into rising or falling energies. Check a current calendar to determine the actual dates of the events listed below, since they vary slightly according to the astronomical calendar. (These events occur six months later in the southern hemisphere; for example, the autumn equinox occurs around March 22 south of the equator.) Choose one of the days listed below:

* The spring equinox, around March 21 in the northern hemisphere, marks the time of equal daylight and darkness, the end of winter, and the beginning of spring and summer's lighter and warmer days. Traditionally, hens begin to lay eggs at this time.

* The autumn equinox, around September 22 in the northern hemisphere, has always been the time of the second harvest. In premodern cultures it was a time of feasts, when the finest fruits and vegetables were given to the gods or goddesses as a petition for sufficient food in the dark days of winter.

* The summer solstice, "the longest day," around June 21 in the northern hemisphere, is a day of pure power, when the sun is at its height.

* The winter solstice, "the shortest day," approximately December 21 in the northern hemisphere, marks the rebirth of light after the darkness of winter. It is interesting to note that, in the Christian tradition, the birth of the Son of God to the Virgin Mother is celebrated just a few days later, on December 25.

You can also walk labyrinths on the Celtic Fire festivals, which were part of the Northern European folk tradition:

* Oimelc (the feast of ewes' milk) falls on February 1; it is both the festival of early spring and of light.

* Beltaine, at the beginning of May, a festival to welcome the old Celtic summer, was the time when men and women would make love in the fields on the eve of May Day to bring fertility to the crops, cattle, and humans.

* Lughnassadh, at the beginning of August, represents the early corn harvest and was a time for honoring the Corn God, who according to Celtic tradition offered himself as a willing sacrifice.

* Samhain, at the beginning of November, is the Celtic New Year and time of the ancestors (see chapter 9), when the deceased members of the family are welcomed at the hearth with their favorite foods.

You can create seasonal labyrinths in ice and snow, or you can decorate labyrinths with ears of corn, dried grasses, flowers, nuts, seeds, or berries. Experiment at these seasonal change points, and at each you will meet a different aspect of the mother goddess.

Meeting the Goddess in the Labyrinth

We all have a concept of a divine mother, who embodies the best qualities of either our own mother or an ideal mother figure— a woman who nurtures and protects but also empowers us to go into the world with courage and integrity. This divine mother is repeatedly linked with labyrinths.

It is conjectured that in Neolithic times the labyrinth, placed outside of or drawn on cave entrances (which represented the womb of the mother goddess), may have been used in goddess worship. Labyrinths may also have been drawn in the earth near sacred wells, which were considered another entrance to the earth mother womb for fertility rituals. The Hopi Indians identify the labyrinth as the symbol of Mother Earth and the center as the belly of the goddess. They have compared it with the *kiva,* the underground home from which, according to their creation myths, the first Hopi emerged (see chapter 6).

If you belong to a particular religion, you probably have your own image of a mother goddess. I know many Catholics, for example, who walk labyrinths reciting the rosary prayers and talking to Mary, who waits for them within. However, you may wish to choose your own mother goddess figure to keep in mind while walking the pathways of a labyrinth. Chapter 11 offers descriptions of some of the earth, mother, and serpent goddesses whose energies form a powerful focus for mother-goddess work in the labyrinth. You may prefer to walk toward the mother goddess or an enclosing, welcoming place of light. You can read of other mother goddesses in the books I suggest in the appendix. Or type Earth Mother Goddess or Serpent Goddess on your Web browser's search page and download images that inspire you.

FINDING YOUR LABYRINTH MOTHER

The labyrinth you will walk in this first ritual will be special, because its pathways are marked only in your mind. If you wish, you may look at the labyrinth forms in chapter 2. Your visualized labyrinth can be as complex or as simple as you wish, a labyrinth with a three-coil spiral like a shell or with fifteen or more coils.

During the ritual, I will talk about marking the perimeter and standing in the center of your visualized labyrinth; however, before you begin the ritual, imagine your labyrinth as a shape created in light upon the ground. Of course, it does not matter if during the ritual you don't follow the exact plan, but your shape will guide you as you start to work with the idea of labyrinth energies. Picture the perimeter, and see the center in your mind. Plan in advance how you will reach this invisible center and the perimeter. It is amazingly liberating to work without physical paths.

If possible, work outdoors in a quiet place on a natural surface: grass, leaves, fragrant herbs, hay, sand, or earth. Sunrise and sunset are especially magical times, as is the night of the full moon. To find your labyrinth mother:

1. The first thing you'll do is mark the boundaries of your sacred space, using a sagebrush smudge stick. Any of the gray sages are especially appropriate, because they are sacred to the mother goddess. Alternatively, use a large, broad-based incense stick containing sage, patchouli, sandalwood, or a fragrance that you associate with mothers.

2. Next, visualize a circle as your sacred space. To begin marking the boundaries of this space, stand in the center of your visualized circle and face east. Moving clockwise, turn south, west, and then north, making a small circle of smoke in the air by holding your power arm (the one you write with) extended and horizontal to your body as you turn. At each direction, stop and repeat the following: "Love, light, and abundance, blessings be. Mother, I greet thee."

3. When you have completed the circle of smoke, face east again. Raise your smudge stick above your head and, picturing a tall

tree rooted in the earth and extending upward to the sky, make another clockwise circle, saying, "Love, light, and loveliness, Father born of the Mother, I greet thee. Blessings be."

4. Finally, stoop down to the ground and, making a third clockwise circle, this one around your feet, say, "Love, light, and abundance, Mother of all that is created, fish, bird, animal, plant, and tree, bless humanity." You have now marked both the perimeter and center of the labyrinth, whose influence stretches deep below you and high above you in sacred union with the sky.

5. Return to the west, the traditional labyrinth entrance on the visualized perimeter, and look inward so you are facing east, the direction of rebirth.

6. Facing the center of the labyrinth, allow your feet to guide you into the center. This may be an easy round with just one or two turns or you may create an altogether more elaborate pathway as you walk (if it helps, picture the labyrinth you created in your mind). As you go, keep your smudge alight and create swirls of smoke above, around, and below you, now allowing it to fall toward the ground, now extending it high toward the clouds. Focus on the vibrations beneath your feet to keep you on the path.

7. As your feet move, visualize the setting for your labyrinth— lit with candles, near the sea, on a mountaintop, in a clearing, in a shady grove, or marked out with crystals and gems. You can imagine your labyrinth as being made of stars dancing through a jeweled sky or spiraling in terraces around a high hill. It may be set in the floor of a high-vaulted cathedral or made of boulders placed within earshot of the crashing sea. Or the labyrinth could be shrouded with mist and allowing you to feel the vibrations of the hidden earth guiding your path.

8. Visualize the mother waiting in the center. She may be magnificent and wreathed with snakes, or surrounded by a circle of flaming torches; she may even resemble your great-grandmother. She will have a sanctuary, a temple, a hut, or a farmhouse kitchen. Now walk by any route to where you imagined your labyrinth entrance to be. Let your feet guide you, and before long you will

know you have reached the center. You will know because your feet will stop and you will feel a surge of energy through your feet. Remember, labyrinth walking is all about trusting yourself to follow the path without thinking.

9. When you reach the center, sit or kneel and allow the mother to speak. She may be swathed in light or be formed from the leaves of the trees, but she will know you and greet you, for she is your special labyrinth mother. She may or may not touch you at this first meeting. After what seems like hours but may only be minutes in earthly time, she will give you a special message. You may hear words spoken in your mind in the voice of a very wise grandmother. Or you may hear words spoken aloud as though from an invisible person. The wind may suddenly pick up and in the rush of the breeze you'll hear words. She may also talk to you by showing you images or scenes in your mind. Or the message may be an impression or something you suddenly just know about your life without realizing how you know. Thank her and take your leave.

10. Look around the spot for a token, a shell, a stone, a dried leaf, or an acorn that you can keep in your purse or pocket and touch when you feel afraid or alone; this will help you recall her love and acceptance.

11. Do not look back as you leave the labyrinth but allow your feet to guide you, perhaps reciting a mantra such as "Above, around, peace surround, sorrow cease, go in peace." You may hear her voice joining with yours on the wind or in the leaves. If you are outdoors, plant a few herb seeds near the perimeter, if the soil is good; otherwise, plant some in a nearby unlovely or neglected place. At a future time, try to find an existing labyrinth that shares similarities to your visualized one and repeat the ritual there.

You may have many guides in your labyrinth work—sometimes animals or birds, sometimes angels—but your labyrinth mother will always be in the background. Talk to her about the matters you hold in your heart; she will not condemn you or dismiss your fears. She will listen to your dreams. When you are sad, anxious, or lonely, you have only to enter your visualized labyrinth or walk an actual spiral and she will be waiting. With practice, you will be able to walk your visualized labyrinth entirely in your mind as you sit on a crowded subway train or in your office.

Keeping a Labyrinth Journal

It can be very useful to create your own journal of labyrinth experiences, since even the most magical moments can soon be swept away by the tide of everyday living. A loose-leaf notebook is ideal because it allows you to add to and rearrange your material. In this journal you can record your own labyrinth visits and experiences in ones you have created. (In the process you may well discover better methods of drawing labyrinths than those I suggest in this book.) You can also add any photographs you take, maps you draw, or postcards of the site you pick up. You may wish to paint or write poetry or stories about your personal experiences and include them in your journal. Note any fragrances, incenses, or candle colors that work well. Write down different settings, meditations, and dreams of myths to which your psyche naturally connects.

The center of the labyrinth is your center, and its paths are your life journey. May your journeys bring joy and regeneration, and reflect your innate radiance.

Chapter 2

THE EARTH MOTHER AND THE LABYRINTH

THE LABYRINTH is based on one of the most ancient mother goddess symbols, the spiral. So simple and yet so profound, the spiral is a symbol that contains all the accumulated power and wisdom of the earth's peoples. In ancient times it was drawn on cave walls and later over doorways in dwellings, temples, and even churches to invoke the protection of the Mother.

The labyrinth and the earth goddess

The Triple Spiral

Why is the triple spiral so important to our understanding of the earth mother and ultimately of labyrinths? As I said in the previous chapter, the spiral, particularly the triple spiral, where three spirals run together, dates to Paleolithic times, twenty thousand years ago. These symbols have been discovered in areas stretching from the Pyrenees to Siberia. The earliest basic labyrinth motif, discovered on a figure in the Ukraine, may date back to 15,000 B.C.E., or even earlier. One of the most striking examples of the triple spiral was found at Newgrange in County Meath, Ireland. These spirals were believed to offer protection and fertility to those who carved them on walls or drew them in the ground.

Triple spiral, as found at Newgrange, Ireland

WHY THE SPIRAL?

Spirals are everywhere in nature—on shells of all sorts and in the serpent, itself an early symbol of the wise, life-giving mother goddess. The spiral developed as a powerful symbol partly because it is such a simple, fulfilling shape to draw in earth or sand. A female creator or walker of a spiral makes direct contact with the earth herself, enclosing the power in a compact form that symbolizes the sacred coil of fecundity within each woman, herself a representation of the earth mother. Men who create or walk spirals reconnect with their first sanctuary, the incubator and shaper of their soul.

DRAWING A THREE-COIL LABYRINTH

The three-coil labyrinth is the most basic labyrinth form; it is remarkably easy to draw yet profound in its spiritual meanings. You can create one in even a very limited space or, as our ancestors did, on a small, portable crystal or stone or in a place close to the threshold of your home.

To draw a three-coil labyrinth:

1. Draw a cross and four dots.

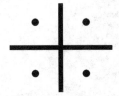

2. Join the top of the cross to the top right-hand dot.

3. Join the right-hand arm of the cross to the top left-hand dot.

4. Join the left-hand arm of the cross to the bottom right-hand dot.

5. Join the remaining dot to the bottom of the cross.

Practice drawing it on paper, on your computer screen, in a small box filled with dirt or sand, or, best of all, on the ground with a stick. Alternatively, make one with stones on grass (see chapter 3 for ideas on making labyrinths).

The Rebirth of Light

The double and triple spirals of the mother goddess are etched on the stones of a number of passage graves in Western Europe. Their purpose was to protect the dead and to lead them to rebirth. The most famous spirals are at Newgrange in the Boyne Valley, not far from Dublin, Ireland. Lying in a small hillock, which is said to represent the Mother, the huge passage grave was originally built about 3100 B.C.E.

One of the triple spirals etched in the rock is found in the small chamber at the end of the passage grave that is directly in line with the entrance. Here, the midwinter sunrise, heralding the rebirth of light and the birth of the sacred child to the Mother, strikes the spiral in a laserlike shaft of brilliance. It has been speculated that millennia ago the high priestess would pour sacred water, symbolizing the breaking of the mother's birthing waters, on the triple spiral as she waited in total darkness for the midwinter solstice sunrise.

The rebirth of light and life is a theme to which I will return a number of times in this chapter, for rebirth is the essential strength of labyrinth work. It is the gift of the Mother, whether you are heralding a new day, a new year, or a new phase of your life. This can be a spiritual rebirth, a new perspective, or a decision to begin a practical change in your life.

A rebirth ceremony, conducted on the morning of the winter solstice, can help you commemorate the return of light to your own world. Christians may prefer to carry out the ceremony early on Christmas morning, and people of other faiths may choose to hold one during their own winter festival of light, for example, Hanukkah or Diwali.

You can do your midwinter rebirth work at dawn (the time of new beginnings) on any day that heralds a major transition in your life. This might be New Year's Day, one of the equinoxes or solstices, the beginning of a new week, or on the first day of a new job.

A MIDWINTER REBIRTHING

This ceremony can mark a transition or celebrate rebirth. To honor a midwinter transition or rebirthing:

1. Choose a spot that receives the morning sun—your front porch, back door, balcony, deck, window, or an interior wall. On this spot, etch, paint, or hang a triple-coil labyrinth. Prepare this after sunset on the night before your ceremony.

2. Make a small dish of empowering water by adding a pinch of sea salt to spring water (still mineral water) and stirring it three

times clockwise with a pointed crystal quartz, saying, "Bless and protect, empower and bring light."

3. Just before dawn, sprinkle your labyrinth with three drops of the water, saying: "Mother Earth give birth. New sun rise, reborn and blessed be."

4. As the sunlight falls on your labyrinth, trace the path of light over the labyrinth with the forefinger of your power hand (the one you write with). Then, after dipping your index finger into the water, trace the labyrinth's pathway from the outside to the center, repeating both chants.

5. As the sun continues to rise, take your favorite crystal (such as a clear crystal quartz) and paint or draw a triple coil labyrinth on it with a permanent marker. Leave it in the open air until noon to absorb the light of rebirth. Carry this in a tiny purse as a talisman.

The Serpent Goddess, the Umbilical Cord, and the Labyrinth

Let us first reclaim the beauty and wisdom of the serpent. In the biblical story, Eve was enticed by the serpent to taste the fruit of the tree of knowledge, which is generally considered to have been a bad career choice both for humankind and for snakes. If, however, we view that serpent not as an external force but as Eve's own realization that without knowledge we cannot make wise choices, the perspective changes. What is more, we can cast Eve in her prebiblical role as mother goddess, who passed her maternal wisdom to humankind.

The Bible tells us that the following occurred after the fall:

> Much labor was created for every man, and a heavy yoke is upon the sons of Adam from the day they come forth from their mother's womb till the day they return to the mother of all. (Genesis 40:1)

Eve's name means "she who gives life," and Adam refers to her as Mother of All. According to a pre-Genesis myth, Adam was created from the menstrual blood of the mother goddess and clay. Other Middle Eastern legends, for example in Babylon, refer to menstrual blood as a source of creation. And in fact, women lose blood from the womb as they give birth. In Genesis, God makes Eve out of the rib of Adam. So if Eve was the creator goddess, Mother of All, and the serpent was part of her, we can think of the serpentine labyrinth spiral as a great umbilical cord connecting us with the great mother. If we follow the serpent/umbilical cord back to the center, we can regain entrance to paradise.

In early cultures, the snake was regarded not primarily as phallic but as the umbilical cord connecting the goddess to her creation. In some cultures, she herself was described as the primal serpent containing all life within her. In a number of African and Australian Aboriginal myths, the Rainbow Snake Mother gave birth to animals, plants, birds, and humans. Indeed, in the ritual death enacted during Aboriginal shaman initiations, the shaman is believed to be swallowed by the great Mother Serpent nearby a water hole (the Mother Serpent is simply one form of the Mother Goddess, and wells and water holes represent entrances to the womb of the goddess). The shaman is then reborn and regenerated from the womb of the Earth Mother. The journey into the spiral labyrinth is essentially a return to the womb, not to die but to be healed and transformed. The whole self is changed. Instead of being wiped clean, body, mind, and spirit, and joy, pain, and suffering, are integrated and restored.

Understanding the Evolution of the Ancient Mother Goddess

One of the most famous labyrinths is the classical seven-coil labyrinth of Knossos in Crete. Images of Theseus killing the Minotaur, the hideous creature that was part man and part bull, in the Cretan labyrinth have appeared in the center of many labyrinths throughout the ages, including some Christian ones, symbolizing the overthrowing of evil by good. The Chartres Cathedral houses probably the world's finest surviving medieval ecclesiastical labyrinth, created around 1,200 C.E.. Until 1792, it had in its center a copper plaque depicting the battle of

Theseus and the Minotaur. Such references to the ancient Greek labyrinth appearing in religious sites speak to the power and resonance of this myth.

Let us continue our labyrinth journey in search of the mother goddess by examining Theseus's mythical triumph over the monster.

THESEUS AND ARIADNE RETOLD

In an alternative version of the Theseus story, more attention is paid to Ariadne as a goddess. In this story, the lovely maiden, Ariadne, daughter of King Minos of Crete and half-sister of the hideous bull man, is also a priestess of the female-centered religion in Crete that worships bulls and honors the Minoan fertility mother goddess Ariadne (commonly pictured with snakes coiling around her arms). As an important priestess, the princess likely took the name "Ariadne" in honor of the goddess she served, as was the practice at the time. Some interpreters see the Theseus and Ariadne myth as a fight between the mother goddess and father god religions. In this interpretation, the Priestess/Princess Ariadne is the mother goddess herself, one who wove the destiny of mankind and to whom rituals were performed in the center of the labyrinth. In this sense, Ariadne was the Lady of the Labyrinth, and the thread that Theseus followed alluded to her magical art and weaving rituals thought to have been performed in the labyrinth.

We learn from Greek legends that the Minotaur was created when Poseidon enchanted Pasiphaë, Queen of Crete, to mate with a snow-white bull that Poseidon had sent to her husband, King Minos. Minos had angered Poseidon by refusing to offer the beautiful animal as sacrifice to Poseidon. Therefore, Poseidon thought of a way to make King Minos kill the white bull in anger. He enchanted Pasiphaë, who then had sex with the bull and gave birth to the Minotaur. Other versions of this myth say that Poseidon, wanting to sleep with Minos's wife, actually turned himself into the white bull and mated with her in her sleep.

In 1900, British archaeologist Arthur Evans unearthed the huge palace at Knossos on Crete. In it was found evidence of a bull-worshipping cult and murals depicting bull dancing, a ritual form connected with bull ceremonies, culminating perhaps in the annual sacrifice of a bull to a goddess, who would most likely be Ariadne.

The complex layout of the palace—actually a number of palace buildings that had been built on top of each other over the centuries— would have made possible the construction of a labyrinth beneath it. Evans concluded that this labyrinth was probably connected with bull and goddess worship rather than with imprisoning a monster.

It would seem that mother goddess/bull-worshipping cults were common not only in Crete but also in other Mediterranean lands, so the cult would have been quite widespread before the Hellenic Greeks (of whom Theseus was one) began their conquest.

Because the Cretans ruled the seas, they had the power to demand from Athens an annual tribute of seven young men and seven maidens, one for each of the coils, who were sacrificed to the Minotaur, or the bull-worshipping cult, depending on the version of the story being told. Theseus volunteered to go with those to be sacrificed, in the hope of killing the monster, or of overthrowing the cult.

The word *labyrinth* derives from the ancient Greek word *labrys,* meaning double-headed axe. This was the symbol of the sea kings and also of the mother goddess and was found in Paleolithic times adorn- ing cave walls. The double-headed axe was also the instrument used to ritually sacrifice a bull.

It is hypothesized that, immediately before the annual sacrifice, the Cretan high priest or king, wearing bull horns or a bull mask (resembling the Minotaur), ritually mated with the goddess Ariadne, in the form of her chief priestess or the queen. He would enter the subterranean labyrinth and walk to the center, which represented the womb of the mother, where Ariadne waited. It was this yearly consummation of the sacred marriage that was believed to ensure the fertility of the land and the sea.

For the king, entering the labyrinth was to go into the tomb to symbolically face death and in mating be ritually reborn of the Mother. An actual bull would have died on the king's behalf (in pre-Minoan times the king may even have offered himself as sacrifice, every seven years being replaced by a strong young man, a Theseus figure, who would kill him in combat).

So if the Minotaur was actually a goddess-worshipping cult, then who was Theseus? He may have been a Greek invader. Floods and an earthquake around 1400 B.C.E. probably weakened Crete so that it fell prey to invaders from the Greek mainland, perhaps led by someone who became personified in myth as Theseus. Given this information, we might wonder what Theseus was seeking from Ariadne when he asked her to hold the thread? It was almost certainly one of many of the things labyrinth walkers have sought from the mother goddess as they have walked the labyrinth in different ages and places. Perhaps it was reassurance, as he entered the darkness of the labyrinth, which was outside the sway of the mighty Poseidon. Perhaps he sought reconnection with the umbilical cord of maternal life.

Whatever his motives, Theseus put an end to the activities of the Minotaur, or the Ariadne cult, depending on the story you choose to believe. He did not worship the goddess; instead he took Ariadne away with him, it is said willingly, to the world where the sky gods held sway.

MAKING A SEVEN-COIL LABYRINTH

The seven-coil labyrinth is only slightly more complicated to create than the three-coil labyrinth. This is the form used most often in labyrinth work because it can be used for many forms of ritual and is easily reproduced.

When drawing a seven-coil labyrinth of any size or making one on sand or soil, you'll begin with the cross and the four dots and build up the structure (see page 28). Practice drawing the shape on paper until it is like second nature. To make a stone labyrinth, use large marker stones for the central cross and smaller ones for the four corresponding dots. Build it up, step by step, keeping a diagram handy in case you go wrong. Make each path wide enough for walking.

To draw a seven-coil labyrinth:

1. Draw an equal-armed cross, with an L shape in each corner, and a dot in each of the L angles.

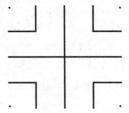

2. Starting at the top of the cross, create an arc up from left to right and end your line at the top of the L.

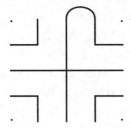

3. Starting at the top of the L just to the left of the last step, make an arch over to the dot on the right. Continue to start on the left, and arch over to the right.

4. Always work from the nearest dot or line to where you finished and follow that around to the next logical point, even if you feel you are going back on yourself (see diagram below). Move the drawing instrument to the first available starting point on the left (the dot) and arch it over to the first available open spot on the right (the other end of the L).

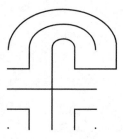

5. The next marker is the other end of the L angle.

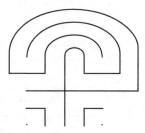

6. Now progress to the left arm of the cross, and curve around to the open end of the lower L angle.

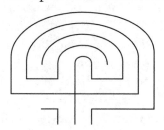

7. Continue to move to the next free starting point on the left, arching over and around to the next free spot on the left until you complete the labyrinth on step 8.

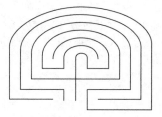

8. The labyrinth is complete when you run out of free spots.

If you do not wish to create your own seven-coil labyrinth, you can use one of the many available on the Internet or in the recommended books in the appendix. Or you can enlarge the labyrinth of Knossos shown on page 4 in the introduction.

Make large labyrinths with chalk, big enough to physically walk in, or paint small ones on your favorite crystal to traverse mentally. Join your labyrinths in patterns and dance from one to the other. I remember one occasion when there were children on my local beach, all quite spontaneously bringing shells and stones to help mark out my labyrinth and drawing their own with spades, dancing them, running them, laughing, chattering. Soon the whole shore was covered with labyrinths. The early-morning skyline glowed with energy and the sand became warm with all the spiraling powers.

Fill your computer screen with a mixture of three- and seven-coil labyrinths; paint them on your pottery, embroider them on your shirts, make them of knitting wool, carve them in wood or metal, and experience the joy and the power in reproducing a shape that has been in human consciousness for more than twenty thousand years. Like opening a compressed data file on your computer, as you create a labyrinth you are releasing into your life the accumulated energies of labyrinth builders throughout antiquity.

Walk, dance, and run in and out of your spiral. Remain in the center for a while, and then go out again so that you can feel the energies of the earth spiraling upward through you.

FOLLOWING Ariadne's Thread

Walking the seven-coil labyrinth of trust is a ritual that is excellent for working with a partner—whether a coworker, spouse, family member, or friend—to learn the all-important lesson of trust and surrender (see chapter 8). You and your partner can help each other resolve your own issues by acting as the other's anchor during this personal journey.

This can be an excellent activity if you have had difficulty trusting others or if you wish to deepen a relationship. In the ritual, you learn to surrender to the power of the labyrinth and the protection of the labyrinth mother and to walk through darkness into light.

Because of the nature of the ritual, a private labyrinth is preferable, but it need be no more than about twelve feet square. Creating it with a partner is the first step toward establishing or re-establishing trust. You and your partner can mark out the labyrinth the night before you intend to do the ritual. Once you have created your labyrinth, you will need a very long piece of thin rope or cord; a laundry line is ideal. Keep it coiled and unwind it as you go. Practice coiling and uncoiling the rope outside the labyrinth before the ritual begins.

One person holds the coil of rope outside the labyrinth and the other takes the loose end. The idea is that the person inside and the person outside establish a rhythm of uncoiling the rope so that it is always quite taut, but gives freedom to explore. When the person inside makes the journey out of the labyrinth, the person outside it slowly coils the rope so that the other person is guided but not dragged. Change places at the conclusion of the ritual.

Rewrite the legend so that it is the power of the goddess within you that is going to the center to rescue the temporarily lost or overburdened person you have become. Or imagine that the goddess's power inside you is leading you to the center to help you learn about mutual trust and support.

Work in a dim light so you can just see the labyrinth pathways. Entering spiritual darkness takes courage, since we all fear that there may be our personal Minotaur waiting in the center to devour us. As you walk inward and the rope uncoils, allow your mind to go blank and focus only on your feet and the umbilical cord, or the thread of Ariadne, guiding you back into the womb.

Remain silent. As you get nearer the center you may feel the rope becoming warm and yourself filled with a glow of well-being, peace, and nourishment.

Once you reach the center, sit holding the rope and allow wisdom of the mother to enter you—answers, enlightenment, healing, peace, reassurance, or whatever you most need. Welcome the inner and outer darkness and stillness as a warm, enveloping blanket. Let yourself become the darkness.

You will find that there was no Minotaur. The only Minotaur you may find is one made of fear, doubt, and lack of trust in the love and protection of the mother, which can be mirrored in earthly relationships. Any fears, doubts, and confusion fall away.

When you feel full and contented inside, as though you have eaten a particularly good meal, begin the outward journey. Close your eyes and, moving slowly, use the rope and the inner light to guide you back, trusting the connection with the person holding the rope.

If you falter, momentarily open your eyes and be assured you are on track. Do not worry if at first you are very hesitant and open your eyes frequently—it takes time to trust the inner light and others, especially if we have often been betrayed.

When you reach the outside of the labyrinth, change places with the other person and become the anchor. Afterward, plant seeds or herbs near the labyrinth entrance or in an unlovely place, as a gift to the earth mother.

The Magic of the Labyrinth

The labyrinth in all of its forms seems to create a state of altered consciousness akin to a light trance or meditation as we walk or trace its coils. In this state, we can more easily manipulate our thoughts and bring them into reality, one of the main functions of what we call magic. The origins of this magic lie in the power of the labyrinth mother.

The first magic goes back to Paleolithic times when early humans made sacrifices to the mother of the animals (a form of the mother goddess) as the fertility mother who gave all life. When humans began to farm from about the third millennia B.C.E., the mother goddess was invoked as the earth mother to bring fertility to cattle, corn, and humans. Magical powers were believed to be held by witches and women who had just given birth, but it was thought that men could invoke them by praying to Nerthus, the earth mother, while walking the sacred spiral. Scandinavian sailors created and walked labyrinths marked out with stones or drawn in the earth in order to try to magically raise winds or control storms.

There are more than thirty ancient stone labyrinths that have survived in Sweden, some dating from the Bronze Age. In Finland and Norway, labyrinths were used as traps for spirits and trolls, who could only travel in straight lines and so would become entangled in the coils. This practice began before recorded writing and certainly continued after the Christianization of Scandinavia beginning around the eleventh century. In remote parts of Sweden, Norway, and Finland people still accept the existence of trolls. This may have been one of the functions of the separate exit path that appears in some labyrinths. Many Scandinavian hunters and shepherds also believed that the power of the labyrinth mother would protect them and their flocks from wolves and other predators. The protective aspects of the mother goddess and the labyrinth remained important devices in folk custom long after Christianity took hold in the land. However, people who lived in inhospitable lands of ice and snow recognized that the mother, though protective, was not always soft and gentle. Indeed it was her fierceness that made her so potent a guardian.

The Dark Mother of the Labyrinth

Consider the average mother: She has to do much of the dirty work and perhaps gets less than her fair share of quality time. She tends to cope cheerfully until she's pushed too far, and then she yells and everyone runs for cover. So it has always been for the mother goddess—she must periodically show her dark side. She then puts on her apron, gives us a spiritual wash and brush–up, and scolds us if we are late or lazy.

The bone or death goddess, or dark mother, is not as popular in the modern age as the glittery maiden goddesses, but we must embrace her if our labyrinth work is to have real significance in our lives and not just become a spiritual ego trip. The first thing we lay down in the labyrinth is our ego. The bone goddess is often pictured with a cauldron of regeneration, boiling away the mighty hero's illusions and his earthly status, leaving a rather uncertain little boy.

In Hindu tradition, the mother goddess may have both avenging and deeply protective facets. For example, the mother goddess form Aindri, who is popular in west India, is depicted with a child on her knee and a thunderbolt in her hand. In my opinion, the most fascinating Hindu goddess is Chamunda, an eight-armed old woman with sunken eyes and skull-like head, wearing a necklace of skulls. She is a death goddess par excellence, but she is deeply protective of her children, defeating armies of demons, with all their weapons and elephants, and devouring them. To those who can look her in the face Chamunda grants rebirth in a new, more perfect form, and to her devotees she offers protection and relief from suffering.

Whether you are president of a bank, a movie star, or a mother struggling to get by on welfare benefits, you are equal to everyone else once you enter the labyrinth—a man, woman, or child on a journey. We have our reasons for beginning our journey. It may be curiosity— we read a book or attended a workshop about labyrinths, or we went into a church or cathedral and saw people slowly walking around on a labyrinth.

Perhaps we wanted some time to think or not to think, or to get away from the person glaring at us from outside the labyrinth, telling us to hurry or we'd be late for the baseball game or the DIY store. Perhaps we wanted to walk a labyrinth with another person in the hope of kindling or rekindling a magic spark. We can, as I have said, work on many different levels in our labyrinths, but at some point we may wish or need to undergo initiation and look into the face of the dark goddess. We should not fear this, for she is kind. Though she may reflect back to us what we are, faults and weaknesses and all, she will nevertheless love and uplift us, wash away our tears and fears, and send us out into the world to try again.

Initiation and the Labyrinth

Our ancestors visited caves, the inner chambers of wells, and passage graves to dedicate themselves to the mother goddess. The most magical of all such initiation sites may have been in the center of the Glastonbury Tor labyrinth in Somerset, England, a site closely associated with the legends of King Arthur and the Holy Grail. This amazing hill rises above the flat landscape, once a flooded area, so what is still referred to as the Isle of Glastonbury was once an actual island. According to legend, the Tor housed Avalon, the Celtic underworld, where the sacred apple tree bearing the golden apples of immortality was guarded by a serpent. The cauldron of rebirth was contained within the magical Tor, also called *Caer Sidi,* the mountain of glass, and was tended by Cerridwen the crone and death goddess, mother of rebirth and magic. Perhaps this is the source of the old rhyme about the goddess: "There was an old woman lived under the hill. And if she's not dead she's living there still."

It is said that the terraces that are built into the side of the hill are the remains of a labyrinth, and that the hill's center leads from the top directly down inside to the Celtic otherworld; other legends say that the Tor is hollow. We know of the existence of various passages and caves leading upward from the mystical white and red springs that are at the foot of the Tor and its sister mound, Chalice Hill. Records as late as the 1960s speak of these tunnels within the Tor. Common also are stories that tell of those who have disappeared within the mound, only to return years later, struck dumb by their experiences or driven mad (or perhaps reborn into a new kind of sanity that can no longer accept the world the way it is).

The seven huge terraces spiraling around the Tor that seem to create a three-dimensional labyrinth may have been cut as early as 3000 B.C.E. Some skeptics deny that the Glastonbury labyrinth is anything more than a pattern of terraces created for farming. But nothing can grow or graze on the steep higher slopes of the Tor, and the terraces do follow the turns of the conventional labyrinth. It is, claim dreamers, mystics, and geomancers, the goddess labyrinth written large.

No one who has climbed the terraces, especially at one of the change points of the year, the solstices and equinoxes, could doubt that the mother lives there or could fail to feel the surge of earth power uniting at the top with the sky. My younger daughter, Miranda, and I walked up the Tor spiral on the autumn equinox in 2001, just before sundown. A kestrel, symbol of the magician Merlin, flew directly toward us out of the sun, so close we could have touched him.

Glastonbury is still called the Isle of Avalon, the Celtic isle of the Blest, home of the nine priestess-goddesses including Arthur's half-sister, Morgan le Fay, Goddess of Winter (sometimes called the Lady of the Lake). It was here that Morgan carried Arthur's body by barge for healing and to await the call for his return.

These goddesses always had a hidden aspect, which is what made them so potent. They addressed something in the human psyche akin to a quest for deep meaningful knowledge. That is why the mysterious labyrinth form can be used to explore hidden aspects of ourselves and the world of spirituality. It is a mixture typical of the mystery religions, as they are called.

The Mystery Religions and the Labyrinth

Goddesses played a strong part in the mystery religions that were popular in ancient Egypt, Greece, and Rome and other parts of the Mediterranean until the emperor Constantine banned them along with other pagan cults in the early fourth century.

In many cultures, secret rites to bring fertility to the land were frequently practiced underground. From what is known of the spiraling dances that were performed in these rites, labyrinths may have been created within mother-goddess caves as part of the rituals involving sacred sex (see chapter 3). Such rites were also part of the death and rebirth initiation rites in which followers dedicated themselves to the Egyptian Isis or to the Greek Demeter, the corn goddess, depending on their culture.

The Cretan labyrinth was used in the mystery cult discussed earlier in this chapter, which was connected with the fertility of the land and the change of seasons. Pasiphaë and Ariadne, the focus of the Cretan cult, also mirrored the Greek mother and daughter Demeter and Persephone in the Greek Eleusian mysteries. Pasiphaë was the mother who gave birth to Ariadne and all creation. Ariadne, here in the role of the maiden, gave herself ritually to the Minotaur, who, like Hades, god of the underworld in the Greek legend, abducted Persephone and took her to his kingdom (representing the coming of winter). Spring came when Ariadne/Persephone was released and appeared as the first green shoot of corn. Theseus, representing the patriarchy, brought an end to this natural cycle.

MEETING THE DARK MOTHER

Find a labyrinth in a shady, wooded place or make one from stones on the floor of a cave if you have access to one or are on holiday in a remote place. I found such a site in southwest England, at Saint Nectan's Glen, near Tintagel in Cornwall. The walk is upward through woods to a waterfall, beneath which are an assortment of half-caves that have been turned into tiny shrines to the Goddess of the Water-fall, as she is now called. Many people had built cairns (piles of stones), and on that damp October day there were no other visitors. In the cave that I chose there was just enough soil to draw a simple three-coil labyrinth.

To fashion your own "subterranean" labyrinth, create a shelter in the center of a homemade labyrinth or even a deserted public open-air labyrinth. Use a blanket or a long coat and branches to make a miniature tepee or bivouac. You could even wrap yourself up Druid style in the blanket so your head is covered (at worst people will think you are eccentric). (The Druids used to cover themselves with a bull hide and sit under a waterfall, but I would not recommend that, certainly not in your local country park.) You could also stay in a campground overnight and draw a labyrinth around your tent, which can sit snugly in the center. I have a long black velvet cloak that, when I wear it in public in the presence of my family, has a strong embarrassment factor. It's sure to give me instant peace and quiet, especially if I threaten to dance in it. A 1960s-style poncho makes a brilliant impromptu shelter; putting one over your head will also make embarrassed teenagers and partners disappear like morning dew. Alternatively, sit in the center of a labyrinth and close your eyes tightly. Creating a miniature labyrinth in your mind, you can visualize the experience.

To meet your dark mother:

1. On a cloudy day, set up your shelter or blanket in the center of a labyrinth. As you enter the labyrinth, allow memories of your life to ebb and flow. Accept the good and bad, the painful and joyous, suppressing nothing but at the same time not dwelling on sorrow and failure.

2. If pain or regrets become overwhelming, say the following to yourself: "All things must pass. The good and the bad times, the kind and the careless deeds and words, all flow back to the mother to be healed and restored."

3. When you reach the center of the labyrinth, enter your shelter or pull your blanket or coat over you so you are enclosed in darkness. Say to yourself: "I am as I am, your child. The gain and the loss, the pain and the joy, the cruelty and the kindness, the weakness and the strength have made me what I am, and so I acknowledge them without shame or blame. Take away what is destructive, outworn, or illusory and give me new birth."

4. Visualize a dark mirror and, holding it in your mind, look at yourself as you are. Few of us are as awful as we imagine—we may be older, sadder, or less optimistic than we used to be, but we are nevertheless people who have done our best with perhaps less-than-promising material.

5. Now hold out the mirror and feel it being taken and cleansed by a dark but benevolent figure, who dips it into a huge, steaming cauldron and wipes it clean with black silk, making it no longer dark but crystalline and bright.

6. Look in it now to once again behold the bright, hopeful, open child you still are inside, smiling or perhaps a little puzzled as to where you have been all these years.

7. Thank the mother, take off the blanket, come out of the shelter, and make your personal pledge to care for another or for your inner self. Walk out of the labyrinth with your inner child skipping within you, no longer lost or wounded.

After this experience, you may be rewarded by glimpsing a sudden flash of sunlight or a rainbow. On the way home do something thoroughly childlike—blow bubbles, fly a kite, play on swings, or sing aloud for the joy of being renewed and reawakened.

The Three-Stage Journey

No matter how many coils your labyrinth has, every journey consists of three distinct stages:

* Entering the labyrinth and walking inward through the coils.
* Pausing at the center of the labyrinth.
* Leaving the labyrinth via the coils to return to the outer world.

There are many interpretations of these stages, and they will vary according to the purpose of your labyrinth walk. Your purpose may be as simple as to reconnect with your own, personal center after a stressful week spent trying to meet the demands of others, or it may be as deep as a decision to make a major life change or transformation.

Whatever you seek, the labyrinth mother will be there to help you, whether you see her as the Virgin Mary, Isis, or a more personalized mother figure. Sometimes she will be gentle, and sometimes fierce, but she will always be supportive and bring healing.

You may want to lay your burdens in the dwelling of the mother in the center. Alternatively, you may bring in your gifts and ask that they be blessed. All of these needs can be filled in the labyrinth, whether it is three or seventeen coils wide.

FINDING PERSONAL MEANING

What is, and will always be, important is what the three stages symbolize to you at the core. You may not be able to express this understanding in words, but it will grow as you regularly visit the mother in her labyrinth. Though you may learn about the various labyrinthine meanings and methods, the labyrinth is as it has always been—essentially a personal, private tool, whether you are walking a cathedral labyrinth or one you have chalked in your backyard before tea. Certain people, expert and otherwise, may tell you how you ought to walk a labyrinth, what you ought to be feeling at each moment, and the questions you should be asking at every stage. For some individuals such guidance may be helpful, but ultimately you should trust your own innate wisdom.

We do not need to be taught how to hold a newborn baby, though there are plenty of books that attempt to do just that. Labyrinth walking is just as instinctive; trust your feet, and allow your heart to expand and your mind and soul to soar free. If you are feeling disconnected and fractious, your walk will reintegrate all the disparate aspects of yourself, so that you come together again when you reach in the center.

As the weeks pass, write down in your labyrinth journal some of the structured ways in which you have used the labyrinth. You may want to use these methods again if they were fruitful. But sometimes, whether you are sad, glad, anxious, or just uncertain, walking the labyrinth entirely without planning may lead to a rich experience that answers questions you did not know you needed to ask.

The following are some ways to visualize or add meaning to the three stages, which I (and many others) have found helpful. In chapter 5, I make suggestions for in-depth work using these stages, but for now, experiment, and above all make every experience pleasurable.

Stage 1: Waxing moon, the maiden goddess stage as you enter, bringing plans, hopes, and dreams with you.
Stage 2: The Full Moon, the Moon Mother in the center of the labyrinth for endowing you with the power necessary to bring those plans to fruition.

Stage 3: The Waning Moon, the Crone, leaving the labyrinth shedding all doubts and all that stands in the way of that fruition.

Stage 1: The question asked while entering.
Stage 2: The decision made in the center.
Stage 3: Action and strategies formulated on the way out.

Stage 1: The sorrow named on the way in.
Stage 2: Healing received in the center.
Stage 3: Shedding the sorrow on the way out (sometimes literally using dead petals or leaves).

Stage 1: Walking toward death in an emotional sense or carrying grief for a loss on the way in.
Stage 2: Transformation in the center.
Stage 3: Rebirth on the outer journey.

Stage 1: Confusion on the inner journey.
Stage 2: Illumination in the center.
Stage 3: Resolution on the outer journey.

Stage 1: Negativity on the way in.
Stage 2: Rechanneling of emotions in the center.
Stage 3: Positivity on the way out.

Stage 1: Seeking.
Stage 2: Discovering.
Stage 3: Communicating.

Stage 1: Fighting the inevitable.
Stage 2: Surrendering.
Stage 3: Gaining true strength through acceptance of what cannot be changed.

Stage 1: Ignorance.
Stage 2: Learning.
Stage 3: Understanding.

Stage 1: Penitence or regret.
Stage 2: Absolution.
Stage 3: Cleansing.

The Labyrinth Revival

The American colonists, who came from many lands, brought with them their own labyrinth traditions. As pioneers ventured deeper into the American continent, they carried their traditions into uncharted territory. Notable was the Harmony Society, an early-nineteenth-century community that planted a labyrinth in each of the three frontier towns they built: Harmonie and Old Economy in Pennsylvania and New Harmonie in Indiana.

The original New Harmonie labyrinth, created using bushes, vines, and plants, was a beautiful place where the settlers might spend time in quiet contemplation. A round log house in the center offered a haven of tranquility. In 1825, the Harmonists went back to Pennsylvania and the labyrinth eventually disappeared. Fortunately, as a result of revived interest, a new labyrinth has been created on the south side of New Harmony (as it is now named), following the earlier design. Now there are privet hedges marking the coils and a stone temple in the center. Like the original, it offers peace to all who visit.

Information is quite scant on the other two labyrinths, but they would have followed a very similar design to reflect the philosophy of the Harmonists. If any readers do know more, I should be delighted to hear. The Reverend Dr. Lauren Artress, the canon for special ministries at Grace Cathedral in San Francisco, has been a key figure in the revival of labyrinths in Christian settings in the United States. She has traveled around America and beyond with a portable fabric labyrinth, giving workshops on its use and writing a number of excellent books on the subject. Dr. Artress was originally inspired after walking a temporary eleven-circuit labyrinth created by one of the pioneers of the American labyrinth revival, Dr. Jean Houston, an author and psychologist. Dr. Artress is credited with the installation of two permanent labyrinths at Grace Cathedral. The floor tapestry labyrinth in the cathedral itself was dedicated in April 1994, and the outdoor paved one was dedicated in September 1995. Their designs are based on the eleven-coil Chartres labyrinth. More than one million people have walked them since their creation.

American dowsers, beginning in the mid-1980s, initiated a secular labyrinth revival. Two of the most influential figures were Sig Lonegren, an author and one of the world's foremost experts on all forms of earth energies and dowsing, and Jeff Saward, editor of the British labyrinth journal *Caerdroia,* which collates and publishes the history and practical knowledge of labyrinths worldwide. A labyrinth movement has also developed in Canada, especially in and around Edmonton.

Church and secular movements have made a happy marriage. As a result, more individuals are creating earth labyrinths of great natural beauty and spiritual power and sharing them with others. For example, in the mid-1980s Toby Evans, an artist, musician, and ecologist, was involved in a prairie restoration project near Kansas City, Missouri. With the help of other earth spirituality enthusiasts, Evans created a wonderful seven-coil labyrinth from prairie grass. The grass now makes high walls between the paths, and in the center are seats where labyrinth walkers can be truly enclosed in the womb of the mother.

As part of the revival movement, labyrinths are being recreated or restored in a number of countries. These include Sweden, Finland, Denmark, the United Kingdom, Austria, Germany, Holland, and Switzerland.

You can work as an individual to raise awareness of labyrinths by creating your own or supporting new labyrinths that appear indoors and out, as well as joining a labyrinth organization (there are many listed on the Internet).

The mother goddess is a core concept for labyrinth work, and almost everyone who works with labyrinths does experience a womb-like comfort in the center. Though as we have seen, the mother has many aspects, all of which are protective and lead to our self-growth.

Over the years, the labyrinth eventually became absorbed into more patriarchal concepts, as I will discuss in the next chapter. It became not only a symbol for the journey to worship male divine powers but, in Roman times, represented the ideal city and appeared in Roman colonies as a reminder of Rome to soldiers far away.

Chapter 3

GOD IN THE LABYRINTH: THE REINTEGRATION OF EARTH AND SKY

ONE OF MY MOST dramatic experiences in a labyrinth occurred when I viewed a sudden flash of lightning in a cloudless sky as I stood in the center of the Miz Maze, which is pictured below. The ancient square, nine-circuit labyrinth stands on top of St. Catherine Down in Hampshire, England, looking down on the town of Winchester, with its ancient cathedral where Saint Swithin is buried. This turf labyrinth radiates strong god energies because it stands right on top of the hills open to the sky.

The labyrinth survived and thrived in the medieval Christian world because it was incorporated as a symbol of the sacred journey to God and to the Holy Land. During the latter part of the twentieth century, the divine mother re-entered Christian philosophy and enjoyed a great revival in nature religions and Wicca. In the new century the labyrinth is once again being celebrated as a mother goddess icon, but its role in the intervening two thousand years or so as a connection with the father forms an important strand in sacred thought and ritual.

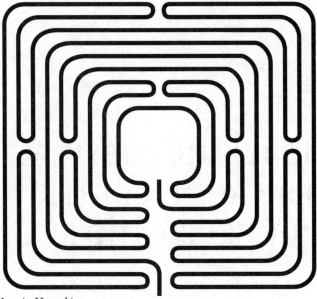

The Miz Maze in Hampshire

We have already worked with the mother goddess; now we will explore the male energies that can be channeled within the labyrinth and how these can be combined with the divine feminine. Through this union of male and female can emerge an immense, galvanized energy—the source of divinity and the generative force behind the universe. This in no way conflicts with the concept of the mother goddess.

Many Wiccans believe all life came originally from the divine mother, who comprised both male and female and gave birth to her son/consort, a view expressed in a number of early cultures and passed down from our Neolithic forebears. (The story of the bull god as the son/consort of Ariadne is an example of this view in an early civilization.) So if we work with the god energy to absorb its most positive powers, women as well as men can benefit from these energies at times when they need a thrust of energy or determination.

The Sky God Enters the Labyrinth

A number of labyrinths originally had a tree in the center, representing the male spiritual power, to balance the dominant female power. The male god played a role that was secondary to that of the mother goddess. The World Tree, an oak, or an ash offered access through its roots to the underworld (in mother-goddess cultures, this was considered a place of healing and rebirth and not a fearsome hell). The Rad Turf Maze in Hanover, Germany, for example, has a mature lime tree in the center.

But, as we know, in most major religions over the last few thousand years the primary figure has been male. So how did the god go from secondary to primary ruler in former goddess-worshipping cultures and so end up ruling the labyrinth? Rad is the Runic name for the wheel, and it symbolizes change. This concept is crucial to our understanding of the evolution of the labyrinth.

From around the second millennium B.C.E., the dominant invading peoples throughout the Middle East, Europe, and Scandinavia were god worshipping, and so the existing goddesses of the invaded peoples were either "married" off to the victorious sky gods or vilified. It is not surprising that the downsizing of even the less contentious goddesses sparked conflict. Take Hera, wife of Zeus, the Greek sky god, who in myth is recalled as a shrewish, conniving female, irrationally jealous over her husband's numerous infidelities and liable to turn her rivals into ugly sea monsters. In fact, Hera was one of the mother goddesses of the indigenous pre-Hellenic peoples of Greece, who are thought to have had matrilineal societies. It is speculated that around 2200 B.C.E. the Hellenes invaded from the north, bringing with them the sky gods and the supreme father, Zeus. The religions merged with the invading religion, becoming superior to that of the previously indigenous inhabitants.

However, the myths reveal the struggle. Hera was not at all willing to marry Zeus, so he shape-shifted into an injured cuckoo, which she held in her bosom. Thereupon he turned back into Zeus and raped her, thus shaming her into marrying him.

For centuries, the seasonal cycle of the land and its fertility had depended on the sacred marriage between the ruler and the goddess of the land, so Zeus and Hera continued to celebrate the divine coupling every year. In this way the combination of male and female powers was preserved, as was the fertilizing power of the earth. In the labyrinth, a wooden post or stone pillar was thrust into the earth or grassy center, representing, like the tree, the sexual penetration of female by male. During the May Day festival the post might be tied with ribbons for Maypole dancing along the labyrinthine pathways.

The Theseus Minotaur design in the center of labyrinths (see chapter 2) also signifies the male power. Some researchers have associated the bull with Asterion ("the starry one"), the indigenous Minoan sun god whom Theseus overthrew; the appearance of the zodiac wheel in the center of later labyrinths strengthens this connection with the sky lord.

The male connection appears also in intricate basket work among southern Arizona's Tohono O'otam and Pima tribes, who weave special baskets incorporating a variation of the seven-circuit labyrinth. The design is called "the man in the labyrinth," House of Iitoi, or Siuku Ki. It is created from dried leaves, stems, and roots of desert plants. Iitoi is the ancestral creator or founder of the people, and his spirit is believed to live at the top of Mt. Aboquivari, a sacred center in the tribal lands. The pathway through the labyrinth is the way home, both for Iotol (the mischievous who still returns to stir up trouble and necessary change) and ultimately the spirits of the people after death.

Working with the Sky God in the Labyrinth

You could create a simple labyrinth around a small tree, either a permanent labyrinth in your garden or a temporary one in a forest clearing. Alternatively, you could draw a bull, antlers or a horn, a knife, a sword, or a spear—all male symbols—or place one of these, a small statue of a bull, or one of the sky gods listed in chapter 11.

A SKY GOD RITUAL FOR POWER

Decide on a relevant sky god focus for your ritual according to the form of empowerment you need. Before choosing one, you may wish to read more about the gods I have described, either in mythology books (see the appendix for suggestions) or on the Internet. If you need to overcome great odds in your life, for example, you might choose the Viking warrior god, Odin, with his gleaming helmet and its magical horns of power. I always visualize Odin with his magical spear, Gugnir, which always aimed true and returned victorious to his hand. Odin rode though the skies on his eight-legged steed, Sleipnir, whose teeth were engraved with Runic symbols of power. Of course, you can adapt this ritual to any god focus according to the specific energy you need. Perhaps you have a special god whom you already associate with power and nobility. You may instead wish to allow your own image of a god to form in your mind, in which case you can use a focus such as a horn or a tall, pointed stone.

To perform a sky god ritual for power:

1. If possible create or find a labyrinth with a tree, a tree stump, or a pillar in the center. Or, on a beach, you can find a tall pointed rock. Or, for a miniature labyrinth, set a small box filled with sand on a table, and create a labyrinth in the sand. Stand a clear crystal quartz in the center, point facing upward, for your male icon.

2. Draw a classical seven- or nine-coil labyrinth. You can also draw one with more coils for a more complex empowerment. Pictured here is a nine-coil creation (see chapter 4 for instructions on how to draw this basic form).

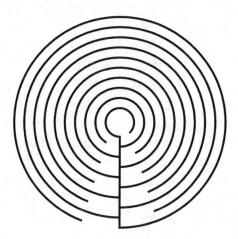

3. As you walk through each coil make an affirmation of intent, weaving if you wish some of the god names into your chant. A god chant tends to be more forceful, more of a warrior song, than the gentler mother-goddess invocations.

4. Enter the first coil, saying, for example, "Odin, All Father, inspire me to battle for what is right."

5. On the second coil, say, "Odin, All Father, fill my heart with courage."

6. On the third coil, say, "Father of Inspiration, Father of Might, empower me."

7. On the fourth coil, say, "Father Odin, with magical spear make my aim true that I may not turn from the challenge."

8. On the fifth coil, say, "Odin, who hung nine nights from the world tree, give me the endurance to see this task through."

9. On the sixth coil, say, "Father of the Northern Snows, who rode through the skies with the wild hunt on Sleipnir, your great steed, with no fear of snow or cold or darkness, guide me as I ride forth, that I may not falter."

10. On the seventh coil, say, "Odin, lord of wise utterances, make my words wise and my deeds just that I may have pride even in this adversity."

11. On the eighth coil, say, "Father, All Father, the World Tree is high, but I know if I look only upward I can cross the Rainbow Bridge with the great warriors."

12. On the ninth coil, say, "Odin, Odin, as I come close to the sacred center, I ask your protection, your strength, and your light."

13. In the center, stand facing the entrance. If there is a tree, hold the trunk with both hands, so that its power enters through your right hand, filters through your body, and leaves through the left, back into the tree in a continuous circuit. Thus, you draw strength from the sky and also deep from mother earth. If there is a stone or pillar, visualize it channeling living power through you. If you are working with a miniature labyrinth, hold your hands around the central crystal to create the circuit.

As you do in your goddess work, allow the god to communicate with you. You may find that your mode of leaving the labyrinth is very different from when you are inspired by the goddess, that you move with long strides as though being propelled—marching, running, feeling as though you could fight any battle and overcome any foe. Because this surge may be quite powerful, you may want to begin your quest at once.

If this is not possible, ground yourself by sitting on the earth and pressing your hands and your perineum downward, or standing with your feet apart and your hands by your sides, fingers downward so that any excess energy can drain through the earth. You will then feel calm and quietly resolute.

The Sky God and the Earth Goddess

When we combine the male and female divine powers in ritual or in lovemaking in a labyrinth, we can momentarily tap into the original power that brought the world into being.

Fertility and the Labyrinth: The Cross within the Spiral

If you go back to the diagrams you have used to create labyrinths, you will see that the labyrinth, with its womblike center, is built around the male symbol of the cross. It is this unity of male and female energies that has made the labyrinth such a powerful symbol of fertility. This fertility power has been expressed through dances and games that may be found in folk traditions from Greece to Scandinavia.

Our ancestors throughout Europe and Scandinavia danced the labyrinths in seasonal fertility rituals, especially grass labyrinths that were cut each spring to capture the rising energies of the season. Recent research suggests that such rites were conducted for reasons that were more than mere superstition, and that dancing and unbridled lovemaking are conducive to conception. Of course, like many other ancient beliefs and actual scientific proof, the connection remains as much of a belief in the mind as a medical fact. Nevertheless, a research team from the University of Wales in Cardiff found that women retained more active sperm when sex had been pleasurable.

The oldest of the danceable labyrinths, made of boulders, may be found in Scandinavia. Generally, labyrinth dancing rituals took place in the spring or early summer according to the climate, usually between the late spring and the summer solstice, in a labyrinth with a leaf-covered tree in the center. In the north of Sweden and in Finland, labyrinths were constructed of ice and snow, along which young men skated to rescue the maidens within, sometimes re-enacting ancient legends about imprisoned maidens. In remote parts of Scandinavia these labyrinth dramas are still performed, especially around the winter solstice, to release the sun maiden who is to be reborn. Obviously the underlying purpose is to claim the maiden and release her from her sexually unawakened state so she can be fertile; the Swedish word for labyrinth, *jungfrudanser,* means "virgins' dances."

Some of these labyrinths had an in-and-out circuit, like the grass labyrinth depicted below, which once existed in Kaufbeuren, Germany. Upon entering, you have a choice of turning left or right. Either path will take you to the center, and then lead you out again.

The Kaufbeuren Turf labyrinth

One of the most important labyrinth sites that have remained unspoiled is Rösaring, which sits atop of one of the largest glacial ridges in the Malar region of Sweden. The site was used by the

Neolithic peoples for burials and ceremonies. The labyrinth here was probably constructed in the Bronze Age and is one of the largest in Sweden. In 1684, Swedish historian Hadorph described "a high hill called *Röra backe,* where there is a *Troijenborg* [labyrinth]; there was here much sacrifice to the gods in olden days." A processional road extends north to south from a point about six hundred yards north of a flattened mound into which it leads, the union of the straight male track and the embracing womblike mound.

The grass labyrinths of England and Germany also attracted fertility rituals. For example, at Saffron Walden (see chapter 9), the huge, seventeen-ring labyrinth was used in an annual race by youths to claim a bride from the center. This tradition continued as late as the eighteenth and nineteenth centuries. Once a world tree stood in the center, but this burned down in 1823 on the annual and traditional bonfire of Guy Fawkes Night (November 5).

Robin Hood's Race labyrinth, on a hilltop near Sneiton in Nottinghamshire, was another scene of an annual abduction and rescue game. This labyrinth, as the name suggests, was linked with the legendary Robin Hood, a version of the ancient fertility and vegetation god Jack o'the Green, who rescued his bride, Marian, the maiden goddess. The labyrinth stood close to a healing well dedicated to Saint Anne, mother of the Virgin Mary, who is also a Christianized form of the Celtic mother goddess, Ana. The labyrinth, which measured one hundred feet wide, had four crosses in its four bastions, symbolizing the male element. Sadly, the labyrinth fell victim to England's agricultural enclosures of 1797, when much of what had been common land where all villagers could graze their stock was parceled up among the wealthy, land-owning classes.

The Glastonbury labyrinth has its own abduction legend. *Gwenhwyvar,* or Guinevere, King Arthur's bride, was abducted by the evil King Melwas and, in a Persephone-type descent into the underworld, was imprisoned in the hollow hill on Glastonbury Tor, beneath the green mound. Her abductor, the evil King Melwas, was none other than *Gwynn ap Nudd,* the guardian of the Tor (see chapter 9). Guinevere was rescued by her love, Lancelot, himself of fairy blood. (See chapter 12 for more information about visiting the Glastonbury labyrinth.)

Dancing the Labyrinth

A number of the labyrinth fertility rites involved dances in which a couple would dance first together then apart along the labyrinthine pathways, in a kind of mating dance, finally coming together in the center.

The most famous is the ancient Cretan crane dance. Wall paintings and vases reveal male and female dancers whirling and forming arcs as part of ritual circle dances. Homer's Iliad refers to the ritual as follows:

> A dancing-floor like one that Daedalus designed in the spacious town of Knossos for Ariadne of the lovely locks . . . Here they ran lightly round . . . and there they ran in lines to meet each other.

Actually, ancient-Greek scholars tell of two Cretan labyrinth dances. The better-known one was the dance of Ariadne, said to have been created by Theseus on the Isle of Delos, to which he sailed with Ariadne (or her high priestess), maidens, and youths, who were probably the surviving bull dancers. Here, Theseus established a shrine to Aphrodite, goddess of love, and created a spiral dance imitating the path of the labyrinth. The dance, which is said to have mirrored the mating dance of the sacred crane (or, as some claim, the path of the planet Mercury), survived for more than a thousand years.

A similar dance was performed in the huge grass labyrinth at Slupsk in Poland. Dancers at an annual festival organized by the Shoemakers' Guild participated in the lapwing dance, in which girls and youths imitated the mating birds.

HOW TO Dance a LABYrinTH

In chapter 6, I write about dancing as moving meditation, a very valuable way of attaining higher consciousness to enhance your psychic powers. Here I am focusing upon the male-female fertility connection. You can work with a partner of either sex with whom you have a sexual connection. If you prefer, you can work alone, holding or wearing a symbol of the opposite sex; a man might, for example, wave a peacock or ostrich feather, hold a spiral shell, or drink from a chalice or goblet in the center of the labyrinth, and a woman might carry a small knife, an ornamental sword, or a horn as she dances. Alternatively, you could place in the center of the labyrinth either a silver candle for goddess energies, or a gold one for god energies, in order to create the sexual circuit with your own polarity. In effect, it is like a natural battery of positive and negative, but attracting, energies.

Work in a classical Ariadne seven-coil labyrinth (see instructions earlier in this chapter), drawn if possible on sand or soil for a powerful earth connection, or work in any grass or outdoor labyrinth. Play music with a powerful drum beat or hang a drum around your neck and bang it as you dance. Shaking a rattle works just as well. Shamans use 240 beats per minute, but you can establish your own rhythm.

Dance under full moonlight, traditionally the time of conception, or visualize the coils and dance it in the shallows of the sea or a river. When you are experienced, try swimming your labyrinth coils in a calm sea or swimming pool.

If you have been feeling stagnation in the relationship, act out with your partner the legend of the unawakened or imprisoned maiden in the center and the rescuing youth (though there is no reason why there cannot be role reversal). Together, define in advance what you are each rescuing the other from. This can lead to a major shift in emphasis—you may discover that what you thought was trapping you is in fact a front for another issue. You may wish to carry out the rescue dance twice, taking turns being the rescuer.

To dance a labyrinth:

1. If you are working with a partner, move into the labyrinth and begin spiraling and whirling. Ask your partner to begin about a minute later.

    The labyrinth will naturally bring you close at times and you can bring your bodies close as you gyrate, but do not touch physically until you reach the center. Make the dance a courting one (visit a bird park to study cranes or flamingos or watch a wildlife video for inspiration). If you allow your feet and body and the labyrinth to guide you, then you will automatically fall into a rhythm.

2. If you have a particular joint of your life in which you need fertility, you can chant a single word or phrase expressing this need as you dance.

Move in and out of the labyrinth two or three times, pausing briefly to embrace in the center until finally you sink down into the center where, if you still have the stamina and the privacy, you can make love.

3. When you are ready, weave slowly out of the center, this time keeping a distance from the other person as the energies reverse.

Sacred Sexuality and the Labyrinth

In the sacred center of the labyrinth, the god and goddess energies unite, as the earth mother powers mingle with the sky father forces. The union is expressed in alchemy as the joining of King Sol (the sun) and Queen Luna (the moon), and in the union is conceived a divine child greater than the two separate energies.

UNITING THE GOD AND GODDESS

Sex between a loving couple in the center of a private or isolated labyrinth is incredibly powerful, not only for creating physical fertility but also for generating energy to bring any endeavor to fruition. Because we all carry within us male and female, yang and yin, the experience is equally potent with same-sex couples. The principle is that the fertile quality of the sexual union transfers to any and every aspect of life.

You can work alone, using traditional male and female symbols in the center of the labyrinth such as a pestle and mortar, a knife and chalice, or a sword and cauldron, the male always penetrating the female. If you are performing the ritual alone, you will dance or spiral your way into the center, chanting your desire with ever-greater intensity until you reach the center, where you plunge the knife into a chalice of wine or juice, a pestle into a mortar filled with herbs (see chapters 7, 8, and 9), or a sword into a cauldron filled with flower petals or water to represent the consummation of love. You may become aware of a god or goddess who has moved close to you and experience a totally unexpected orgasm—a momentary bliss beyond normal sexual fulfilment—and you may even sense yourself rising from your body and merging with cascading light.

You may identify with a particular pair of deities (see chapter 11), or you may decide to allow the universal god and goddess energies to enter you and your partner as you lie in the labyrinth center. This very spiritual experience should be attempted only when you know you have total privacy and when there is no coldness or hostility between you, because it involves soul-to-soul contact.

To unite the god and goddess:

1. Walk slowly together into the center of the labyrinth in silence and, standing or lying, face the other so that you can see your self mirrored in the other's eyes.

2. Let silence and stillness wash over you, maintaining deep eye contact. Begin slow, gentle breathing so that one inhales as the other exhales, creating a circuit.

3. Touch each other lightly, first with the brow, the tongue, the heart, and then the navel, sending love to the other person through eye and skin contact.

4. Speak words of love, trust, and fidelity, and visualize the center of the labyrinth being filled with enclosing light, filling the gaps between you so you are truly one flesh, mind, and spirit.

5. Now make genital contact, slowly and, maintaining the same rhythmic breathing pattern, make slow, deep, circular contact movements rather than thrusts. This allows you to flow within the circular center and become the center, the tree, and the well—the earth and the sky commingled. Allow the energies to flow between you, rising through one body and descending through the other so that you are one organism in breathing, lifeblood, and sexual feeling. If the energies become too intense and you are not ready to climax, move slightly apart so that you are still touching, but using gossamer strokes.

6. Rise and fall together. When you are ready, look into the other's eyes and momentarily exchange souls as you rise upward, returning to your own body, while together, hand in hand, your spirits ascend in a glorious array of stars and rainbows to experience a cosmic out-of-body orgasm.

7. This is the point in tantric sexuality when the human pair link with Shiva and Parvati, or in the Western tradition, the earth goddess and sky god unite to fertilize the earth and all within. As the orgasm subsides, remain quietly together and, when you are ready, recreate the experience in words. You may discover you saw the same visions.

The Labyrinth and the State

As the patriarchal religions and states continued to conquer the remaining matriarchal societies, the labyrinth came to represent the ideal state or city. Its journey became a rededication of loyalty or, in a more spiritual sense, a journey to an ideal way of life. In Roman times the labyrinth symbolized the *omphalos,* the sacred center of the city, and

The Harpham labyrinth

so was depicted on mosaic pavements in a number of towns throughout the Roman Empire. For example, one showing the battle between Theseus and the Minotaur has been found in Roman paving near Fribourg, Switzerland.

Roman labyrinths tend to be square with four quadrants, each with a triple meander or spiral that must be walked in order to reach the center. One of the most famous labyrinths in the United Kingdom comes from Harpham, Yorkshire, and dates from the year 304. It was removed and is now in the city hall in Kingston-upon-Hull in the Humberside region of northeastern England.

Others have appeared in Romanized cities, such as Caerleon in Wales, but one of the most poignant labyrinths is the one found in the ruins of Pompeii. It was probably drawn by a child with the inscription, in childish Latin, stating, *Labyrinthus hic habitat Minotaurus* ("The Minotaur lived in this labyrinth"), which suggests that the labyrinth had entered folk tradition.

Labyrinths may often be found in places called, locally or colloquially, "Troy Town." Such finds in England range from the seven-coil turf labyrinth on the grass verge beside the road from Dalby to Terrington in Yorkshire, to the five-coil boulder labyrinth at St. Agnes in the Isles of Scilly, a small group of islands off the coast of Cornwall. These sites are also called Walls of Troy, or the City of Troy. These names may refer to the ancient city that was the glory of the ancient classical world. Or this name might derive from the Welsh phrase *caer y troiau*, which means not "city of Troy" but "city of turns." Either way, they represent a model city, our perfect home.

A Home of Your Own

Labyrinth work can address the need to return not only to the sanctuary of the mother or the father but also to the ideal home or place we would like for ourselves. This need can be as abstract as feeling not quite at home in ourselves or our present environment. It can reflect a desire to attain that physical nest in which we can feel safe and fulfilled and from which we can go forth into life.

Take a few minutes to think about your ideal setting. It may be the place where you are now; in that case you can use the following ritual to strengthen your personal base and center. But you may have a dream to live in the country with dogs and horses, to become a desert dweller, to acquire a loft in the center of the city, to have a family or stepfamily, or to live solo after years of child rearing. You may have already made plans to acquire your own special place or you may know that it will be a number of years before you can change your dwelling.

For this ritual you might be more comfortable using a secular rather than ecclesiastical labyrinth. Perhaps you could work with a labyrinth near your favorite part of town or one that typifies your ideal lifestyle; if possible, work with the same labyrinth over a period of time so that it becomes imbued with personal significance. I use my garden stone labyrinth to work on plans for my future (a Spanish apartment overlooking the sea where I can work once my children grow up—or where I can go if I need to escape from my creditors; visualizing the sunny, blue skies of Spain from my labyrinth center has helped me through many cold, damp days, of which the Isle of Wight has its fair share).

I do believe that such is the power of the labyrinth that you can use its psychokinesis to draw toward you what it is you need. As you walk the labyrinth you are not just visualizing your personal Troy Town in the center, but also drawing it toward you as you devise all kinds of ways in which you can improve your present life.

To create a home of your own:

1. Create a seven-coil (or more) labyrinth or create a sandbox or clay coil labyrinth.

2. If you are working in a small labyrinth, place a symbol or picture of your personal City of Troy in the center: an ideal house, a family, or a spiritual community. In a large labyrinth, carry the symbol with you as you walk; make it as personal and idiosyncratic as possible, since this is your dream.

3. Wearing a pocket recorder with a buttonhole microphone can be useful. Because much of what you say will be spontaneous, having a recording of your reactions gives you a personal record

of your inner journey as well as your physical journey. The inner journey can be edited to form an empowerment tape if you become discouraged. The outward journey casts up solutions from your deep unconscious wisdom, with a little help from the cosmic well of wisdom that flows into us all when we touch the deep center of the labyrinth.

4. As you stand at the entrance, see in your mind's eye the unfolding pathway toward your ideal home, lined with trees, tall hedges, or flowers, and paved with stone, bricks, or concrete with steam rising from the grilles.

5. Now project the vision as though you were throwing a ball or shooting an arrow from a bow, casting it from the inner to the outer world. This takes practice, but when you have walked to your labyrinth home many times over a period of weeks or months, you will begin not only to see the flowers but also to smell the fragrance of the blossoms or hear the hiss of the steam. It helps to verbalize as you walk through your dream.

6. As you enter your Walls of Troy on a continuous stream of words, those words call to the place where your home or your yet-unborn family waits. If others are around, whisper the words but speak them in your mind clearly and with confidence. For some of us the path is harder than others, littered with discarded dreams or unfulfilled plans, but walk in faith. "Magic is the art of making things happen," says my friend Lilian, white witch, clairvoyant, and healer.

7. Enjoy every step of the way into and through Troy and when you reach the center, sit in your mind in your special chair by the fireside or against the warm wall with the hum of the bees and the sleepy sun-kissed lizards to keep you company. Hold your symbol and let it speak through your fingertips, your mind, through sight, hearing, fragrance, and even taste, perhaps the tang of the ocean or salt marshes. You are for now the mother or father of your Troy labyrinth city and can invite who you please to visit, take tea, walk, talk, and smell the flowers. Sometimes, you will find the Troy in the center is not the Troy you planned or are working toward. There may be a good reason, so while

you should not abandon your plans, do not dismiss this alternative unprompted vision out of hand, but explore it in this and subsequent visits. This may be a staging post in the master plan or you may have a change of perspective round the corner.

8. When you find the vision fading or you are simply ready to leave, begin to walk outward, allowing your mind to make suggestions for moving forward or making your present life even more enriching. You do not need to force these ideas.

If you continue to speak or whisper on your outward journey, the inspiration gained in the center will continue to flow until you reach the outer world. Thereafter it will re-emerge through your dreams and in moments of reverie in the days to come.

When you have time, listen to your recordings and perhaps edit them to create an ongoing saga. Use your inspirations to make practical plans for bringing your dreams closer to fruition.

As with many other non-Christian symbols and practices, the labyrinth came to be associated with the Christian concept of pilgrimage.

Labyrinths and Christianity: The Journey to Jerusalem

The first known Christian labyrinth is in the Basilica of Reparatus in Algeria, dating from the year 328. It was dedicated to Ecclesia (which means "mother church"), another name for Sophia, goddess of wisdom, whom some less-orthodox sects called the Mother of God and all creation. The first known European church labyrinth was a small paved labyrinth in the Church of St. Vitale in Ravenna, Italy, dating from the sixth century.

It is not surprising that the Christian church adopted the labyrinth, for it incorporated a number of pagan practices and would ease the transition from the pagan religion to Christianity. The church was known to have incorporated pagan traditions into religious events. For example, Easter was grafted onto the old spring equinox celebrations and the equinox fires, in which a straw man representing the corn god was burned and his ashes scattered on the fields to bring fertility was replaced by the burning of the straw Judas man.

To early Christians, a pilgrimage to Jerusalem, the Holy City, or to Santiago de Compostela in Spain, was an important quest. It was probably the Roman Christians who began the idea of the labyrinth as the symbolic path to Jerusalem. In the early Middle Ages, the rise of Islam led to conflict among religious groups in the Middle East and also sparked the Crusades, making travel in the Holy Land dangerous. As a result, in the eleventh and twelfth centuries cathedral labyrinths became an important substitute for pilgrimages.

The labyrinths in Rheims, Amiens, and Chartres in France were three of the finest. The Rheims labyrinth was destroyed in 1778 because a clergyman was dismayed that children played in it. The octagonal labyrinth at Amiens was likewise destroyed but fortunately was restored during the nineteenth century to its position in the nave (see chapter 12). A shaft of light strikes the center at the winter and summer solstices. Countless other labyrinths in churches and cathedrals were destroyed during the sixteenth, seventeenth, and eighteenth centuries, now only represented in woodcuts in old books or not at all.

The Amiens labyrinth, an octagonal version of the Chartres labyrinth

In addition to symbolizing a pilgrimage to the actual city of Jerusalem, labyrinths represented a journey to the heavenly Jerusalem described in the book of Revelations:

I saw the holy city, New Jerusalem, coming down out of heaven from God . . .

The construction of its wall was jasper. The city was pure gold, like pure glass.

The foundations of the city's wall were adorned with all kinds of precious stones. The first foundation was jasper; the second, sapphire; the third, chalcedony; the fourth, emerald; the fifth, sardonyx; the sixth, sardius; the seventh, chrysolite; the eighth, beryl; the ninth, topaz; the tenth, chrysoprasus; the eleventh, jacinth; and the twelfth, amethyst.

The twelve gates were twelve pearls. Each one of the gates was made of one (21:2; 21:18–21).

It is hard, in the modern world, to understand how important pilgrimages were to Christians or the hardships involved—traveling on horseback across hills and wild moorlands, sleeping on roadsides for those not wealthy enough to pay for the rooms at hostelries. A pilgrimage, even within one's own country, would take weeks, and one across the sea and many lands to Jerusalem would take months. The sacrifices and hardships of the journey were the substance of the experience, whether the destination was a sacred healing well, a saint's relic housed in a cathedral, or Jerusalem itself. Many who undertook such a journey believed that the city would be like the one described in Revelations, glittering with jewels. Other pilgrims who journeyed to pay homage to ancient relics housed in great cathedrals expected miracles to occur when they touched the relics. I have no doubt that, because of their intense faith combined with the accumulated spirituality of the places, miracles did occur.

Entering the huge cathedral, the pilgrims would have been overwhelmed by the profusion of stained glass, the gold and jeweled crosses and statues, the golden candlesticks and altars. Churches were, until the Reformation of the church in the sixteenth century, treasure houses from which not even the poorest would steal for fear of danger to their soul. The air would be thick with exotic frankincense, sandalwood, and myrrh and a choir singing so harmoniously it might seem as though they were angels on high. Then, in the jeweled light, would be the labyrinth, its path winding inward to a glimmering mosaic.

For those who walked the labyrinths in the great cathedrals, the sacred geometry of the buildings ensured that they saw jeweled colors glittering from the windows and casting rainbow light on the labyrinth. As they followed the paths of the labyrinth, the pilgrims would mentally walk toward the heavenly city on the hill, with different prayers in their heart. Mothers, temporarily relieved of their infants, might ask for patience and dream of rest and freedom from worry about feeding the family. Older people might look to the heavenly land of rest and comfort after a lifetime in the fields, the men seeing themselves as warriors in Saint Michael's golden army. Young girls might be distracted momentarily by dreams of jewels, castles, ribbons, and handsome princes. Every pilgrim, rich or poor, would create in his or her vision a splendor probably beyond anything we in the modern world could conjure.

Making a Labyrinth Pilgrimage

Today it is remarkably easy, using cars and freeways, trains, or buses, to reach places that were virtually inaccessible to our ancestors. If we are not careful, this ease of travel can diminish the value of a spiritual journey. I am not advocating trekking over muddy fields or camping under a bush to recreate the experience, but since we do have far more leisure time than our forebears did, we can fit pilgrimages into even the busiest schedule, and they need not be expensive. Children love to plan adventures and, when you include a visit to a theme park, this kind of journey can be something they talk about for months. I have tried it with my own offspring with some success.

Alternatively, you may decide to go alone or with a friend or family member who is undemanding emotionally and whose presence will enrich your experience. While pilgrimages are almost always enriching and healing, dealing with sniping relations, cynical friends, or even a spiritual know-it-all will sap too much of your psychic energy.

Choose the labyrinth you will visit with care so that the pilgrimage involves at least a few hours of travel and takes you to a special setting of great natural or architectural beauty. I have listed a number of labyrinths in different regions in chapter 12, but this represents just the tip of the iceberg. Contact tourist information offices in areas to which you feel drawn or conduct an online search.

During your research, you may find mentions of private labyrinths; and by making a phone call or sending a letter you may have the opportunity to work in a rarely visited chapel or grounds of a house where a labyrinth is located. Before I traveled to the privately owned Troy Town near Somerton in Oxfordshire, which houses a beautiful fifteen-coil grass labyrinth, I called ahead to arrange my visit. I was then able to spend a morning and an afternoon in the secluded grove of trees where the labyrinth lies hidden and was able to work and research on a very private level for a number of hours.

Find out as much as you can about your chosen labyrinth—its history, its uses, its location; also investigate local legends, healing wells in the vicinity (a feature around most European cathedrals), and any saints or holy figures who are associated with or have been adopted by the region. Find images of the site on the Internet if possible, or write in advance for a brochure so your mind can begin to visualize the experience.

Don't forget to research in advance the mundanities, such as how you will reach the labyrinth, when church services take place, if you are visiting a labyrinth housed in a religious building, and when the labyrinth is open. My plans to visit particular labyrinths have many times been thwarted by a local saint's day that I didn't know about or the fact that the custodian closes every June 2 because it is his mother's birthday. In churches and cathedrals services can prevent access, although you may find that they help you to tune in to the sanctity of the place. The real ecclesiastical hazard is chairs—a number of people have made journeys to Chartres Cathedral only to find the labyrinth covered with rows of chairs (see chapter 12 for dates when this labyrinth is open).

Outdoor labyrinths can also close at certain times or be fenced off, especially if owned by a trust. For example, the beautiful eleven-coil Chartres-type grass labyrinth set in woodland in Hampshire is fenced off. (Worse still, on a hot day during the recent outbreak of foot-and-mouth disease among British grazing farm animals, I went to St. Catherine's Down in Hampshire to walk the Miz Maze, only to find the whole down fenced off with barbed wire.)

Allow plenty of time for travel and perhaps stay overnight nearby. If you go to the labyrinth early in the morning on a weekday you are more likely to have privacy, even in a cathedral. If possible, leave your car a mile or so from the labyrinth and walk there, whether through old streets with names such as Pilgrim Way or through woodland. Ignore rain or wind; wear boots if it is muddy.

If you arrive just before opening time, find a place to sit and observe the setting. If you are visiting a church or cathedral labyrinth, perhaps reread the description of the new Jerusalem; if you are visiting one close to the sea, read the early-twentieth-century American visionary Edgar Cayce's writings about Atlantis with its crystal pyramids and golden statues.

When you reach the labyrinth, remove your shoes if possible or practical so you can walk barefoot and absorb the energies through your feet as well as from all around. Walking shoeless also helps to preserve delicate labyrinths for posterity.

Focus only on the heavenly or otherworld city, allowing images of this ideal place to build up in your mind. For you it may be the jewel-colored Jerusalem pictured in the stained-glass windows towering over the labyrinth, filled with golden angels and illuminated by beams of brilliant light. Or it may be a city of pure white marble with flowing streams or fabulous water gardens. I always visualize the multicolored, domed cathedral of Basil the Blessed in Moscow's Red Square. Here I add in my own imaginings the staircase of water overhung with orange trees in the gardens at the fabulous Moorish Alhambra in Granada, Spain, with its intricate stone lacework. Others might add images of Atlantis, with purple crystal pyramids and a huge golden statue of Poseidon in his chariot atop the highest hill, or of *Caer Sidi*, the palace of glass, in the Celtic paradise.

If you allow the images to form in your mind, you will draw on places actual and dreamed, pictures from books, and scenes from films and mold them into a place of beauty. You may be aware of increasing light all around you, even on the grayest day, or rainbows dancing, as you move from your real-world surroundings to the spiritual dimensions.

When you reach the center of the labyrinth, you will envision the Tree of Life; on its branches will be many kinds of fruit, more exotic than any you have ever seen or tasted. Each represents a gift you may take back with you into the world, so choose one that seems to symbolize what it is that would fulfill you spiritually as well as materially.

In the next chapter I'll discuss ways that you can create your own temporary or permanent labyrinths based on designs of your own making or existing labyrinths around the world.

Part Two

LABYRINTH WORK

Chapter 4

MAKING A LABYRINTH

I AM LUCKY ENOUGH to live near
the sea, on the Isle of Wight, a county-sized island a few miles off
the shore of Portsmouth and Southampton on the south coast of
England. It is very easy for me to slip down to the beach in the early
morning or evening and draw a labyrinth in the sand, looking out
at the waters of the English Channel.

Sometimes, if I need time away from everyday worries and
pressures, I will mark a labyrinth out in stones and shells collected
from the beach. At other times I may have only a few minutes between
maternal taxi runs, as I keep up with my family's frantic social whirl;
then I create a simple three-coil spiral with a stick in the sand.

Yet there is always a timeless period of peace as I reach the center,
looking out to sea and feeling the combined powers of earth, sea,
and sky flowing in and through me. Even the ever-present seven plagues
of Israel, waiting like my hungry cats on the doorstep for my return,
suddenly seem less daunting.

You have already learned how to create the basic three- and seven-
coil labyrinths. In this chapter I suggest a basic method that you can
use to create any circular labyrinth with five to seventeen coils.

Although labyrinths are enjoying a long-overdue revival in many
countries and so you may actually have a public labyrinth nearby,

using a public labyrinth will not always meet your needs. Sometimes you'll require a place for a private ritual, a place that is yours alone; other times you'll want an instantly accessible labyrinth for meditation or decision making.

As I've mentioned, the entrance to a labyrinth is traditionally in the west, the direction of death in a number of cultures including the Celtic, so that you walk toward the east, the direction of ascending light and rebirth. However, if you were to follow the Western magical tradition, you would set your entrance in the north, the realm of midnight, magic, and mystery, and walk toward the powerful south, place of the noonday sun.

In medieval cathedrals, labyrinths were usually sited near the entrance at the west end of the nave, close to the baptismal font. This is also the location of later examples, too, such as the nineteenth-century creation in Ely Cathedral in eastern England. The symbolism driving this location choice encompasses many aspects of spiritual rebirth and initiation. You may wish to incorporate a water feature or small pond in the west or in any spot close to your labyrinth (see chapter 2), since water is a symbol also of the mother goddess.

However, you can set your labyrinth with its entrance in any direction that has significance to you, perhaps orienting it so that you walk toward an inspiring view or a powerful tree. In the center you may face different directions in turn or face just one, perhaps looking at the ocean or an open vista that fills you with peace and harmony.

Temporary Labyrinths

Creating a personal temporary labyrinth, one that is either miniature or full size, can be an integral part of labyrinth ritual. It should not be thought of as a chore, but instead as a chance to connect with the powers of the earth; the creation marks the gradual withdrawal from the everyday world to a sacred center as your spirals unfold.

The materials and locations of personal labyrinths are limited only by your ingenuity. Vacations and holidays spent away from the city and weekends spent in the wilderness offer great opportunities for creating labyrinths in beautiful earth settings—on a hilltop, in a forest clearing, or by the ocean or a lake. Below are some ideas:

* Draw the largest labyrinth imaginable on a beach, fill it with all of your emotional clutter and garbage and allow one of the sea mothers to carry it away. My own favorite sea mother is Mama Cocha, the Peruvian whale goddess, who was originally worshipped by the Incas and has been revered throughout the ages by the people living along the South American Pacific coast.

* Create a forest labyrinth from pliable fallen branches and greenery, if necessary binding them with twine. Use oak for power, ash for healing, hazel for wisdom, redwood for strength and courage, rowan for protection, olive for peace, and palm for fertility.

* In a rocky place, create a labyrinth with large stones, harnessing the energies of friends or family members to help you haul boulders into place.

* Draw a labyrinth in a large sandpit or in damp soil with a stick.

* Chalk one on a concrete play area in the local park in the early morning—children love finding them.

* In a paved area, use masking tape of different colors.

* Indoors, fill a tray or dish halfway with sand and trace the circles with your fingers; this can be incredibly therapeutic.

* Make a labyrinth on a tray using nuts. Use Brazil nuts for power, hazelnuts for wisdom, almonds for fertility, cashews for creativity, and walnuts for abundance in all things.

* Use small crystals or white stones on a tabletop.

* Create a labyrinth on your desktop computer in order to still your mind before a meeting or at times when you feel angry or anxious.

* On a bulletin board, create a labyrinth using a long piece of string or cord, securing it at regular intervals with pins or tacks.

* Twist thin coils of copper wire for a table labyrinth and place votive candles around it.

★ Make a labyrinth with coils of dough or pastry and bake it.
Afterward, walk between the coils with your fingers and then
eat the coils one by one, absorbing the energies. This is a wonderful exercise for stressed, anxious, or hyperactive children
(and adults) or those who are being bullied. They can name
their fears and turn each fear into a strength by eating it.

Permanent Labyrinths

Making a permanent labyrinth is like any act of creation: it's a statement about yourself and your spirituality, a gift to the world and a gift
from the earth to you.

You should not hurry or feel pressured to finish your labyrinth
during a single session. However, a day spent labyrinth building either
alone or with family and friends is a power- and energy-enhancing
exercise that brings harmony as you mark out your personal or collective sacred space. Have a picnic in the center to celebrate its completion.

Creating a labyrinth in a garden or yard, or on a floor does subtly
but positively alter the energies of the place, filling the surrounding
space with spiritual peace and sanctity.

The creation of a new public labyrinth, in either a secular or
religious setting, brings life as well as people to an area, and the accumulation of the spiritual energies of labyrinth walkers gradually brings
sacredness to a new labyrinth site.

You can bring the same blessings upon your home or office with
even the smallest labyrinth. I would suggest creating two labyrinths,
if possible, a small one for your work area and one for a special place
in your home. Surrounded by crystals, herbs, and candles, a labyrinth
is an oasis in the most bustling office or household.

You may even find room for a walkable labyrinth in your home
or garden. You will be surprised at how easily you can fit a compact
labyrinth (if you make the walkways between the coils quite narrow)
on a patio, in a garden or yard, or on the floor of a garage or storage
shed, attic, or basement. Over the weeks and months you may notice
the atmosphere at home improving, with fewer quarrels or unthinking
behavior. Visitors who are unaware of your labyrinth may comment

on how light and bright your home is, possibly asking whether you have had it professionally decorated. The labyrinth will provide a haven for you, your place in which you are protected and can regain inner harmony.

CREATING MINIATURE LABYRINTHS

If you do not have room for a large labyrinth, you can make a special miniature labyrinth to form the spiritual focus of your home, and build a sacred place to enclose it.

* Use shells or stones within a small box or deep crystal or glass bowl filled with sand or pale earth. Rather than securing them, allow them to rest in the sand and have a small box of similar shells or stones nearby so you can add to your labyrinth at any time or re-create it as a meditative exercise.

* Using acrylic paint, create a labyrinth on canvas in bright colors or on wood, painting traditional mother goddess symbols in the coils: birds, butterflies, bees, crescent moons, snakes, lozenges, and spirals. In the center place a grandmother spider in her jeweled web, or Ariadne, coiled with snakes.

* Make silver or gold coils on black cardstock or a large dark stone.

* Embroider the labyrinth coils onto canvas or similarly appropriate material.

* Build a mosaic labyrinth with tiny tiles, Roman style.

* Hammer nails in wood to form the coils and weave threads in and out of them.

* Glue seeds to stiff cardstock in a labyrinth formation. Use sunflower seeds for hope, sesame seeds for courage, pumpkin seeds for fertility, lavender seeds for love, and poppy seeds for magical awareness.

* Make the ultimate earth mother labyrinth out of clay. If you make a clay base, you can fire it in a kiln. Otherwise place the coils on a stone slab or a piece of wood, rolling out the coils between your fingers and molding each into place as tiny walls.

HONORING YOUR SPECIAL PLACE

Take time to find the right setting for your miniature labyrinth. You may decide to make a small altar or shrine for it, which need be no more than a table covered with a cloth that you can change according to the seasons or your current focus. By rotating the incense, candles, and crystals that surround your labyrinth, you can subtly change the mood and intent. Following are some ways to make the setting for your labyrinth special:

* Set out candles—a single white one for the mother goddess, a silver one for the goddess, and a gold one for the god—so that their light shines on the labyrinth. You can use other colors, too: yellow for communication and logic; orange for health and happiness; red for courage and power; green for love and all matters concerning the environment; blue for wisdom and leadership; purple for spiritual awareness and magic; pink for healing and reconciliation; and brown for acceptance, children, and animals.

* In the room hang suncatchers or rainbows in the windows to reflect the light during the daytime so your labyrinth is a focus of light energy.

* Keep ceremonial incense close by, using myrrh for healing, frank-incense for power, sandalwood for spiritual awareness, lavender and rose for love and gentleness, orange for confidence and deepening relationships, and patchouli for prosperity and environmental concerns (see more incense meanings in chapter 9).

* You may wish to have two or three large crystals that you can keep near the labyrinth or, on occasion, place in the center. Crystals in unpolished form or still enclosed in the rock are just as powerful as highly polished crystals, and they may be much cheaper. Crystals that work well with labyrinths include clear crystal spheres for energy and the flow of the life force; agate for balance; amethyst for spiritual power and tranquility; carnelian for courage and confidence; citrine for joy and optimism; jade for love, especially self-love; and rose quartz for healing and harmony. You may have other favorites that work well for you.

* Some people keep a goddess and/or god figure in the center (see chapter 11), but you can also use a spiral shell to represent the goddess and a horn made of bone or wood to represent the god.

CreaTInG Your Own Large LabyrinTH

For a labyrinth in which you can walk you will need an area of ten to twelve square feet minimum. You may want to make the center slightly larger than stated (throwing the labyrinth out of proportion) so you can sit or stand there more easily. Following are some ideas for creating a large labyrinth:

* Make a labyrinth of grass and paving stones. Dig small trenches to create the paved paths, and then, to make the coils, cut the grass to the length you desire. If you wish, you can instead make the grass be the pathway and the stones be the coils. The earth you dig out can be molded as earth mounds, which will soon be covered with grass. I have even heard of skilled people using a diagram to mow the labyrinth paths, leaving the grass in between uncut. Of course, they have to keep mowing regularly in order to maintain the labyrinth. Alternatively, work straight on the grass by marking out a labyrinth with medium-sized stones, available at garden centers (see later in the chapter for precise instructions). Pure-white stones will glisten in sun and moonlight.

* Work directly on the earth, and plant fragrant herbs or flowers to mark the coils. This will take some time, especially if you are using seeds, but the result will be a beautiful garden feature. With small starter plants, purchased from a garden center, you can make a labyrinth in a day. Or you can buy a larger plant and separate the roots to create individual shoots to save money. Leave some space for herbs, especially fast-growing herbs such as mint, to spread. As you trim your labyrinth herbs, dry the cuttings on racks or crush or chop them for protective or healing sachets (see chapters 9 and 10 for more about the magical and healing properties of herbs).

* Buy very small wooden posts (no more than a few inches high) from a garden center and hammer them into the ground (on

grass or soil). If working on soil you may want to lay small paving or stepping stones on the pathway to avoid getting muddy feet.

* Paint a labyrinth in an outbuilding or in a room with a wooden floor. Arrange furniture outside of the labyrinth or in the outer coils, and add a water feature and some green plants in the center. In this way you can create an oasis of calm in your home. For rituals, just move the furniture out of the room. An attic or basement can be cleared of junk or old family treasures for this purpose; an outbuilding can be reclaimed and repainted.

* For a portable but permanent labyrinth, paint one on canvas using waterproof nonporous paint. An old boat sail or any porch, camper van, or trailer awning works well. Paint your design on it and let it dry. You can store it rolled up under a waterproof cover against a wall in the garage. You could also stretch it over a frame (large circular trampolines can be pirated for this purpose) and paint your labyrinth on it. Or you might also be able to obtain a very large rubber mat, the kind used in gyms at school, on which to draw your labyrinth. Garage or yard sales can yield all kinds of useful materials.

* Create your own indoor or outdoor temple for your walkable labyrinth, enhancing it with statues, tall plants, crystals, and candles. Insist that anyone who visits your sanctuary is quiet and leaves their quarrels and demands outside.

If you do not have room for a large labyrinth at home, you can do your quiet work with a miniature one. For more active work that involves larger movements, create your own temporary labyrinths outdoors in parks and play areas or use existing public ones at quiet times. Seek out or create labyrinths of special natural beauty or those that are in settings of particular sanctity.

How to Draw Labyrinths

The following is an easy method for drawing a labyrinth of any size containing five to seventeen coils. You will recognize parts of the process from when you made your three-circuit labyrinth in chapter 2.

To draw a five- to seventeen-coil labyrinth:

1. Begin with a shepherd's crook shape. The bow of the crook forms the heart of our labyrinth.

2. Next draw a broken circle around the inner circle. This forms the last circuit, which will lead to the heart of the labyrinth.

3. Draw another broken circle around the first, leaving a gap on the opposite side.

4. Draw another circle, again broken on the opposite side. By now a pattern may be appearing.

5. You should be into the swing of this by now, so draw another broken circle.

6. Now close the pattern with a final broken circle.

This is a very simple design, but its beauty is that it can be adapted to produce as many coils as you require. Just keep adding broken circles and extend the vertical line of the shepherd's crook where necessary.

You can also go bigger, as in the nine-coil labyrinth below. This is an alternative method for drawing the classical seven-coil labyrinth you practiced in chapter 2. See which method you prefer. You can use either to create even the massive seventeen-coil version, which you can make on a beach to serve the most complex rituals or meditative work.

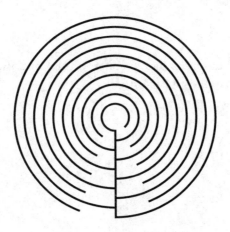

Read on for some variations on the theme, a few different methods of drawing labyrinths.

THE TARRY TOWN LABYRINTH

It is very easy to recreate the Tarry Town labyrinth, a four-coil labyrinth like the one that once stood in the village of Temple Crowley, just two miles outside of Oxford in England. The land is thought to have been owned by the Knights Templar, a mystical order begun in 1118, after the first Crusade, whose purpose was to guard the Holy Grail and protect pilgrims in Jerusalem. It has been said that members of the order used to walk the labyrinth as part of their initiation. The order, created in 1118, after the First Crusade, was originally based in Jerusalem to protect pilgrims. The labyrinth survived until 1852, when it was destroyed. All that remain are old diagrams. Because of its mystical associations it is an excellent labyrinth to create when you are engaged in a spiritual quest (see chapter 5).

Because this method involves erasing lines, you'll need to use a smooth medium such as chalk, sand, or earth. You can mark out the borders with small stones, if you wish. For a miniature labyrinth, draw it with pencil, paper, and eraser or pen and erasing fluid. The Tarry Town laybrinth is also an effective computer screen labyrinth (you might even incorporate one as your screen saver).

My husband, John, and I chose to draw this labyrinth on our local beach, Whitecliff Bay. We set off early on a Sunday morning when the tide was on the ebb, leaving a good stretch of firm, moist sand. We chose an isolated stretch of beach and drew the labyrinth using a long stick we had picked up on the way.

You can do the same following these easy steps:

1. Draw five concentric circles. Start at the center and work outward, giving yourself enough space to walk in between each circle. The circles need not be geometrically precise. If you are concerned about precision, use a length of rope or clothesline: each of you can hold an end of the rope, and one person can stand in the center while the other walks in a circle and draws the lines.

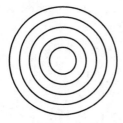

2. Choose an entry point. We chose to face the sea, but you can opt for any point that seems right for you at the time, of course. Then, using your foot, hand, or a spade, smooth over the sand to make gaps in circles one, two, three, and five.

3. Using your stick, join up the center and the outer circle and lines one, two, and three.

4. Smooth over the sand again. Make gaps in lines two, three, and four.

5. Use your marking stick to join lines two, three, and four to the left of the entrance.

6. Finally, smooth the sand to make a gap in line three on the left side of the entrance, and your Tarry Town labyrinth is complete. Happy walking.

A Garden Labyrinth

Because our garden is so long and narrow, the obvious choice when we decided to build our own labyrinth was Tarry Town. It can be as narrow as ten feet in width, yet it is still satisfying to walk or contemplate.

We chose to lay out our labyrinth using ornamental stones from the local garden center. For this labyrinth we used three twenty-pound sacks of pebbles about the size of a child's fist. A larger design would, of course, require more. Ours took almost two hours to build, with the help and advice of our thirteen-year-old son, Bill. But by using larger stones you could use far fewer of them and complete the labyrinth quicker. We placed the stones on top of our lawn, rather than cutting a shape into the grass, because it gave us the option of easily changing the labyrinth later.

The first problem with making a garden labyrinth is laying it out. It's not as easy to draw out your design on grass as it is on sand, in dirt, or on a floor. So, in laying out the design we used two tent stakes (garden stakes would also work), a length of rope (you could substitute garden twine), and a tape measure. It is possible to build this labyrinth on your own, but it is much easier if you are working with one person or even a team of people. In our case, Bill and I did the hard work while John acted as the foreman and took pictures.

To make a garden labyrinth:

1. Choose an area for your labyrinth and measure it. Drive a stake into the center point.

2. Measure off a length of rope or twine about two feet longer than the radius of your labyrinth. (For example, if the labyrinth is going to be a total of ten feet wide, with a radius of five feet, then you will need about seven feet of rope.) Make a loop at one end of the rope, so you can attach it to your central stake.

3. Divide the radius of your labyrinth by five in order to give you the width of each pathway. (For example, if you are building a ten-foot-wide labyrinth, the width of each pathway will be one foot.)

4. Starting from the loop end of the rope, make five knots, each one pathway-width apart (say, one foot, in the case of our example). These will be the guides for your walls; the extra rope at the end gives you a place to hold onto it.

5. Take a second piece of rope and prepare it in the same way, and put it aside along with the second stake. You'll use them later.

6. Slip the loop over the central stake and pull on the rope so that it is straight.

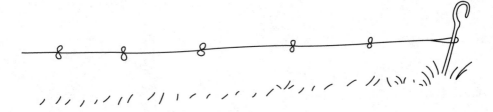

7. Decide where you want to place the entrance for your labyrinth, and line the rope up with it. Keeping the rope taut, lay a line of pebbles from the fifth knot (the knot farthest away from the peg) to the first knot (the one nearest the peg). Think of the labyrinth as a clock face with the stake in the center and the line of pebbles pointing down to six o'clock, where your entrance is. This gives us our first vertical line.

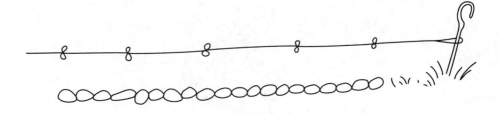

8. Move up to the first knot. Keeping the rope taut, begin to slowly move it clockwise. As you do this, follow the movement of the knot with a line of pebbles. This gives you the circle

enfolding the heart of the labyrinth. Don't get too carried away—remember to leave a space for the entrance.

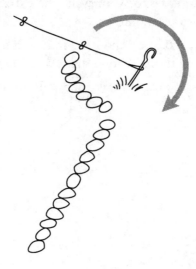

9. Line the rope up with the vertical line of pebbles. Move to the second knot and begin slowly turning the rope counterclockwise, laying pebbles on the circular path indicated by the moving knot. Leave a space. This will form our second broken circle.

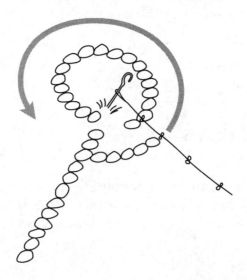

10. Now we need to make our second vertical line, which is where the other piece of rope and the second stack come into play. Put the second peg in the three o'clock position, as near as possible to the first wall. Attach the second rope to it and pull it taut so that it is parallel to the first vertical. Now lay a line of pebbles from its third knot to the fifth knot.

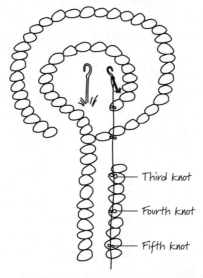

Third knot

Fourth knot

Fifth knot

11. Move the second tent peg to the nine o'clock position. Pull the rope taut, and, starting from the second broken circle, build a line of pebbles from the second knot to the fourth knot. This gives us our third and final vertical.

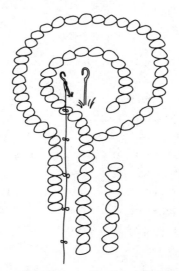

12. Remove the second tent peg, and put it and the rope aside. Line up the third knot on the central rope with the right-hand vertical line of stones and, moving the rope counterclockwise, build the third broken circle of stones, leaving a gap between it and the left-hand vertical line.

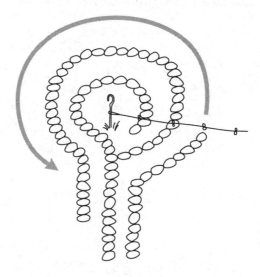

13. Using your fourth knot marker, start from the base of the left-hand vertical and, turning the rope clockwise, make a broken circle.

14. Now, using the fifth knot as your marker, turn the rope clockwise, and build a wall of pebbles from the base of the right-hand vertical to the base of the first vertical wall we made—and Tarry Town is complete.

This basic method is highly adaptable. If you want to make a permanent turf labyrinth, then you could use this technique to cut away the turf and sink a permanent path into your garden. Or you could choose to plant flowers to mark out your labyrinth. However, I would suggest laying pebbles first to see how you like the effect. Pets or kids may scatter them, but the damage is easily repaired. You can also make the path wider, if you wish.

If you have the space and are more ambitious, you could expand the labyrinth by adding coils to the basic Tarry Town structure. To figure out how much space you'll need, use the following formula:

decide how wide you want the path to be, multiply that number by the number of coils you want, and then multiply by two (you are multiplying by two because the coils lie on both sides of the center). So, if you want a twelve-coil labyrinth with a two-foot-wide path, you will need an area at least fifty feet wide, or 12 x 2 x 2 = 48. So why did I say fifty feet? Well, you'll need a little space to walk around the outside of it.

A CLASSICAL LABYRINTH

Once you have mastered the simple formula—beginning with the cross and four dots—you'll find that the classical seven-coil labyrinth is easy to create (see chapter 2). You can build one in your backyard if you have the space, or on a beach that has lots of pebbles. This labyrinth tends to be fairly wide. For example, if you want the path to be one foot wide, then you will need a space about 20 feet square. This allows for a central space two feet in diameter plus the surrounding coils, which are two lots of seven feet whichever way you look. You will also need some space to walk around the outside of the labyrinth and also to allow for bulging. I would recommend building this labyrinth by laying pebbles; this way you can make sure it is what you want before you commit to making a permanent installation.

To make a classical labyrinth:

1. First, measure out your central cross and lay it out in pebbles, stones, or bricks. Tent stakes and lengths of twine can be used to measure out the spacing of the cross, the L shapes, and the four marker stones.

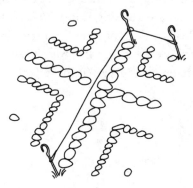

2. Now join the top of the cross to the top of the right-hand L to make the heart of the labyrinth. The diameter of this area determines the overall size of the labyrinth. Remember, the center is two times the pathway width you've chosen. If you are tight for space, you may decide to go for standing room only in the center. You may find it useful to measure the central space by putting a tent stake in the center and attaching a length of twine to it. Mark the center radius you want on the twine with a knot, then use it as a marker to lay the central wall.

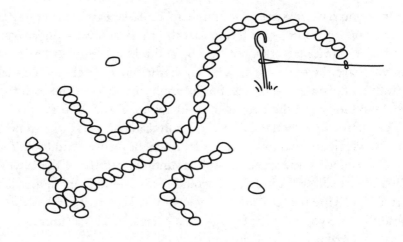

3. Now, continue working around the labyrinth—join the top right-hand marker stone to the top of the left-hand L (see also chapter 2, which contains instructions for drawing this classical labyrinth). You might choose to use a ruler or length of wood to ensure that you are keeping the correct distance away from the center wall or you might decide to trust your judgment. Don't worry if there are slight irregularities in the walls, as they will give this ancient design an antique feel.

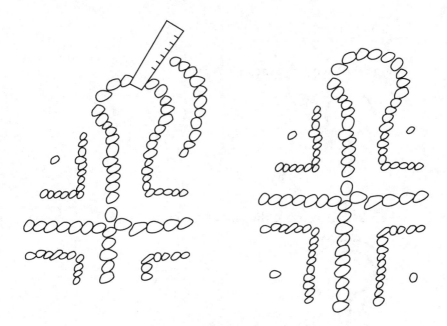

Reread the steps for creating the basic seven-coil labyrinth on pages 35–38 so you can monitor your progress as you create this stone labyrinth. Before long the process will become automatic and you'll no longer require a diagram or set of instructions no mattter where or how you create your labyrinth.

A SIMPLE LABYRINTH

It is indeed possible to build something as complex as the Chartres labyrinth in your backyard if you have the time, patience, and space. Although that design is beyond the scope of this book, the labyrinth described below is within reach and is just as beautiful.

This example is also featured in chapter 8 on healing. It is very simple to draw, yet it obeys the "rule" that a labyrinth should draw you into the center and then tantalize you by taking you away again. With this simple labyrinth, you walk along the track from one point to the center, either with your finger or on the ground. If you are creating this design in your garden, for example, you might cut into the grass and lay bricks or paving stones down to make a track.

To draw a simple labyrinth:

1. Begin by drawing the shepherd's crook.

2. Take a loop back from the end of the crook.

3. Loop back again.

4. Keep looping.

5. Continue until you run out of path.

6. Then dash up to the center.

You can, of course, elaborate on this design by making a longer path and adding as many coils as you require. In a garden, the invaluable tent stake and length of twine will help you mark out the circular paths.

An Indian Labyrinth

This simple labyrinth comes from Hallebad in India.

To draw an Indian labyrinth:

1. Start with a simple spiral to form the center of the labyrinth, ending at the top.

2. Let the upper arm continue to form a loop, then circle back around the center of the labyrinth.

3. Inside the left-hand loop, draw a new line and take it around the center.

4. Continue the line to loop it around the labyrinth and join it to the initial spiral.

Moving into a Labyrinth

Now you have created a space in which your spirit can dwell and soar. In chapter 13, I have suggested a blessing ceremony that you can use to dedicate your labyrinth before you begin your walk or ritual. Or you can offer a simple prayer of your own filled with light and blessings to a goddess, a god, or your favorite angel.

The greatest blessing you can give to the labyrinth is to work with reverence and with an open heart. Whether you follow the path of silence—one important way of walking the labyrinth—or chant aloud or in your heart, it is important to give love to the labyrinth, whether public or private, and to all you meet there. Open your heart to those of this world who are rushing, feeling troubled, or following their own private path. Offer blessings to the wise ancestors from another century who may brush against you as they tread the path and to those spirits yet unborn who frolic within the coils like butterflies.

Within even the smallest labyrinth lies a piece of eternity and one of the interconnected cells that make up the universe. This is why it can also be a pathway to divinity.

Chapter 5

PATHWAYS TO DIVINITY

T HE LABYRINTH IS A sacred place, a sanctuary and source of spiritual power in which we can reconnect with ourselves and with the world of spirit. As we walk toward the center of the spiral, we are symbolically moving closer to our personal spiritual center and to the core of divinity, no matter whom we worship. If you are not comfortable talking directly to a divine source in your labyrinth explorations, talk with and pray to archangels, angels, and saints, as people have done for centuries to tap into divine powers and healing.

The Labyrinth as a Spiritual Journey

From early times, the labyrinth has been regarded as a symbol of the mother goddess. We see this connection in Christianity through the Virgin Mary, and in Hinduism through Parvati, the gentle mother goddess, wife of Shiva, who protects women in childbirth.

Before joyousness was finally banished from churches, medieval priests would form a chain and dance their way to the center of the labyrinth, three steps at a time, sometimes tossing a ball to represent the sun or moon at such festivals as Easter and Christmas as a way of

greeting and honoring the deity. This is why a labyrinth can be seen
as both a physical path to trace and an inner spiritual journey.

RECONNECTING WITH DIVINITY

On September 11, 2001, I was in Ely Cathedral in Cambridgeshire in
the east of England, walking the labyrinth there. This labyrinth was
created in 1870 by Gilbert White using a unique design, a five-circuit
square with protruding three-circuit octagons, marked out in black tiles.

Inexplicably, I was drawn to buy a rosary, the prayer beads that
have become a part of Anglican and Episcopalian faiths as well as the
Roman Catholic tradition. As I walked the labyrinth, surrounded by
glorious stained glass windows and painted angels, I counted beads
as I recited prayers to the Virgin Mary, which I had last chanted in
childhood. I realized that these prayers could just as easily be directed
to a mother goddess or, indeed, to any source of divine love.

I focused, perhaps aptly though I knew nothing of the disasters
that had occurred in the United States, on the protective Hail Mary
prayer as I walked toward the center of the labyrinth.

> Hail Mary, full of grace, the Lord is with thee. Blessed art thou
> among women, and blessed is the fruit of thy womb, Jesus. Holy
> Mary, Mother of God, pray for us sinners, now and at the hour
> of our death. Amen.

In the center I prayed silently, talking to Mary, whom I visualized in the form of an elderly version—careworn, and infinitely
compassionate—of the Black Madonna statue that I had seen in the
Museum de Cluny in Paris. I discussed problems that were worrying
me and for which there seemed to be no answer. Though I had not
prayed like this in years, I was able to leave my burdens, piece by
piece, with Mary each time I returned to the center. On the way out
of the center each time, I alternated the Gloria with the Hail Mary.

> Glory be to the Father, and to the Son and to the Holy Ghost.
> As it was in the beginning, is now and ever shall be, world
> without end. Amen.

These prayers carried me back to the secure world of my childhood. I remembered coal fires, curtains drawn against the darkness, and Sundays in church rich with the smell of incense, brilliant-colored windows, and choirs singing words that resonated in my heart even though I did not then understand them. After five or six cycles of the labyrinth, I felt not exhausted but at peace and at home in my body for the first time in ages. Afterward, while driving back to my home on the Isle of Wight, I heard on the radio the news of the tragedies in the United States, and I recited the same prayers for all those affected. Then, later still, at the end of the day, while sitting on the midnight ferry home and watching the waves, I walked the labyrinth in my mind and knew that the world would never be quite the same.

LABYRINTHS AND PRAYERS

You may find it helpful to walk a labyrinth or visualize the pathways in your mind, counting beads on a rosary or a Buddhist prayer bead circle to keep the rhythm of traditional prayers. Alternatively, you may prefer to create your very own prayer chant to a chosen deity.

I believe we should feel free to adapt spiritual practices from faiths that may not be our own, for we all walk the same path to reconnect with the spirit. There are many Buddhist and Hindu Internet sites where you can listen to chants and perhaps find one that resonates for you. The Old Testament, too, has wonderful psalms that carry the spirit upward and create a natural flow inward as well as outward in a more traditional, celebratory, or worshiping form.

You may find that labyrinth work strengthens your existing faith or draws you back to the faith of your childhood. You may even open yourself to a new form of spirituality as a result of walking labyrinths, especially in sacred buildings.

Whether you walk your labyrinth in a sacred setting or under the stars, you can develop within its coils a sense of prayerfulness—for world peace; for healing the planet, a loved one, or yourself; for the lightening of your burdens; or for connection with the source of divinity.

The Threefold Path to Enlightenment

In chapter 2, I wrote about the three stages of labyrinth walking. The same three stages can give structure to spiritual work. The Reverend Dr. Lauren Artress, author of *Walking a Sacred Path: Rediscovering the Labyrinth as a Spiritual Tool,* has described walking the labyrinth as a threefold process, and the result of this spiritual journey as the experience of "the presence of something holy." She describes the first stage as entry and purgation, followed by the stage of meditation and prayer in the center. Finally, she says, comes union on the outward journey as the seeker integrates the new spiritual awareness into his or her life. It is worth considering each of these stages in more depth.

SURRENDER AND PURGATION

In spiritual work, I personally find the inward walk to be the most difficult stage. I suspect that the individualistic nature of modern living can make relinquishing control of ourselves and our lives much harder than it was for our ancestors, who were part of a more inclusive community. So much connects us with the material world as we walk into the labyrinth—all the trappings and achievements with which we seek to clothe ourselves and protect ourselves from our innate fears of being ultimately alone, as described by the psychologist Erich Fromm. This walk involves releasing ourselves from those connections. We experience a personal cleansing of all the strong emotions we may have been experiencing, including fear, bitterness, anger, and envy. In essence, one undergoes a process of surrender and purgation.

The only time we are physically a part of another human being is when we are in our mother's womb or when we carry a child of our own. It may be for this reason that the mother goddess labyrinth experience is like returning to the womb and why so many personal encounters within the labyrinth are with a female deity form, even within formal religious contexts. A number of Jewish women have told me that in the labyrinth they welcome into their hearts Shekinah, the female face of God, just as they do every Sabbath in their homes, with the lighting of the candles.

PRAYER AND MEDITATION

While the walking may be a public process, this quiet time is the private aspect when you talk to the mother, father, son, or daughter of God or ask for intercession by one of the angels or saints. Rather than using any set prayers, you may prefer to speak the truth in your heart, or to close your eyes and listen to the silence, finding a sense of connection with the source of divinity of which your own soul is a living part. You may find it helpful to connect with your own center of divinity by using such words as "I am within the god (the goddess) and he (she) within me. So am I blessed and ever shall be."

LEAVING THE LABYRINTH

This stage, integrating your newfound spiritual peace with your life in the everyday world, can be quite sad, like going home after a lovely holiday. But, as with a perfect time away from everyday concerns, you carry within you not only the memories of the experience but also the knowledge that you can return.

Formal prayers do seem to work on the outward journey, but you might like to intersperse them with other utterances: the names of people, animals, or places in need of healing, or the special blessings you have received, such as peace, reconciliation, or courage.

Praying the Labyrinth

You can walk a labyrinth and pray with or without tools. If you use prayer beads, which can be as simple as a special bead or crystal necklace, make a knot where you begin and recite a prayer for each bead on the necklace. Many people choose one or two basic prayers to say repeatedly or to alternate. You can create your own or borrow prayers from your childhood or newfound faith.

Countless websites offer traditional prayers from many faiths; if you choose ancient ones with a natural rhythm and simple form, you'll find that the many people who have spoken them over the centuries increase their spiritual potency. Most of the prayers described in the pages that follow are ones that I heard and recited in my childhood during the long Sunday church services when I often thought more about my afternoon tea than about spiritual matters. Others I have learned throughout life, usually at change points or when my outer world seemed to lack meaning and so I was more receptive to unexpected sources. For example, I learned Native American prayers from people who had spirit guides and had close connections with this form of spirituality. I have adapted these slightly for labyrinth work. You may decide to collect prayers, ones that you have either discovered or created, in your labyrinth journal.

Choose short prayers you can easily memorize, weaving one or two favorites into a continuous chant. Recite the prayers continuously as you walk into the labyrinth, counting on your beads, if you wish, each individual prayer. Seek not to consciously channel wisdom, but instead to open the pathway between yourself and a higher power.

When you reach the center, sit or kneel and speak in your own words as though to a wise, gentle mother or father. If there are other people around, you may prefer to have this prayer conversation silently. Talk of your dreams, your hopes, your fears, your failures, and your successes.

You may find that the mother you have already encountered in other labyrinths takes on an altogether more glorious, Sunday-best appearance. You may be deeply moved and awed, rediscovering true reverence, a quality rarely seen in our modern, quick-witted society. You may hear replies to your prayer in a gentle yet pervasive voice, or, as is more usual, be filled with a sense of peace, self-love, humility, and wonder at the universe we have not managed to totally despoil despite humankind's worst efforts.

You may see lights or wonderful colors or hear music that is so harmonious it could not be earthly. This is what you will carry out of the labyrinth, the unity with the smallest flower, stars thousands of light years away, the wind, the rain, the sunshine, and cantankerous relations or colleagues.

As you chant your prayers on the way out, your words and the rhythm may become more upbeat, as you experience the flow of love to and from all creation. Give yourself time before returning to the world, the noise, and the traffic. If you've been working in a religious setting, sit in the cathedral or church, wander around looking at icons and windows, or read a few lines from a sacred book.

You may find small prayer books in the cathedral or church bookstore; if you choose to, sit and read one in the refectory before leaving. Partake of the delicious coffee and homemade cakes sold in the cathedral café, if there is one. This grounding process helps the transition from the spiritual to the material planes.

If you feel very tangled in your life, you may benefit from weekly prayer sessions in the labyrinth, perhaps walking it in your mind and reciting your special prayers before facing the day (or under the stars at the close of the day). If you cannot return to the ecclesiastical labyrinth where you had this experience, you can surround your miniature labyrinth with candles and use that as a focus for weekly prayer.

The Magnificat

This is the Virgin Mary's hymn of praise to Elizabeth, mother of John the Baptist, after Gabriel told her she was to conceive a son. It is a joyful prayer that, for women of any age, taps into the heart of creative love and fulfillment in many aspects of life and is especially powerful when said in a large labyrinth in a sacred setting. You may be lucky enough to have a choir in the distance. You can easily substitute the feminine form of God if you wish.

> My soul doth magnify the Lord
> And my spirit hath rejoiced in God my savior
> For he hath regarded the lowliness of his handmaiden.
> For behold from henceforth all generations shall call me blessed
> For he is mighty that hath magnified me
> And holy is his name
> And his mercy is on them that fear him throughout all
> generations,
> According to our forefathers,
> Abraham and his seed forever.

A Prayer of Saint Ignatius of Loyola

I learned this prayer as a child, but it has helped me in times of doubt or when I have needed to make a great effort or to be unselfish, especially in caring for my children. Ignatius, founder of the order of the Jesuits, was a Spanish soldier who converted to Christianity after being wounded in battle.

> Teach us, good Lord, to serve thee as thou deservest;
> To give and not to count the cost;
> To fight and not to heed the wounds;
> To toil, and not to seek for rest;
> To labor, and to ask for no reward,
> Save that of knowing that we do thy will;
> Through Jesus Christ our Lord.
> Amen

Saint Bridget's Prayer

Because Saint Bridget is the Christianized version of the ancient Irish Triple goddess (see chapter 11), this prayer has been used over many centuries by women of Celtic descent in many parts of the world during labor. It is a very potent prayer for men as well as women for strength at times of sorrow or grief, for bringing change and removing obstacles or stagnation, and for help with mothering and family issues. This prayer was sent to me by an American friend.

> Come to my help.
> Mary fair and Bride,
> As Anna bore Mary,
> As Mary bore Christ,
> As Eile bore John the Baptist
> Without flaw in him.
> Aid thou in my unbearing,
> Aid me, O Bride.

SAINT PATRICK'S PRAYER

Patrick is said to have converted Ireland to Christianity in the year
431. There are many legends attached to him, including the story
of how he drove the snakes from Ireland and performed magic to
defeat the Druids, whom he drove from the sacred Celtic hill of Tara,
lighting his own festival fires there. He is quite a stern saint and not
particularly female friendly, but he is a good focus for courage and for
defending ideals.

My own great-aunt, Bridget, who brewed potato whiskey in a
copper pot in her washhouse, taught me this prayer when I was being
bullied at school.

> I arise today
> Through the strength of heaven,
> Light of sun,
> Radiance of moon,
> Splendor of fire,
> Speed of lightning,
> Swiftness of wind,
> Depth of sea,
> Stability of earth,
> Firmness of rock
> Through the creator of creation.

THE DRUID/DRUIDESS PRAYER

This is my own special favorite. I work as a solitary Druidess though
I have trained with the Order of Bards, Ovates, and Druids and in my
practice I have found that this prayer is one that is especially potent
in open-air labyrinths. I was told this prayer by a Druidess I met at
Avebury, and recently I have noticed a similar version being used in the
growing Druidic peace movement, prompted by these troubled times.

> Deep within the center of my being,
> May I find peace
> Silent within the center of my Grove.
> May peace increase

Still within the great circle of humankind,
May I radiate peace and reconciliation.

A CELTIC PRAYER

Because the Celtic tradition has continued orally, some of the very
ancient prayers and blessings have been translated and recorded only
in the last century, and the work is ongoing.

There are many similar versions that vary according to the trans-
lator and the specific region from which they come. My favorite
Celtic prayer that I have used many times in labyrinth work was
introduced to me during a concert by the British singer-songwriter
Ralph McTell. His song featuring a version of the prayer can be
found on his album *Sand in Your Shoes*. There is another popular version
sung in folk clubs, often without accompaniment.

This prayer is especially helpful if you are far from home or if
a friend or a member of your family is absent or estranged. It is also
a useful prayer to say if you face a challenge or are embarking upon
an emotional or spiritual journey. You can, of course, substitute the
name of your goddess or other deity form.

God be with you on every pathway
Each step walk with God beside.
May the roads rise to meet you,
May the wind be always on your back,
May the sun shine warm upon you
May the rain fall gently on your fields
and until we meet again
May God hold you in the hollow of his hand.

PRAYER FOR THE HOME

This is another Celtic prayer that is very potent for bringing protection
to the home and loved ones, and for reconnecting with our roots at
a time when we are feeling alienated from others or our essential self.
I first heard it on the Isle of Skye in Scotland at a traditional folk
evening. At the time I desperately wanted my own home and family,

my parents having died when I was still quite young. I scribbled down the words, and the next day, as I recalled the prayer, through the rain appeared a double rainbow. Years later, when I recite the words as I walk a labyrinth, I remember the blessings of my own children. There are many versions, but this is the one I use.

> I kindle my fire this morning
> With this good peat, without fear or envy of any
> Who walk beneath the good sun this day
> I kindle this flame in my hearth and my heart
> For food on my table, health in my home and a gentle parting
> when my days are ended
> I kindle in my heart this morning
> A flame of love to my neighbor
> My foe and my kindred
> And God over all protecting.

A NATIVE AMERICAN TRADITION

Native American prayers are especially powerful in labyrinth work. I have used this prayer, by Black Elk, Holy Man of the Oglala Sioux, in a classical, circular seven-coil labyrinth. My late friend Doris, a wise medium, believed that she was guided by Black Elk, and she would close meetings with his prayer.

This prayer is especially good for use at any gathering concerning the environment or pollution, and when there is a need for reconciliation, whether at home, in the workplace, or throughout the world. Black Elk, who as a child was present at the massacre of Wounded Knee, had nevertheless lived at a time when his people were free. Later, in 1930, he explained that "everything the Power of the World does, is done in a circle. . . . Birds make their nests in circles, for theirs is the same religion as ours. The life of man is a circle from childhood to childhood and so it is in everything where power moves."

In his prayer he asked:

> Grandfather, Great Spirit, once more behold me on earth and
> lean to hear my feeble voice. You lived first, and you are older

than all need, older than all prayer. All things belong to you: the two-legged, the four-legged, the wings of the air, and all green things that live. You have made me cross the good road and road of difficulties, and where they cross, the place is holy. Day in, day out, forevermore, you are the life of things.

THE HEBREW TRADITION

Surprising though it may be, I was taught this chant by a clergyman of the Church of England when I worked as a teacher in London. I have used it many times for labyrinth prayer at times of conflict, either national or international, and at times when my personal world has become painful and discordant. (*Shalom,* of course, means "peace" and is much used as a form of greeting.) This prayer can form a round for a group of friends or people working together for peace especially when the participants carry candles in a labyrinth ritual or vigil (see chapter 13).

Shalom, my friend,
Shalom my friend,
Shalom, shalom, shalom my friend,
Shalom my friend, shalom, shalom.

PRAYERS FROM THE FAR EAST

This is probably the most famous mantra, or chant, to pass into Western spirituality.

Om Mani Padme Hum

Originating in India, the mantra was brought to Tibet, where it is now central to Tibetan Buddhism, containing, it is said, all the teachings of the Buddha. Its basic meaning is "the jewel is in the lotus," the lotus flower being a manifestation of divinity.

The pronunciation has changed from the original Sanskrit, and the version I give may be found with the following variations:

Om, the sound that is said to have brought the universe into being, is pronounced "ohm."

Ma is pronounced "mah" or "meh;" *ni* is pronounced "nee."

Pad is pronounced "pah'd" or "peh;" *me* is pronounced "may."

Hum is pronounced "hoong" ("oo" as in "book").

Chant it a few times and the sounds will flow.

Candles and the Labyrinth

Candles have always been associated with religious ceremonies. Those made from beeswax are linked with the Virgin Mary and her mother, Saint Anne, especially in Eastern Europe. Lighting a candle is itself an act of prayer that carries our petitions into the cosmos. Candlelight can increase the spiritual vibrations of the universe, even in dark times or in the face of deeds of spite or cruelty. This practice began when tallow torches were made from juniper twigs to illuminate the inner caves in Paleolithic times in honor of the mother goddess.

I was once given a photograph of Chartres Cathedral labyrinth encircled by candles and realized how powerful candlelight work could be when done within the sacred labyrinth. For example, prayer vigils for peace or planetary healing could be held in a large labyrinth, creating a spiral of constantly moving light as suppliants pass in and out of the coils carrying candles. The energies of the labyrinth combined with the power of light and prayer can amplify any petition to the divine source whether for individuals, for one or two people, or for a larger group.

I often work with candles in the labyrinth of stones I have created in my garden, either alone or with my younger daughter, Miranda. The labyrinth is just about big enough for both of us to move round. I use garden torches around the outside so we can work after dark. We carry small nightlights in heatproof holders into each of the five coils, offering a prayer as we light the candles in each coil.

Recently we carried out the ritual described next to ask that relief be sent to lands where the people were starving and without shelter because of civil war. You can ask for protection on behalf of individuals who may be in danger, a group of people, a species, or a whole nation.

This ritual works well with one person, but you can adapt it to include more participants quite easily. I have based this ritual on a seven-coil labyrinth. You and your participants should devise prayers to be said in each coil upon lighting a candle and in the center. For this ritual we are setting four candles at the outside of the labyrinth, one in each quadrant, a candle in the center, and one candle for each coil. The coil candles will be carried into the labyrinth during the ritual. (If you are working alone, use a labyrinth with no more than seven coils or you will get tired of carrying the candles to the different coils.) The coil candles will be set, unlit, in a group near the entrance to the labyrinth so participants can collect and light them before the labyrinth walk.

Choose in advance the people who will light each labyrinth coil. If you have more people than coils, put extra candles near the labyrinth entrance for the extra people. They can stand around the edge and light their candles from the nearest directional taper after all of the coils are lit. If you have fewer people than coils, decide in advance who will light which coils so the rite moves smoothly. In this case, the coil lighter will stand next to the candle in the innermost coil he or she works with after he or she has lit its candle. For instance, if you light coils three and six, you would stand in coil six after lighting that candle. You would then be responsible for saying the prayers for both coils three and six.

Your local church might allow you to use its labyrinth when no services are planned, or you could create a temporary labyrinth on the shore on a windless night or in chalk in an urban square. I am using a classical seven-coil labyrinth, but you can use a more complex formation, especially if there are other participants.

To work with candles in a labyrinth:

1. Work after dusk or at the time of the most magic, for instance, just before dawn so that as you extinguish the final candles, daylight floods the sky.

2. Place unlit pure-white candles in floor holders, or garden torches if outdoors, around the perimeter of the labyrinth at each of the four cardinal directions, north, south, east, and west.

3. Next to each perimeter candle place a lighted taper in a tall holder. Place a large, unlit white candle in the center.

4. Circling around the perimeter of the labyrinth, sprinkle sacred water over it. This can be water that you have obtained from a holy well or spring water in which you have stirred three pinches of salt clockwise using a silver or stainless steel knife or a pointed quartz crystal. To do this, begin at the north. Light the white candle from the lighted taper next to it, and sprinkle a clockwise circle of sacred water around the base of the candle, saying, "May there be peace in the north. Lord (Lady), bless and protect."

5. Continue to sprinkle water around the labyrinth perimeter until you reach the east. Light the white candle from the lighted taper next to it, and sprinkle a clockwise circle of sacred water around the base of the candle, saying, "May there be peace in the east. Lord (Lady), bless and protect."

6. Continue to sprinkle water around the labyrinth perimeter until you reach the south. Light the white candle from the lighted taper next to it, and sprinkle a clockwise circle of sacred water around the base of the candle, saying, "May there be peace in the south. Lord (Lady), bless and protect."

7. Continue to sprinkle water around the labyrinth perimeter until you reach the west. Light the white candle from the lighted taper next to it, and sprinkle a clockwise circle of sacred water around the base of the candle, saying, "May there be peace in the west. Lord (Lady), bless and protect."

8. Each participant who has been chosen as a coil lighter should light a candle to carry into the coils (from those candles set by the labyrinth entrance). Use the lighted taper located closest to the labyrinth entrance to light the coil candles. With the lighted candle in hand, walk to the first coil and say a prayer.

9. Repeat these steps for the rest of the coils. If you are working alone, leave the candle burning in coil one, return to the entrance

to collect the candle for coil two, and then walk to coil two and say a prayer. Each person from coil one onward will have to pass through the earlier coils to get to their designated coil.

10. Take the candle from the last coil and light the central candle. Say a prayer and then remain in the center, praying, meditating, or just gazing into the flame as you choose. When you are ready to leave the center, extinguish the central candle, saying, "Send light into the darkness. Blessings be." As you make your outward journey, extinguish the candle in each coil in turn, repeating your labyrinth prayers at the end of the ritual. If possible, let the candles on the perimeter continue to burn or extinguish them in the reverse order of lighting, repeating your labyrinth prayer.

11. If there is more than one person in the labyrinth, they should all follow the person who extinguished the central candle out of the labyrinth, having each extinguished their own candles.

If you do not have room for a full-size labyrinth, you can carry out this ritual on a labyrinth you have created in a sand box or drawn on flame-retardant paper using small tealights, visualizing your walk along the pathways.

Labyrinths can also form the focus of candle rituals to mark different stages of your life, from dedicating your love to another, naming a child, or holding a vigil to ease or mourn the passing of a beloved friend or well-loved religious or national figure.

A candle ritual can also banish any personal darkness, whether caused by sorrow, betrayal, fear, a natural ending, or a devastating trauma. It differs from a magical labyrinth ritual in that the focus is on using the candles for prayer. You can also use this ritual alone or with a group of friends or family members to ask that sickness and suffering be taken from a loved one or yourself. You need only create a relatively small labyrinth or even, as I described previously, a miniature one to walk with your fingers.

To walk a labyrinth using candles and healing prayers:

1. Just before dusk, in the center of the labyrinth place a large pure-white or beeswax candle that will burn right through the

night. (If you buy a "church candle," the label will tell you how many hours it will last.) Next to it place a white taper.

2. Stand outside the labyrinth entrance, and light a small, dark-colored candle in a deep heatproof container and carry it into the labyrinth, saying, "Even in the darkest hour a small light burns bright. I ask you, Father (Mother), to take away my fear and sorrow (or this sickness) as this candle burns likewise away."

3. Move from coil to coil, saying, as you enter each one: "I pray that light and health and joy return to my life (our lives) and to the world."

4. When you reach the center, sit in the candle's glow until all the light has gone from the sky, offering silent prayers. When it is dark, light the white candle from the dark one using the taper. Say: "I (we) pray that the new light may ever grow and become more glorious and with it healing and restoration."

5. Remain in the center. If you are working with other people, they can each carry a small candle through the labyrinth in turn and light it from the central candle, making a silent prayer for the future, perhaps adding a flower or crystal to create a circle around the white candle.

6. Afterward, they can return through the coils one at a time and sit or stand around the perimeter in the candles' glow. Then you, or the last person in the center of the labyrinth, should extinguish the dark candle, saying, "Blessings be. I thank you for lighting the darkness. I pray that as your light fades, so may past sorrows (illness) fade away. I ask you, Father (Mother), to take away my inner darkness (the darkness of pain and suffering)."

7. Send light to all who are in sorrow or in spiritual darkness. Gaze into the white candle and recall blessings that have fallen upon you and your family, naming each and offering thanks. If you wish, add a second white candle to increase the positive energies.

8. When you are ready, take the extinguished dark candle and walk slowly out of the labyrinth. Leave your candle or candles in a safe place until morning and they are quite burned down.

The preceding chapter has been a journey through which we have explored the idea of divinity manifesting through the channel of the labyrinth. We have used prayers and candles to direct our own healing energies and to create a place of personal sanctity during our rituals.

In the next chapter we will build on these concepts of divinity and personal sanctity by working with meditation within the labyrinth, especially miniature labyrinth forms, to explore our own inner world and touch the divine core that I believe is within us all.

Chapter 6

PSYCHIC DEVELOPMENT WITH THE LABYRINTH

TRACING A SMALL labyrinth with your finger or eyes creates an altered state of consciousness, akin to a light trance. The power of a small labyrinth is no less than a large one. Over the centuries, it has been accepted that even a tiny labyrinth can create a site of magical energy and become a center of spirituality. Therefore, you should not worry if you can work only with a table-sized structure. For example, two of the most magical labyrinths I have come across are each barely a foot wide. They are two classical seven-coil labyrinths carved into a rock wall near a ruined mill in the wooded Rocky Valley in north Cornwall, England.

There is some dispute over their origin, but they may date back as far as the Bronze Age. The Rocky Valley, near the magical little port of Boscastle, is said to be the most haunted valley in Cornwall. Reportedly almost everyone can, when touching the labyrinths, see fairies and nature spirits and beings. Certainly the wooded valley has a very magical feel, as the narrow river rushes past to meet the sea, less than a quarter of a mile from where the labyrinths are etched into the rock.

On the trees around the labyrinth carvings are hung offerings of ribbons, jewelry, messages of petition, and thanks. Here, as I traced the classical labyrinths with my finger, I was aware of the power of all those who had come to this spot in pilgrimage over the millennia. I felt that their accumulated emotions had created an otherworldly place where the dimensions of time had no meaning.

The labyrinths felt electrically charged but in a gentle vibrating way. Psychic images and sounds filled my mind with impressions, vivid colors, and fragrances, not only familiar scents of the wild herbs that grew around but also new, unfamiliar scents.

The sound of the river merged with birdsong in that deserted valley imbued my fingertips with psychometric power; I detected warmth from the sun that had filtered through the trees over centuries. There grew in me, too, an instinctive awareness that I was no longer alone but was commingling with the essences both of the natural world and of the spirits of those now passed to other realms. Their prayers may have been to the goddess of the labyrinth; to the deities of the water, the woodlands, the rocks, and the sky; or to the Christian God, but all carried lingering kindness, compassion, and an over-whelming love for the natural world and all its creatures.

Developing Your Psychic Ability

Why should such magical power exist in and around labyrinths? Simply because of the very act of surrendering to the labyrinth that I described in chapter 5. For whether a labyrinth is very old or newly created, it helps us to shed our conscious thoughts and barriers as we move closer to the center to work within an otherworldly space.

Before I visited the rock labyrinths, I had gone to Boscastle's Museum of Witchcraft in North Cornwall, itself set in a valley between rocky hills and moorlands where the river tumbled over rocks to challenge the incoming tide. Donning my newly acquired black velvet cloak, I walked around entranced by the beautiful exhibits and the spirituality (my husband skulking behind to avoid any association with the wild-haired, black-cloaked figure who, despite attempts at mystique, had more in common with a jolly, rotund Disney witch than with the ethereal mysterious raven-haired beauties of modern movies about witches). Included in the museum's labyrinth exhibition was a classical labyrinth carved into a flat rock brought from Michaelstow Farm, a remote farmstead not far from Penzance, which was shrouded in mist when I passed it the next day.

This labyrinth had been used for divination, not just for preparing the mind to receive information from the cosmic well of wisdom but as a divinatory tool, an alternative to tarot cards or a crystal ball. What is surprising is that even people who normally find it hard to direct their psychic abilities into divinatory work experience a blast of multisensory psychic awareness when drawing and tracing a labyrinth for the first time. The labyrinth reopens the channels that often close with the ending of childhood. Once the channels are open again these powers remain accessible and will enrich all your psychic explorations, not only those amplified by labyrinth ritual. In chapter 7, I describe more formal methods of divination using the labyrinth.

A Miniature Power Source

Let us begin by walking a small labyrinth with the index finger of your power hand or with your eyes. You can use any labyrinthine form, though the Bronze Age designs I found in Rocky Valley were classical seven-coil labyrinths. The complexity or simplicity is not important.

I would suggest that at some time you try a five-circuit formation, which works well for miniature labyrinths and can be quickly and easily drawn or traced. The prototype is the full-size boulder labyrinth with five coils at Troy Town at St. Agnes in the Scilly Isles. This type of boulder labyrinth consists of stones varying in size from a tennis ball to a man's head and is often associated with magic. The labyrinth at St. Agnes, rebuilt twice, is said to have been made by the lighthouse keeper in 1729. However, an earlier one may have occupied the same site. It cannot be called a "pure" labyrinth, since you do, at the end, get a choice of routes—but both of them lead you to the center. You may decide to take one route in and the other out. In chapter 4, I have described how to draw a five-coil labyrinth. However, the following is a very quick alternative method.

To draw the Scilly Isles Troy Town labyrinth:

1. Begin by drawing the shepherd's crook. The length of crook you draw depends on how big you want your labyrinth to be. Experiment to get the proportion right.

2. Draw a half circle around it.

3. Starting a little way down on the right-hand side of the shepherd's crook, draw a loop and let it double back on itself.

4. From inside the loop you have just drawn, start a new line that will loop around the third line and join up with the bottom of the crook.

You can draw or trace this five-coil labyrinth in chalk or paint, on black paper, slate, or dark stone. Make it about three-feet square. Set it on a low table or supported on bricks or stones so that you can sit on the earth, grass, or floor and look directly into the center. Work in pale sunlight or moonlight, perhaps with light filtering through trees, or by candlelight so that the light illuminates the coils.

1. Focus on a question or an issue that you can summarize in five or six words. Create a very simple chant, for example, "Choose to leave, choose to stay, spiral inward show the way."

2. Begin at the entrance. Chant as you follow the pathway with the index finger of your power hand (the one you write with), allowing your mind to clear itself of any other thoughts. If you find this difficult, picture a star in each coil, and, as you reach the coil, watch it fade and leave only the white outline in velvety darkness. Move your finger even more slowly, and let the chant taper away to a whisper.

3. When you reach the center, be silent and wait, with your finger still connecting with the heart of the labyrinth. At this point you may see images or scenes in your mind's vision or hear words or lines of poetry from some great work such as the Bible, the *I Ching,* or a Shakespeare play. There may also be less concrete impressions—fleeting joy or a sense of peace or a sudden desire for change or movement—accompanied perhaps by colors, fragrances, sensations of heat or cold, rushing water, waves, or sand beneath your feet. Do not analyze these impressions or images; simply let them flow into your mind.

4. When you are ready, allow your finger to move outward again as you repeat the chant, this time beginning in a whisper and gradually increasing the volume until you reach the outside world.

5. Now sit quietly, focusing on the labyrinth, and allow the impressions and images from your labyrinth experience to form a pattern. As they come together, you will understand perhaps not the answer to the particular question you were grappling with but instead your issue in a wider context, pathways you could take and possible outcomes.

Celtic Labyrinth Stones

Because the Druids did not leave permanent monuments or written records of their practices, much of their magic has been lost. We learn of their ways mostly from Greek and Roman writers of the time who were hostile toward them, and from later Celtic writings. We do, however, know a little about one of their ways: the custom of carrying stones etched with labyrinths and used for meditation by the Celts. These were traditionally carried in a pouch or purse for day- and nighttime use.

These small flat stones were used in Wales, England, and Ireland to induce a light trance and to create that altered state of consciousness that would allow wisdom to be channeled from other dimensions. Focusing on them made it possible to step outside linear time; visions of other times and places could be induced, and the mind could be directed to bring thoughts into actuality. Such powers can still be induced by meditating on Celtic labyrinth stones regularly over a period of months.

With these stones, the pattern was traced with the eyes rather than the finger. Ordinary people as well as the Celtic priests used these labyrinth treasures, handed from mother to daughter as tradition tells, and therefore perhaps dating back to the pre-Celtic Neolithic traditions when the labyrinth was a powerful connection with the mother goddess herself.

Those created and used in sunlight were called "serpent stones" because the spiral represented the magical serpent. Sun stones are intended to be used in sunlight and are very good for meditating about matters concerning power, success, ambition, and the external world. Moon stones are intended for moonlight work and are concerned with matters of the inner world, spirituality, and dreams.

MAKING YOUR LABYRINTH STONES

In order to create a sun (serpent) labyrinth stone, find a round, flat, white stone, the size of a very large coin or round pendant. Draw or paint in black the classical seven-circuit labyrinth (see chapter 2) on it. (Alternatively, use the simple three-coil labyrinth that resembles a serpent, also shown in chapter 2.)

Use an awl or a screwdriver to scrape out the design to make the labyrinth three-dimensional, and then paint it if you wish. Work on sunny days especially around noon. Most powerful is the day of the summer solstice, the "longest day," around June 21 in the northern hemisphere.

Keep your serpent stone wrapped in white silk or in a light-colored purse made of natural fabric from dusk till dawn.

Your labyrinth moon stone should be created at night during the waxing moon period (check your diary or the weather section of your local newspaper) by the light of the moon or a pure beeswax or white candle. Alternatively, look in the sky. Each night, a waxing moon gradually increases in size from the right. The most powerful night for using a labyrinth moon stone is on the full moon and the day just before and just after it. Walk your moon stone labyrinth in your mind, rather than with your fingertip. When possible, work in moonlight, but if that isn't possible, work by candlelight. When your labyrinth moon stone is not in use, wrap it in dark silk or keep it in a dark purse made of a natural fabric from dawn until dusk.

MEETING THE WILD MOTHER OF NATURE

There are many ways in which you can use your labyrinth stones. They hold the key to many realms and many psychic experiences. The more you work with them, the greater connection you build up, so that gradually it takes less time to pass through the labyrinth center into other levels of awareness and dimensions. The following method is a way of working with Mother Nature and encountering a different face of the labyrinth. The wild mother of nature holds a great store of potential energy that is akin to the power of the wind, to thunder-storms, and to cleansing torrents of rain. It is a vortex of energy that brings cleansing, a tossing up of all the components and ingredients, or the swirl of a kaleidoscope that re-forms the pieces into a new integrated picture. Unlike sky god energy, which flies like a rocket or arrow and which you can (to some extent) direct if you hold on tight, the wild mother of nature's energy is like a whirling pool that requires surrender and trust that she will release to us the gifts we need.

I use this method when trouble has me backed up against a wall, when the figures just don't add up no matter how I rearrange them, and a drastic solution is needed.

In chapter 11, I have listed wild mothers from a number of traditions, which may prove to be a focus for your explorations. However, you may prefer to allow the figure to build up quite spontaneously.

To work with the wild mother of nature:

1. Hold your labyrinth stone so the sun or moon shines on it. Sit somewhere comfortable and quiet where you will be safe if you fall asleep, as sometimes happens during meditation.

2. Focusing on the labyrinth's center, stabilize your breathing pattern so that it becomes smooth and regular. Try breathing in through your nose for a count of four (one and two and three and four), holding your breath for two (one and two), exhaling for four, and resting for two before beginning the cycle again. Continue your breathing cycles until you feel calm and relaxed.

3. Still focusing on the labyrinth stone, walk the shimmering pathways in and out several times in your mind until you feel as though you are floating along them. Traditionally, people would chant a deity name, the name of a tree or stave made from it, or some other word of power as they worked, but I find that this is most effective as a silent process. Experiment.

4. Concentrate only on the pathways and the light, and after a while the pathways will blur as your instinctive senses take over. If you are working with the sun (serpent) stone, you may find yourself on sunlit pathways, perhaps floating through rainbow-hued clouds or over seas. You may see a tree at the center of the labyrinth. There may be tree spirits or forest deities and, presiding over all, the mistress of the herds, untamed but benign, or a wise tree mother or Druidess who will share with you the secrets of the sacred groves.

5. With your moon stone, you may pass through the labyrinth entrance to the otherworld that leads to fairy palaces, like the

Glastonbury Tor. On the other hand, your labyrinth entrance may take you deep within the sea. Here you may encounter sea spirits, mermaids, deities, and the sea mother, old and wise. To some, the sea mother is frightening, but to those who approach her with courage to comb her tangled hair she offers abundance and kindness (see "Sedna" in chapter 11). These initial experiences may be relatively unstructured but rich in symbolism and otherworldly beings.

6. Gradually the outer world, with its sounds and fragrances, will return. Sit quietly and allow the magical experiences to wash over you. They may continue in your dreams.

Contact with Mother Nature in this way can help you develop a strong connection with the natural forces that provide you with a sense of connection to all forms of life. You may feel as though you have access to a whole repository of powers that have become blocked in our high-tech, industrialized world. If you work with the wild mother through your labyrinth stones over a period of months you will come to love this connection with the labyrinth mother, who will always be with you in the most tangled forest or fiercest battle.

DEVELOPING AND DIRECTING YOUR AMAZEMENT

Although there may be times when you want to work in an unstructured way, you can also use your miniature labyrinth stones in a more ordered way.

To visualize a particular symbol representing a quality you need:

1. In your mind, picture a fiery dragon for courage, a flower for self-love, a rock for stability, or a butterfly for regeneration.

2. Project the image so that you can see it in the center of the labyrinth on your stone.

3. Picture it getting larger as you move nearer the center in your mind, and visualize it getting smaller as you focus on your outward journey through the coils.

4. Continue to visualize the image becoming larger or smaller as you weave in and out of the labyrinth with your eyes. This sets up a spiral dance in your mind.

5. On the final entry, your mind will blend with the symbol, transferring the symbolic strength to you, which you can carry within you on your final outward path.

CHANNELING WISDOM AND CONNECTING WITH A LIGHT BEING IN THE LABYRINTH

You can also channel knowledge and insight from a wise source using your small labyrinth stones. Find a place of nature in which to work if possible. Many towns have small woodlands or wildlife gardens, botanical gardens, or quiet flower gardens. At night, you can work at home, in your garden, on a balcony, or near an open window.

Before you begin, take time to remove yourself from the world, perhaps by having a bath with fragrant herbs or flowers, or going for a walk in a wild setting.

To channel the wisdom from the labyrinth:

1. Light any candles you need, and, if working indoors, add myrrh or sandalwood incense for increasing psychic awareness. Sit quietly in a safe comfortable place, holding your stone but not yet focusing on it, allowing any thoughts to float away on imaginary helium balloons or clouds.

2. Breathe gently and rhythmically, and, when you feel quite relaxed, hold your stone and focus on the center, allowing a figure to form in your mind, surrounded by light.

3. Allow your mind to float along the labyrinth pathways, as though your feet are not touching the ground. You will be pulled gently through circling, colored, vibrating energies, like a gentle carousel or vortex. See golden light flooding toward you so that you are also enclosed within it. Retrace your steps mentally to leave the labyrinth, and then repeat the process several times.

4. Now, make only one journey into the labyrinth. This time, it may seem to take an incredibly long time, because you are moving

toward a different level, to the inner or psychic labyrinth that is
accessed through the physical one.

5. The figure you encounter here will be too bright to see, but
    you can feel its peace and love. This is not your labyrinth mother,
    the wild mother of nature, or the sky god. This is another wise
    guardian who resides in the world beyond the labyrinth, an angel
    or being of light who may be more challenging than the mother
    of the labyrinth and less externally focused than the sky god but
    is equally kind and will help you to evolve spiritually.

6. If you wish, ask for guidance in matters that concern you, for
    we cannot evolve spiritually until we have resolved earthly prob-
    lems that divert our energies. Then wait. A soft but powerful voice
    will speak in your mind, and you may enter into a dialogue.

    Allow the being of light to direct the encounter; he or she will
    tell you what you need to know and hear. This may not be what
    you thought you needed, but it will make perfect sense and fill
    you with confidence and optimism.

7. Ask whether you may see the being of light. If he or she agrees,
    close your eyes. Open them, blink, and you may have a glimpse
    of your guardian, surrounded by radiance. You may not learn
    his or her identity for several more encounters. Close your eyes
    once more and you may feel a gossamer touch first on your
    head and then on your heart. Let your own hand follow the
    path of the angelic touch down your body, and you will experi-
    ence the magical sensation of being touched by a divine form.

8. Now allow yourself to be gently pushed out of the spiral, again
    floating or flying or even swimming in the colored energies.
    After the experience, you may wish to record the words you
    heard in verse or as a series of symbols, or you may be inspired
    to paint, draw, or create with clay, metal, or wood.

In time, as you continue to work with your labyrinth stones in this
way, you may see the figure of light for longer periods. The channeling may become more complex and profound. You may then identify
your guardian as an angel, an archangel, or a being who perhaps never
lived on earth but has chosen to guide those who travel a spiritual

pathway. Shortly after this revelation you will usually encounter the image of your angelic visitor at a time when you least expect to, in a picture in a shop window or in a book, for example.

Once you establish a pattern, windows of time, ideal for channeling, will unexpectedly open up. These windows usually occur when the physical light is especially suited for your channeling. An appointment you did not really want to keep gets canceled on a sunny morning or your family members suddenly decide to go out on the night of the full moon. If you do not have a chance to channel for a while, then accept that and wait.

If you record your channeling you will discover that without any conscious structuring by you, the material does follow quite naturally from the previous encounter.

If you use both your sun (serpent) stone and your moon stone to channel your being of light, you may initially have two different light guardians. After initial encounters, however, you will be drawn to one or the other as your natural source of wisdom. After all, to expect both Saint Michael, Archangel of the Sun, and Gabriel, Archangel of the Moon, to keep a regular date is asking rather a lot of cosmic forces.

On the whole it is better to allow your labyrinth angel to show himself or herself to you. However, if you want to find out more about your angel, you can find a whole heavenly host of images online and in the books listed in the appendix. In chapter 7 I have listed a number of archangel forms that are often encountered in labyrinth work.

LABYRINTH STONES FOR MAGIC

You can, with care and sensitivity, use your labyrinth stones for magic. But before you write your cosmic wish list, run through the basic rules for responsible labyrinth power:

* The unbreakable rule is this: ask for enough to meet your needs and only a little more. This means that if you ask for a new car to replace your old, broken one, or money to fix your roof or to take the children or yourself on holiday, that is quite legitimate— you may have enough left over for a new bikini or three. However, state lottery wins really have to be left to old Lady Luck.

* The next rule is that you can work magic for any purpose as long as it is not harming anyone else, which is not as easy as it sounds. If the job or guy you crave is someone else's, then you have to add "if it is right to be." As a result, the person in *your* job might get a promotion or move abroad, or your object of desire's wife might fall in love with someone else. However, happiness built on another's loss or sorrow tends to have a foundation of sand, and so you may end up empty handed and alone.

* The third and final rule is that whatever you send out comes back threefold, so be sure that what you are requesting is what you really want. If you are trying to influence others, make sure that your intentions are entirely honorable and pure.

So you can now go ahead and use your mind powers amplified by the labyrinth to translate thoughts into positive effects for use in everyday life.

To use the labyrinth stone for magic:

1. Before you begin, light a sagebrush (desert or mountain white or gray sage), cedar, or rosemary smudge stick or broad-leaved smudge herbs set in a flat ceramic dish. You could also use a broad-based pine or rosemary incense stick.

2. Face north (you can use a compass if you wish) and draw a clockwise circle of smoke around where you will be sitting. You can leave the smudge to burn down in a safe place. This circle will protect you while you are manipulating energies, although, of course, the labyrinth itself also offers natural protection.

3. On a cushion or blanket, sit in the center of a circle of candles or in a pool of moonlight or sunlight.

4. Then, holding your sun (serpent) stone or moon stone according to the time of day, stand in the center of the circle you created with smoke. In your own words and facing the north, east, south, and west directions in turn, ask the sentinels of the four directions for protection as you work. Raise your labyrinth stone for blessing at each.

5. Sit in the center of your magic circle and, holding the stone so that you are looking down on it, breathe gently until you are relaxed and have sent away all irrelevant thoughts.

6. Now, concentrating on the center of the labyrinth, state what it is you want or need as fully as you wish, and, as you do so, visualize your dream or need coming to fruition.

7. Returning to the entrance of the miniature labyrinth, begin the inward path toward the center in your mind, seeing in the center the fulfillment of your goal. You practiced this when you were absorbing different strengths using symbols. In magic, you need to raise and release the power to create the cosmic explosion that will cause your desire to become manifest in actuality (though maybe not straight away).

8. In your mind, return to the entrance again via the coils. Move inward again, chanting a single word to represent the wish, then outward like an amusement park swingboat, coming out faster propelled by an unseen impetus. Then turn in again, ever faster.

9. Continue to chant faster and faster, still moving in and out, until you feel quite dizzy and suddenly there is a flash in the center as the energies fuse and cascade from the stone like colored stars flowing upward. You may spontaneously utter a cry such as "It is free," or "Come to me." This time you will find yourself outside the labyrinth.

When you feel quiet again, make plans for bringing those dreams into reality. The magical impetus is like a plane taking off from the tarmac, but you need to fuel and pilot your dream to a happy landing.

Moving Labyrinth Meditation

Some people find it incredibly hard to forget their bodies and be still. You may decide to leave your small labyrinth work for a while if it does not seem fruitful. Alternatively, you could try conducting the miniature-labyrinth rituals and methods in this chapter in a large labyrinth, walking or running the coils rather than visualizing your progress. Moving through a large labyrinth naturally induces a meditative state in even the most hyperactive individuals, like me—before long you are floating along in that altered state of consciousness in which the deeper powers of your mind can re-emerge from their adult atrophy.

There are a number of ways of walking or dancing a labyrinth. Some people walk very slowly, head down, step in front of step, focusing on the path in the manner of the early pilgrims. Others sway, chant, dance, smudge the path, or do a mixture of all of these. Earlier in the book I talked about the Cretan labyrinth mating dance and applied this to relationship issues. Next I discuss a number of these themes to suggest ways you can enter meditative states and, by moving rhythmically, dance your way into other dimensions.

The Rhythm of the Labyrinth: Surrendering to the Earth Dance

I have swayed, chanted, and danced my way through a number of public labyrinths both indoors and out. Working by moonlight or in the early morning or evening light is especially powerful. The key to attaining higher states of consciousness is to lull the conscious mind into allowing the deeper unconscious and psychic parts to emerge.

Try all or some of the following suggestions as you aim to merge with the sacred form of the labyrinth. Once you can move between worlds on the pathways, you'll be able to call into being specific powers to answer questions, channel wisdom, help you make decisions, or travel to other realms.

The act of making your own labyrinth can become part of the meditative process. Choose a simple drawing method, such as chalk or a stick marking out earth or sand. Use a fairly simple form, probably not more complex than a classical seven-coil labyrinth, unless you are an experienced labyrinth maker or you majored in geometry.

Find a quiet place and time. You can combine the following methods to create the one that is right for your own labyrinth meditation, or you can devise your own.

USING MUSIC

If, like me, you are easily distracted, for your initial forays play some gentle but upbeat music, perhaps dolphin song or slow drumming, using a portable stereo, or a portable headset if there are others present who are not participating. (However, communal partying in labyrinths is to be recommended.)

Even better, find or create a labyrinth near a source of natural sound, such as a beach or a river. If you are working in a church or cathedral labyrinth, choose a time when a service or choir practice is being held. This method helps especially to develop your clairaudience, the ability to detect sounds from other times and dimensions, not only in the labyrinth but also generally in your life. Chanting (see chapter 5) also enhances these abilities.

The focal point of your journey, if you need one, is a piece of music. A snatch of a song will enter your head in the center, and if you sing or hum it on the way out it will trigger memories or give a message that becomes crystal clear in the hours or maybe days after your experience.

THE PILGRIM WAY

This method is all about taking your time. Even the smallest labyrinth walked slowly represents a pilgrimage to that sacred place we visualize in the center. You might like to re-read the section in chapter 5 on pilgrimages, though in this section it is the journey rather than the destination that is the focus.

This method seems to enhance the ability to channel angelic and higher spiritual guides and increase your power to connect with past lives and worlds. You'll find that these abilities are strengthened not just during your labyrinth work but in your life and dreams. Here are some guidelines:

* For pilgrimage meditation, make each step measured, one foot in front of the other as though walking over a narrow bridge. Keep your eyes on the pathway and your arms either raised slightly before you in an arc (as though holding an imaginary precious object) or by your sides, fingers pointing to the earth.

★ Allow the paving stones, the path, or the grass to take on its own form, a pathway through a valley, winding upward and around to the top of a hill, like the Glastonbury Tor labyrinth, which would carry you into the magical otherworld in the center. You may see your pathway as gold, silver, crystal, flowers, or beneath the water between shoals of shining fish. Even in a relatively small labyrinth the journey may seem to take forever once you move out of linear time.

★ You may find that you do not walk alone but are accompanied by or part of a procession. When I walked the labyrinth at Ely in Cambridgeshire, I felt that I walked in procession with the Anglo-Saxon nuns who lived quietly among the marshlands of the English fens, chanting to the Virgin Mary. Also present with me were the earlier mother-goddess priestesses who looked over the misty flat landscape to a golden land of peace and healing just beyond the horizon, where the marsh geese flew into the setting sun.

★ In the center, you may feel that you have entered a heavenly city. Yet often the pilgrimage center is a place of radiance filled with symbols of beauty and joy but with no identifiable focus.

★ The voices you hear, the images you see, and the impressions you sense may seem otherworldly or may be symbols of what it is you need to know.

★ Often a single word will be the culmination of the experience. If you recite this both in the center and on the way out, you will make numerous associations with it, answering a yet-unasked question.

DANCING IN A LABYRINTH

Dancing a labyrinth on a regular basis is an excellent method of increasing clairvoyance, the ability to see into the future or distant places and become aware of nature essences and other magical beings who share our planet. For this, you will use your psychic, or inner, third eye, located on your brow above and between your eyes. It throws your physical eye off balance so you can see glorious things just over the horizon or even a universe away.

There will be times when you will dance your labyrinth joyously like a child, perhaps with a friend, your own child, or a lover. In doing so, depending on the speed you dance, you may attain a state of ecstasy, akin to a peak experience in which the world is gloriously spinning and you feel connected with the whole of nature and the universe.

Or you may choose a more measured, meditative tread so that you are gently uplifted as you spiral. This allows you to connect with the earth energies beneath your feet as your upraised arms connect with the powers of the sky. You become your feet and your hands, the earth and the sky, the crawling insects, the tiny scurrying animals, and the birds soaring above.

Join with a chain of friends, or even strangers, chanting, stepping and treading, and creating your own labyrinth of movement. If you are working alone and find it hard to tune into the labyrinth rhythm, in each hand hold a fern stem, a long frond of other greenery, or a peacock feather (with its magical eye, it is a symbol of intuitive vision).

Either alone or with others, stand at the entrance with your feet apart, gently swaying from side to side, allowing your mind to flow free until you make connection with the earth energy. You may be aware of nature's essences joining you in your sacred dance. Greet them and follow their movements, and you may momentarily see the world and even fairy realms through their eyes.

You may even dance out of your physical body quite spontaneously and see your spirit dancing ahead of you, leaping in and out and circling around you, laughing. You may have forgotten how happy you can be in your own company and what delight you can take in your body and its movements.

SMUDGING YOUR LABYRINTH

Fragrance is a powerful tool for inducing states of altered consciousness. Smudging the paths of a labyrinth, using a smudge stick or broad-based incense stick, will enable you to pass easily into a light trance state as you weave your way with the smoke. Smudging the labyrinth is especially powerful for developing clairsentience, the power to pick up psychic impressions from past and present settings. It also helps you to travel in your etheric or spirit body to other places and times.

This method is best used in a labyrinth created in sand, soil, or chalk, to avoid the risk of fire to grass. Use no more than seven coils, so that even the most recalcitrant smudge will stay alight until you reach the center. You can place a lighted candle or torch in the center to relight the smudge for your outward journey if necessary. Set a deep container in the center to hold your smudge.

Smudging a labyrinth is especially magical in a sheltered place on the shore, on a calm day or night, since the fragrance from the sea mingles with the smudge.

If you are working indoors, make sure the room is well ventilated. Avoid smudging while you are pregnant and when small children or those with chronic respiratory conditions are present.

Use commercially prepared sticks of sagebrush—desert or mountain sage—rather than small-leaf culinary sage unless you are expert at making smudge sticks. Sagebrush sticks are particularly robust, light easily and well, and tend not to flake in use.

To smudge your labyrinth:

1. Face the entrance to the labyrinth, and light your smudge from an outdoor torch or candle. Ignite the center of the stick so that a small flame appears; it will naturally die down, leaving a glow.

2. Holding the smudge in your power hand (the one you write with), fan the smudge with a feather in your other hand until the center is glowing and the smudge emits a steady stream of smoke.

3. Holding the smudge at waist height, move rhythmically and slowly around the coils, fanning the smoke upward and downward to form spirals. Allow your feet and the smudge to dictate the rhythm.

4. Once you reach the center of the labyrinth, place your smudge in the container and sit for a few minutes, allowing the smudge to weave pictures and patterns with its smoke.

With a gentle, slow breathing pattern allow yourself to be carried on the smoke to wherever your psyche and spirit body wish to travel. Alternatively, you may enter into the heart of silence, where you may experience unity with all life and the creator.

5. When you feel yourself stirring inwardly, relight the smudge if necessary and weave your path outward.

After this ritual, you may reach conclusions quite spontaneously or make connections between disparate aspects of your life. You may also experience the expansion of your psychic awareness so that colors seem brighter, sounds seem more harmonious, and fragrances seem more pervasive. This awareness will bring your intuitive abilities to the fore, and you will see beneath the surface to the true situation in many aspects of your life.

CHANTING THE LABYRINTH

For me, this is the most effective method of labyrinth meditation, which can be done alone or with friends or family. As well as increasing clairaudient and mediumistic abilities, chanting the labyrinth also bonds you psychically to those with whom you work, helps you have significant dreams, and allows you to be aware of the energy fields around yourself and others.

Work in a more complexly coiled labyrinth such as an open-air one, in the early morning or evening when you will not be disturbed. If you can, find one with a tree in the center, the tree representing the world tree and the union of earth, water, and sky.

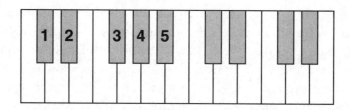

You only need to use the pentatonic scale, traditionally used in shamanism, to create altered states of consciousness and out-of-body travel. The pentatonic scale uses five notes instead of eight in an octave. One example of the pentatonic scale can be found by playing only the black notes on a piano. The simple chanting tune given below is in the pentatonic scale (the numbers correspond to the marked piano notes on the previous page).

1 2 2 2 3 2 2 5 2 4 2 3 2 2 2

If you prefer, you can allow your voice to rise and fall naturally. You will find that whether you work alone or with a group, a chant emerges quite spontaneously and may build up as you traipse the circling pathways. You can, if you wish, link hands as you spiral inwards.

Keep a steady chant and move with a slow skip-and-tread rhythm toward the center. Begin with just three or four words and repeat them as you step, for example, "We are one" or "Light, life, and loveliness, blessings be." One of my favorite chants comes from the soundtrack used at the Museum of Witchcraft in Boscastle, Cornwall, sung by Liz Crow and Heike Robertson:

The river is flowing, flowing and growing
The river is flowing, down to the sea.
Mother Earth carry me,
Your child I will always be,
Mother Earth carry me down to the sea.

You can focus on a single natural force and add a new elemental force for each coil. For example, in the first coil say, "I am the light and the light sanctifies me." Next, add, "I am the wind, I am the light and the wind and the light sanctify me." Continue, adding, "I am the rain, the fire, the sea," and so on, until you have a complex chant that can be sung by different voices in harmony when you reach the center.

In the center, circle the tree, if any, either alone or with your group, still chanting and stepping as before, and then spiral slowly out again. On a special occasion, such as the night of the full moon or the summer solstice, you can chant your way in and out of the labyrinth several times, until at last, you sit or lie within the center, closing your eyes and experiencing rainbow-colored, swirling out-of-body sensations. If you are working with others, you may form a collective vision, each one of you adding your images and experiences.

This has been a significant chapter because the labyrinth has become a doorway to higher levels of awareness. Physically walking or dancing the labyrinth coils, or meditating using labyrinth patterns will lead us to our inner world but also to those higher planes that we can only access when our conscious minds are still.

In the next chapter, we will work further with these higher energies, using them to uncover the right pathways for our future.

Chapter 7

Planets, Archangels, and the Labyrinth

Seven heavenly bodies visible to the naked eye move across the fixed constellations of stars. In ancient times, Mercury, Venus, Mars, Jupiter, Saturn, the sun, and the moon were seen as rulers and directors of the universe, guiding the lives of people and nations on earth. These celestial bodies have become central to magic and astrology in many lands, associated with great deities whose attributes seem to mirror the influences of these planets upon humankind.

In the ancient Greek and Roman cultures, each planet was believed to have its own layer, like a series of concentric spheres, around the earth. As a result of this concept, the planets naturally became associated with the traditional seven coils of the labyrinth. It was believed that the soul progressed through each planetary layer or sphere before being incarnated. Medieval magicians and mystics would trace the planetary path to discover auspicious times for ritual.

The Planets and Empowerment

There can be few more magical or empowering experiences than walking through a seven-coil labyrinth under the stars, recreating the journey of the soul through the seven planets. As you pass from one planetary layer or sphere to the next, you can take strengths and qualities from each until you reach the center of the labyrinth for "reincarnation." Then, moving outward from the center to the periphery of the labyrinth, you reascend the starry passage in reverse order through the Milky Way to the heavens.

At sundown on a clear night, make a seven-coil labyrinth on the beach, in the earth, or in chalk in your yard. Watch the stars come out and the planets move among them: brilliant Venus, for example; the morning and evening star, most dazzling next to the sun and moon; and fiery Mars, with his red glow and who, at certain times, moves close to the earth. Each can, once identified, be easily recognized and used as a focus as you walk inward in the labyrinth.

Use a sky map or consult your computer beforehand to identify which planets you will be able to see. For each planet that you see, you can utter a wish as you leave its coil on the upward path out of the labyrinth.

If you work close to sunset during a full moon, it will rise in the east almost as the sun sets in the west, a powerful moment of cosmic transition. But there are many other times during the waxing period when moon and sun are in the sky at the same time; using their dual influences, make your labyrinth, and then wait for darkness to perform your ritual. A moon diary or the weather section of a newspaper will give you sun and moon rising and setting times.

IDENTIFYING THE PATHWAYS

The following diagram shows the pathways of the classical seven-coil labyrinth, each labeled with its planetary influence.

Numbered from the inside out:

8 Earth

7 Moon

6 Mercury

5 Venus

4 Sun

3 Mars

2 Jupiter

1 Saturn

In this diagram the planets, moon, and sun are arranged according to their positions as seen from earth, which is of course how the ancients viewed the cosmos as well. Following is a list of the qualities and strengths of each planet, which you can tap into as you move through each coil.

Coil 1: Saturn is potent for setting the parameters of what is possible given the constraints of the immediate situation. In this way, he dispels illusion and unrealistic dreams; he brings patience, perseverance, and a practical focus to any endeavor, plus the ability to overcome any obstacle step-by-step. Saturn is the planet of self-control.

Use this coil as a focus for all slow-moving matters, such as the home, property and security; the finding of lost objects; concerns over animal welfare; exploration of the unconscious of the individual and the collective psyche; and past-life work. Saturn can be used to slow down the outward flow of money and encourage repayment by those who owe you favors or money.

Archangel Cassiel

Color Purple

Crystals Fluorite, hematite, jet, lodestone, obsidian, and smoky quartz

Herbs, incense, and oils Aconite, bistort, comfrey, cypress, horsetail, mimosa, patchouli, Solomon's seal, and vetivert

Coil 2: Jupiter brings increase in every aspect of life—material, emotional, intellectual, creative, spiritual—so that horizons and opportunities expand. He encourages principled leadership and nobility of thought and deed. Jupiter promises joy through giving, receiving, and exploration.

Use this coil as a focus for improving one's fortune, career prospects, and worldly success; for extending one's influence in the wider world and for matters of justice and the law; for the need to either follow tradition or the more conventional path, authority, and for encouraging altruism; long-distance, permanent travel; and home or career moves. Jupiter also rules marriage, permanent business and personal relationships, fidelity, and loyalty.

Archangel Sachiel

Color Blue

Crystals Azurite, laboradite, lapis lazuli, sodalite, and turquoise

Herbs, incense, and oils Agrimony, borage, cinquefoil, coltsfoot, honeysuckle, oakmoss, hyssop, mistletoe, sandalwood, and sage

Coil 3: Mars represents courage, initiative, survival instincts, protection of the vulnerable and loved ones under threat, and strength to fight injustice through action. It is the focused expression of righteous anger.

Use this coil as a focus for areas of your life where change is needed or desired. Particularly, you might want to use it to help you assert your individuality and independence; improve your physical health and resolve any issue that is central to your livelihood or your essential self; and encourage passion, male potency and fertility, and the consummation of love.

Archangel Samael or Uriel

Color Red

Crystals Bloodstone, blood agate, garnet, ruby, and jasper

Herbs, incense, and oils Basil, coriander, dragon's blood, garlic, ginger, mint, pepper, tarragon, and thyme

Coil 4: The Sun represents male/animus/yang energies in both men and women, and the pure life force. It brings illumination and inspiration, the restoration of optimism, self-esteem and self-confidence, and originality and creativity. It speaks of the need to seize the moment and use every available opportunity for happiness while the sun is at its height; this is the time and place of peak power, when anything is possible.

Use this coil as a focus for the fulfillment of dreams, for the realization of hidden talents, and for a new beginning or sudden transformation of any aspect of life, for all matters concerning fathers and fatherhood, for enhanced spiritual development, and for inspired solutions to old problems.

Archangel Michael

Color Gold

Crystals Amber, carnelian, diamond, clear crystal quartz, tiger's eye, and topaz

Herbs, incense, and oils Bay, benzoin, copal, frankincense, juniper, orange, rosemary, saffron, and St. John's wort

Coil 5: Venus represents sexual and romantic love, the love for family and friends, and beauty. It also symbolizes arts, crafts, and music; blossoming sexuality; the acquisition of beautiful possessions; harmony; fertility; and gradual growth in every aspect of life.

Use this coil as a focus for attracting new love, for love magic, the mending of quarrels, and the slow but sure growth of prosperity; for women's health matters, for rituals concerning horticulture and the environment; and for healing wisdom using herbs and crystals.

Archangel Anael

Colors Green and pink

Crystals Amethyst, calcite, emerald, fluorite, jade, moss agate, and rose quartz

Herbs, incense, and oils Echinacea, feverfew, geranium, lilac, mugwort, pennyroyal, rose, strawberry, thyme, vanilla, vervain, yarrow, and ylang-ylang

Coil 6: Mercury represents the powers of the mind, logic, and clear thinking; focus and concentration; and clear and persuasive communication. He also rules honesty, adaptability and versatility, business and scientific acumen, healing powers, and the ability to see through illusion and deception and repel spite or envy.

Use this coil as a focus for money-making ventures, for learning and preparing material for examinations and tests, for mastering new technology, and for conventional methods of healing, especially surgery. It is also potent for divination, business negotiations, and overcoming credit problems; for short-term or short-distance travel and house moves.

Archangel Raphael

Color Yellow

Crystals Agate, citrine, falcon's eye, jasper, malachite, and onyx

Herbs, incense, and oils Dill, fennel, ferns, lavender, lemon-grass, lily of the valley, mace, parsley, and valerian

Coil 7: The Moon represents primarily female/anima/yin energies in men and women, plus intuitive abilities, clairvoyance, mystical abilities, mediumship, the inner world, and the power of dreams. It represents inner powers and insights, the spiritual side of life, and the natural, seasonal ebbs and flows of life.

Use this coil as a focus for rituals concerning the home, family matters, mothers, children and animals, female fertility, and all the ebbs and flows of the human body, mind, and psyche in both men and women. It is also potent for protection for the home and for psychic self-defense.

Archangel Gabriel

Color Silver or white

Crystals Calcite, moonstone, mother of pearl, pearl, selenite, and opal

Herbs, incense, and oils Chamomile, jasmine, lemon, lemon balm, lotus, mimosa, myrrh, poppy, sandalwood, sweetgrass, and wintergreen

WALKING THE COSMIC LABYRINTH

Of course, the sequence of one to seven is *not* the order in which you walk your seven-coil labyrinth. You actually start on coil three. Using the diagram on page 146, trace your potential pathway in advance. For each coil, create an empowerment to absorb that planet's power according to what you feel you need. An empowerment is a statement or chant that you make to focus on, in this case, the particular strengths of each planet and archangel. By speaking a statement aloud or focusing on it in your mind, you trigger psychic and psychological connections with these powers. One of the basic tenets of magic says that speaking an intention or desired state aloud allows you to absorb the particular strengths and powers you need.

You seem to be going out again in the early stages of labyrinth walking, but the energies are increasing with every coil. In labyrinth work, as in life, plowing straight to the center not only means that you miss the pleasures of the journey but also that you are not prepared to use the gifts you receive along the way. It is a bit like starting off down the interstate in a car before you've located *drive, reverse,* and, most important, *stop,* on the gear shift.

If you are working with a public labyrinth, arrive early or late in the day to allow more quiet space and time for your walk through the planets. You can speak words in your mind if you feel self-conscious about chanting out loud. In a labyrinth you have created yourself, work by starlight with candles or torches to illuminate the coils. Below I've inserted empowerments that I use, but feel free to use your own—they will be even better for you, since they relate to your unique worldview.

To walk the cosmic labyrinth:

1. Stand at the entrance to the labyrinth facing the center. Begin with a slow but steady pace, putting one foot in front of the other.

2. In coil three, Mars, the first circuit to be walked, say, "I enter with courage. I take into myself the fire of Mars to cut through fear that keeps me from achieving my destiny in the world." Scatter a few Mars herbs as you walk, for example, basil and mint, naming fears to be shed and areas where courage is needed.

3. In coil two, Jupiter, the second circuit to be walked, say, "I open myself to the power. I grow in wisdom and vision as I see before me the purpose of my journey." You seem to be moving outward, but the energies are growing. Scatter a few Jupiter herbs on your pathway, for example, sage or hyssop, naming ways of bringing your dreams to fruition. Your steps will increase in length and become more deliberate.

4. In coil one, Saturn, the third circuit to be walked, say, "I must persevere and not be impatient if the journey seems never ending, for there is a purpose." You may have been swung to the outside by Saturn, who rules the outermost coil and reminds us that there are no easy ways to achieve true fulfillment. Now you slow your pace again, being aware of the sound or rhythm of each tread. Scatter a few Saturn herbs, for example, mimosa flowers and patchouli, naming obstacles you have already overcome.

5. In coil four, the sun, the fourth coil to be walked, say, "I walk into the light and am filled with joy as the way and purpose suddenly become clear." Scatter a few sun herbs, for example, rosemary and dried bay leaves, casting away indecision and all doubt. Now you may want to raise your arms slightly, lift your head, and do a simple skip-and-tread movement.

6. In coil seven, the moon, the fifth coil to be walked, say, "I open myself to the mysteries of darkness, seeking meaning in the shadows and in the clarity of light." Scatter moon herbs, for example, sweetgrass and sandalwood, naming secret dreams and unfulfilled desires. You may find yourself swaying slightly as you walk.

7. In coil six, Mercury, the sixth coil to be walked, say, "I surrender to the cosmic dance and do not hesitate. Mind, body, and soul walk as one." Scatter Mercury herbs, for example, lavender and fennel, and express the truths in your heart that have been dammed up. At this point, if not before, people often begin to dance or spiral.

8. In coil five, Venus, the seventh and final coil to be walked, say, "With love and harmony, I enter the sacred spiral and join with all the powers of the labyrinth." Scatter Venus herbs, for example, rose petals and thyme, and offer messages of love and peace, especially to those from whom you are estranged. Let your feet be guided by the harmony of the energies beneath them.

9. Finally, enter the center of the labyrinth, saying, "Mother earth, mother home within your sanctuary, womb and tomb." Sit in the center, drawing up red earth energy through your perineum, your Root chakra, or psychic energy center (see chapter 10). Then, as my late mother used to say, take time to count your earthly blessings. If it is sufficiently dark and clear, watch the stars overhead and know that you are part of them and they you. Otherwise close your eyes and visualize them. If you are working in the early morning you may see Venus, Mercury, and maybe even the moon if it is waning, as well as the rising sun.

10. When you are ready, walk out, pausing at each coil to make a wish on its planetary ruler. In your own words, give thanks for the qualities of each planet that you will carry back into the world with you. Your feet will know how to respond, as they link with the feet of those who have walked or danced labyrinths throughout the world and through the millennia.

You can also create a miniature labyrinth, etching the planetary glyphs (shown on the next page) in the coils and walking it with your fingers. If you want to work in darkness, stick glow-in-the-dark stars and planets to the ceiling and wait for a bright moon to shine in through the window on to the coils.

⊙ Sun

☽ Moon

☿ Mercury

♀ Venus

♂ Mars

♃ Jupiter

♄ Saturn

♅ Uranus

♆ Neptune

♇ Pluto

The Labyrinth and the Archangels

Each of the planets is associated with an archangel whose energies can give quite a different feel to the labyrinth pathway. Each coil of the classical seven-coil labyrinth is ruled by a specific archangel, whose energies may fill you with light and harmony as you walk inward to the place of stillness, the center.

IDENTIFYING THE PATHWAYS

The diagram below shows the pathways of the classical seven-coil labyrinth, each labeled with its archangel influence.

Numbered from the inside out:

8 The point of stillness

7 Gabriel

6 Raphael

5 Anael

4 Michael

3 Samael or Uriel

2 Sachiel

1 Cassiel

This order is one of the most commonly used in the Western magical tradition, but if you use another archangel system it can easily be adapted to the labyrinthine formation.

I have named the archangels from the outside in. Of course, you will not walk them in this order but, as before, you will begin with coil three, Samael or Uriel. I have deliberately left the descriptions of the archangels vague, since we all have our unique visions of their physical appearances and personalities. As you work with this ritual, the archangels will become clearer to you. If you wish, consult the books listed in the appendix that offer information about the archangels. Alternatively, you can download images of famous paintings of angels from the Internet if you prefer to begin with a more clearly defined focus.

The archangels' focus includes more than just the planetary energies, encompassing the needs of others and global and spiritual concerns. However, under the threefold laws of magic, the good wishes we send out and good works we do all return threefold from the cosmos, so you need not fear that your personal needs will remain unnoticed by the angels. For this reason I have included personal needs under the specific archangel energies even though they are not strictly spiritual.

You can work with the archangel's associated fragrances in the form of incense, oils, or smudge. You can also focus on the archangel's specific crystal and, holding it, connect with the angelic powers. To find out each archangel's color, herbs, and crystals, refer to the earlier descriptions of the planets, each of which corresponds to a particular archangel. The colors I have given are from the Western magical tradition and also correspond with planets and chakras, or psychic energy points (see chapter 10).

Though I have referred to the archangels as male, and some esoteric traditions identify corresponding female angel energies, they are often seen as androgynous.

> **Coil 1: Cassiel** is the conservator, the angel of stillness, quiet contemplation, and moderation in all things. He will help with earthly matters, especially those concerning money, property, and lands where there is poverty.

In this coil, focus on the reversal of bad fortune, the conservation of ecological resources, the return of places to their natural state, and the preservation of history and tradition. See the description of Saturn earlier in this chapter.

Coil 2: Sachiel, the divine benefactor, is the angel of charity, who works constantly to help others and improve the lives of humankind. He restores rundown areas or cities where employment has been lost, and lands where there is famine, blending new skills with traditional knowledge. He encourages expansion and moves into new areas of activity, of a beneficial kind.

In this coil, focus on the increase of abundance in your own life or in the lives of those in need; better harvests; the physical, intellectual, and emotional; and all charitable works. See the description of Jupiter earlier in this chapter.

Coil 3: Samael or Uriel Traditionalists may prefer the name Uriel, for Uriel, Raphael, Michael, and Gabriel are regarded as the four core archangels in a number of religious and magical systems, representing the four directions and the four ancient elements. Samael forms, however, the direct magical correspondence with Mars, who also rules coil three in the seven-coil labyrinth.

Samael is sometimes called the "severity of god" and, as such, is an angel of cleansing and of righteous anger. Samael offers protection to the weak and vulnerable and cleanses doubts and weakness, replacing them with spiritual courage to stand against the corrupt. He also aids those in war-torn lands, minorities who are being oppressed, and endangered species.

In this coil, focus on obtaining the moral courage to stand against injustice and for your principles; the release of those who are unjustly imprisoned and who suffer under harsh regimes; those who are deprived of equality and who are not accorded basic human dignity because of their beliefs. See the description of Mars earlier in this chapter.

Coil 4: Michael, the initiator, brings illumination and inspiration. He is guardian of all who stand alone with a unique vision for bettering the world and who will not compromise their ideals for money or fame. He protects those who work for civil rights and peace, and those who seek to unite nations or abolish arms, and nuclear and biological warfare. He also protects those affected by drought, fire, and air pollution.

In this coil, focus on increasing creativity, spiritual and intellectual inspiration, and contact with the source of divinity and the higher self or spirit guides. Perform rituals for reviving barren land despoiled by industrialization, for international peace and unity, for irrigation programs, and for cleansing air pollution. Focus on the prevention of corruption and the creation of a good standard of living for those in need. See the description of the sun earlier in this chapter.

Coil 5: Anael, the regenerator, represents pure altruistic love for humanity, animals, and plants, healing sorrows and abuse, restoring rainforests, bringing wildlife habitats to the city, protecting animal and bird sanctuaries, and helping the regeneration of greenery everywhere.

In this coil, focus on fertility in any aspect of life, inner harmony, reconciliation with others, the restoration and preservation of the planet, the use of natural medicines, organic methods of farming and husbanding the earth, animal rearing, and prevention of cruelty to any creature, however small. See the description of Venus earlier in this chapter.

Coil 6: Raphael is the healing archangel, bringing protection, especially of children and the vulnerable, and the healing of mind, body, and spirit. He helps to clear away technological and chemical pollution and the adverse effects of modern living.

In this coil, focus on guidance and sustenance for all who are lost, emotionally or spiritually, and those who are on pilgrimages. Also focus on healing rituals for people, animals, or the planet. Raphael can be invoked for preventing the destruction of natural areas by industrial, chemical, or nuclear plants. See the description of Mercury earlier in this chapter.

Coil 7: Gabriel, the integrator, brings increased spiritual awareness through prayer and meditation and increases spirituality within the family and work environment. Gabriel also protects water creatures and cleanses polluted seas, lakes, and rivers.

In this coil, focus on mystical experiences, astral travel, significant dreams, and the cosmic memory bank. Gabriel can also be invoked to assist in industrial disputes, especially those where workers are being exploited or may lose their livelihoods, and to help with negotiations in places with a history of discord between people of the same nation or of opposing religions and doctrines. See the description of the moon earlier in this chapter.

WALKING THE ARCHANGEL LABYRINTH

You may wish to walk a seven-coil labyrinth in an ecclesiastical building or you may choose to create one of your own at dawn or dusk, in the open air or indoors. My favorite time to construct the labyrinth on a beach or in the earth is just as dawn is breaking, with the entrance in the east. For an indoor labyrinth, you may even decide to paint a silver and gold one on a floor in your home, if necessary placing a carpet or a large rug over it so you can use the room for other purposes. Alternatively, use a miniature one.

Mark the entrance to each coil beforehand with a crystal for the angel who rules it, for example, a jade in coil five for Anael (Venus). As I spiral through I pick up the crystal and place it in a drawstring bag I hang from my wrist. Afterward, I use the crystals for divinatory purposes if the questions I have are especially important or I feel in need of guidance. When I leave the labyrinth, I walk out toward the newly risen sun.

Alternatively, in a sheltered place, I make the labyrinth with the entrance in the direction of the setting sun. I then place garden torches or small nightlights in containers in each of the archangel colors at each of the coil entrances. When I leave the labyrinth, I walk out toward the last rays of light or into the welcoming dusk.

Within your own labyrinth, place a circle of small white candles at a safe distance around the perimeter coil (ideally twelve candles, each thirty degrees apart, to represent the zodiac wheel or the twelve months of the passing year). Alternatively, place four large candles for the four elements and directions: green or brown in the north for the element of earth, yellow in the east for the element of air, orange or red in the south for the element of fire, and blue in the west for the element of water.

Some people carry a beeswax candle in a very deep holder that will not get hot, a lit sagebrush smudge stick to smudge the coils (see chapter 6), or a crystal sphere between their hands. The sphere, my chosen object for angelic labyrinth walking, will give you reflections of your angel as you walk. The offering is then placed in the center of the labyrinth. Others rely on different rhythms of movement and chants to connect with the sanctity. You will not walk the coils in numerical order but in sacred order.

If possible, have a bath to which a few drops of lavender or rose essential oil have been added, and spend some quiet time before beginning your walk.

To perform an archangel connection ritual:

1. Stand at the entrance to the labyrinth, facing the center. See the cross that forms the axis within the labyrinth as a shaft of pure life linking heaven and earth, time and space. You will link your chakras, or psychic energy points, within your body to the labyrinth energies.

2. Touch the center of your brow with your power hand (the one you write with) and say, "Before me the pathway."

3. Touch the center of your throat and say, "Before me the utterances of the truth within my heart."

4. Touch the center of your chest between the breasts and say, "Enter my heart as you inspire my mind and my words."

5. Touch the area of your womb or genitals and say, "With all my being—body, mind, and soul—make me a vessel of truth and purity."

6. Place your right arm and hand across your left shoulder and say, "Cassiel, Sachiel, Samael, Michael, Anael, Raphael, Gabriel—archangels all." Move your hand across to the left shoulder in a horizontal line, completing the cross on your body and say, "Protect, inspire, guard, and guide me lest I fall." Of course, you can also create and substitute your own archangel invocations.

7. Beginning with coil three, Samael (or Uriel if you wish), visualize spirals of red-colored mist. In the mist, see Samael hovering above and enclosing the coil, formed from shades of red, from pink and scarlet to ruby and damson, in intricate light patterns that are themselves many tiny labyrinths. Invoke Samael with this chant (silently if there are strangers around and you feel self-conscious): "Samael, protect the weak, make me strong in pursuit of justice as I fight the foes within and beyond that beset me and would keep me from fighting on behalf of the oppressed." You may feel power entering you like a shower of warm rain or light bubbles. When you reach the end of the coil, turn and thank Samael for his gifts.

8. In coil two, Sachiel, visualize brilliant blue rays flooding this coil and, in a deeper blue, Sachiel himself, who is the pathway and the sky above. Invoke Sachiel with this chant: "Sachiel, bring abundance to those who have little, and help me to succeed in my chosen path, so I may help others on their way." You may feel the power entering you like a shimmering, shiver-inducing waterfall. When you reach the end of the coil, turn and thank Sachiel for his gifts.

9. In coil one, Cassiel, visualize deep indigo and amethyst light as filtered through stained glass windows and, just visible, the outline of Cassiel above the labyrinth, his hands raised in blessing. Invoke Cassiel with this chant: "Cassiel, conserve the ancient wisdom of the ancestors. Help me to work within the external constraints and limitations, preserving what is of worth whether from the old or new worlds." You may feel the power entering you like gossamer threads. When you reach the end of the coil, turn and thank Cassiel for his gifts.

10. In coil four, Michael, visualize golden rays cascading all around and Michael himself framed by the sun, his halo drawing and reflecting the rays. Invoke Michael with this chant: "Michael, bring light to all who are in darkness; fill me with inspiration that I may create what is of beauty and so express the half-formed visions within me for the good of my fellow creatures." His power may enter you as shafts of light or you may feel an inner flame kindling. When you reach the end of the coil, turn and thank Michael for his gifts.

11. In coil seven, Gabriel, visualize a silver shimmering mist resting on the surface of water and Gabriel reflected within it, like a fire opal or the iridescent, multicolored effect of light on pearls. Invoke Gabriel with this chant: "Gabriel, reveal your mystical wisdom to a world jaded by materialism; help me to understand and interpret the hidden world I see reflected dimly in my dreams, the ripples in the water, and the voices in the wind." His power may gently penetrate you like dancing moonbeams and tiny stars. When you reach the end of the coil, turn and thank Gabriel for his gifts.

12. In coil six, Raphael, visualize rays of pale yellow like early-morning sunlight filtered through trees and Raphael himself, a gray-winged form with a halo of buttercup yellow enclosing his whole body like a sphere. Invoke Raphael with this chant: "Raphael, heal all who cry out in sorrow and pain; let me, too, learn to bring healing to creatures, people, and places and make me a channel of your blessings." His power may enter you through thousands of tiny crystalline balls of pale yellow light. When you reach the end of the coil, turn and thank Raphael for his gifts.

13. In coil five, Anael, visualize pink and green light flooding the coil and Anael swathed in flowers and greenery. Invoke Anael with this chant: "Anael, bring peace to the world and to all nations; help me experience harmony and unconditional love that I may enter the sacred center of stillness." His power may enter you as herbs and flowers that shower down in fragrant

softness. When you reach the end of the coil, turn and thank Anael for his gifts.

14. Finally, move into the center and sit or stand entirely motionless. Breathe gently in through your nose and visualize the pure light pouring down all around from above and the rich ruby radiance of mother earth rising through your feet, or your perineum if you are sitting. Exhale through your nose any darkness.

15. As you establish the rhythm of breathing, say in your mind on every inhalation, "I see the light, I am the light," and say on the exhalation, "There is nothing but the light."

16. When you are quite still in your mind and soul, open yourself to the light. You may experience a connection with all life and perhaps the source of divinity; you may see angelic realms, hear words that relate to your innermost self, or be prophetic and global in focus. You may smell the fragrances of a thousand unseen flowers or be filled with peace and a sense of coming home.

17. You should not feel sad on your outward journey, for you carry within you the blessings of the archangels. As you walk out of the labyrinth, maintain your inner stillness and do not structure the experience; instead flow from one archangel color and sensation to the other and accept any channeling or visions as a bonus.

18. Outside of the labyrinth once more, sit quietly in the cathedral gazing at the stories illustrated in the stained glass windows or outdoors watching the waves or the grass blowing in the wind. Spend time drawing, painting, or writing down your experiences in your labyrinth journal. Start a page for each archangel that you can add to when you repeat the exercise. As you continue to work with the labyrinth, you will find that each experience becomes increasingly meaningful.

Divination with the Seven-Coil Labyrinth

Labyrinths have been associated with divination since Roman times. Virgil, in his epic, *The Aeneid,* which told of the travels of the hero, Aeneas, described an image of a labyrinth at the entrance to the cave of the Sibyl, the prophetess at the Cumaean temple of Apollo.

Because walking or meditating on a labyrinth does induce an altered state of consciousness, it is a good method of cutting through the conscious blocks that can prevent us from making wise decisions. It alerts us to the calling of the inner voice, which has knowledge of factors beyond the immediate context. However, sometimes we may wish to focus specifically on divining the answer to a question, and you can use a labyrinth as the medium for this kind of divination. The seven-coil labyrinth is by far the most successful, since it corresponds directly with the planets and the archangels who may indicate the best course to take. There are a number of ways you can use a seven-coil labyrinth specifically for divination.

Focus initially on either the planetary energies or the archangels, depending on whether your questions relate to earthly matters and relationships (planetary energies) or spiritual development and the inner world (archangels). Orient yourself before beginning divination, toward either the planetary or the angelic energies. For each planet and archangel I have listed a specific crystal that works especially well in this kind of divination. Use the same colored crystals for either method (except when you are working with Uriel, whose stones differ from those of Mars, with whom he shares a coil).

You may also prefer to create separate sets of stones for each method. Start with pure-white stones about the size of a medium-sized egg. You can find these stones on a shore, a river bank, or a hillside. For your planet stones, mark each stone with a planetary glyph (see the list of planetary glyphs earlier in this chapter). The archangel stones can be painted or engraved with the name of each archangel. You can use anything from a permanent marker to proper etching tools. You could also paint tiny angels in their appropriate colors on the stones.

Stones and crystals in your divination set should be of uniform size and shape to make conscious identification difficult. The conscious mind is like a curious child and can be very determined to interfere in the adult process of unconscious wisdom. Keep your crystals in a drawstring bag made of a natural fiber.

I have found the following seven crystals to be especially potent for labyrinth divination:

The Moon/Gabriel: moonstone

Mercury/Raphael: citrine

Venus/Anael: rose quartz

The Sun/Michael: clear crystal quartz

Mars/Samael: carnelian (with Uriel, I use amethyst)

Jupiter/Sachiel: lapis lazuli

Saturn/Cassiel: obsidian

CHOOSING YOUR METHOD

There are two methods of casting the stones. The first method is to cast from the center outward as you stand in a full-size labyrinth. The second method is to cast from the outside in, sitting or kneeling outside of a miniature labyrinth. Both are equally effective.

With either method, the coil names and meanings are the same as those you have already learned for the planets and archangels. You may wish to alter or add to these meanings as your divination work progresses, keeping a special section in your labyrinth journal for recording these alterations or additions.

The coil into which the crystal falls tells you the area in which any change or decision should be made (it may not be the area you expect), and the crystal itself tells you the qualities or strengths you need to galvanize to bring about fulfillment, success, and happiness.

CASTING THE STONES

Create a seven-coil labyrinth on sand or in earth, or draw one on a large piece of cardboard or canvas. You might like to reserve this particular labyrinth for your divination work. It should be just large enough for you to kneel or stand in the center, roughly eight to nine feet square. Before you begin, decide which crystals you will cast (planetary or archangel) according to the nature of the question (earthly or spiritual).

To cast the stones:

1. Travel to the center of the labyrinth, clearing your mind of all clutter, including the issue on which you will be working, to allow the unconscious mind to resurface.

2. As you sit in the center facing the entrance, formulate your question and, if possible, translate it into symbols in your mind. Visualization is a powerful way of connecting with your unconscious wisdom.

3. Take one stone out of your bag, allowing your fingers to choose the stone that feels right in your hand, there being no reason to look at it. Repeat your question either aloud or in your mind and focus on the symbol in your mind as you ask it.

4. One at a time, take two more stones from the bag, again being guided by your hand, and cast the stones one at a time onto the labyrinth.

5. Now, look at the stones and see where they have landed. The first stone will define the issue. The second will give you a course of action or a suggested path. The third will show you the possible outcome if you follow that path. I say *possible* because the future is not fixed; it changes because of your own action or inaction.

To use the second method of casting:

1. Draw, paint, or otherwise create a miniature labyrinth.

2. Closing your eyes to focus on the question, take a stone from your bag and cast it on the labyrinth.

3. Take a second and a third stone and cast them in the same way.

4. Look at the stones and see where they have landed. The significance of each is the same as those discussed in step five, above.

Divination (the practice of consulting the goddess or god within us all) can be very valuable in allowing us to understand, and thereby control and direct, our destiny. Through it we can tap into the wisdom of the ancestors and go beyond the constraints of linear time.

INTERPRETING YOUR READINGS

Interpreting your reading is largely an intuitive process. Though I explain what each stone means in each coil, everyone must attach their own personal significance to the basic ideas. Once you have read through the basic meanings, relax and just let the ideas, words, and images flow through your mind.

To interpret your reading:

1. Whether you are working with a walkable labyrinth or a miniature labyrinth, begin by interpreting the first stone cast. This stone will define the issue or question you have asked. Note that this issue or question may end up being different from the question you posed—it may very well end up being a question that you must resolve before moving on to your stated concern. There are, as stated earlier, two factors for each part of the reading: the significance of the stone and the coil in which the stone fell. Sometimes, this information is immediately clear; if it isn't, just work on the significance when you have the whole picture. Sometimes when you cast a stone in a particular coil, you know exactly what it means. But if it doesn't seem to make sense, wait until you have cast all the stones. When you have all of the pieces, like a jigsaw puzzle, the reading will make sense.

2. Next, consider the second stone cast. This one tells of a decision you should make or actions you could take to resolve the situation and maximize your opportunities. The stone itself represents the energies you will need, and the coil in which the stone fell represents the area of your life at issue or the way the energies will be manifested.

3. The third stone suggests a potential outcome of any change or decision you make as a result of the messages sent by the second crystal. Again, the coil shows the area of your life that may be affected or the way the decision will manifest itself in the real world.

4. After you have made this initial interpretation, beginning from the center, pick up and hold each stone in turn in your cupped hands. Stand in the coil in which the stone fell (or hold it over

that coil on your miniature labyrinth). You may receive information psychically in the form of sensations through your fingertips that may be expressed as images or words in your mind. These may be symbolic and unclear; the full significance may come to you in your dreams that same night. Note these extra insights in your labyrinth journal.

5. Keep notes about your readings and illustrate them with diagrams to help you keep track of predictions, which may come true in months rather than weeks. If the reading seems incomplete, cast a final stone from the outside of either kind of labyrinth, in order to clarify the reading.

If more than one stone falls in a particular coil, then this coil is central to your life and will continue to be so. If a crystal lands in the coil ruled by its own archangel or planetary deity, it suggests that you should transfer all your energies temporarily to that area of life. Giving extra energy to that area now will have beneficial results for your long-term as well as immediate future.

Because interpretation of the results of these methods may at first seem very abstract, I include two sample readings and their interpretations below so you can see the techniques in action.

Susanne's Planetary Reading

Susanne had reached a crossroads in her life. She was in her late thirties, was divorced with no children, and had a successful career in banking in London, which allowed her to enjoy a comfortable lifestyle. But she felt that time was passing and something was missing. Her sister, Megan, owner of a struggling alternative health center in Australia had asked Susanne if she would come over for six months to help her expand the business with a view to creating a partnership if the venture did well. However, Susanne would receive only a small salary, housing, and food for those first six months. If the venture were to fail, Susanne would have given up her London home and job for nothing. What should she do?

Susanne went to the seaside for a weekend and built herself
a labyrinth on the sand. She edged it with shells and stones, a
task that took her about an hour and a half. She felt that this task
centered her and enabled her to pour her essential self into the
process so that the reading would reflect her true state.

She placed her labyrinth near (but not too near) the waves
so that afterward the labyrinth would be washed away by the sea
to help her energies merge with the cosmos. She also left the
crystals in the labyrinth as an offering to the sea. (Personalizing
a reading really helps. Some people will work with a small labyrinth on a table but will form it from clay. Others color each
coil with intricate patterns to connect with the energies inherent
in the sacred form. Whenever you create a labyrinth, large or
small, you are creating a place of power in which altered states
of consciousness will follow as you use your creation for the
purpose you choose.)

Susanne cast:

The sun, an amber, in coil five, Venus

Mars, a red jasper, in coil three, Mars

The moon, a pale blue moonstone, in coil four, the sun

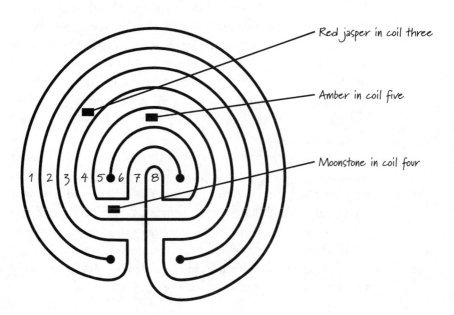

Red jasper in coil three

Amber in coil five

Moonstone in coil four

The Sun in Venus The amber sun crystal speaks of the need to seize the moment and to make a new beginning. Venus talks about relationships; Susanne realized that she had been missing her sister, her only surviving family member, but she felt that she was always too busy at work to visit.

In the short term, money was not a problem compared with her personal harmony, but it was a big step to transfer her area of living into the sphere of Venus, as she was very cynical about love and had difficulty trusting even her own sister.

When Susanne stood in the coil and held her amber stone between her hands, she felt what she described as electricity surging through her, as though she was coming alive after a long sleep. Susanne found herself crying, which she had not done in a long time—even when her husband deserted her for a woman with young children, despite having insisted to Susanne that he wanted to remain childless.

Mars in Mars Mars speaks of courage and the need for change; when the Mars stone falls in the master coil, the effect is doubled. Susanne acknowledged that she had a lot of unexpressed anger about her husband's betrayal that had, she felt, taken away her chances of having the family she so much wanted. She realized that she had recently become interested in alternative therapies, after scorning them for years, when a healer cured her of a series of allergies that conventional medicine had failed to alleviate. She also acknowledged that her older sister, who had cared for her after their mother died when Susanne was twelve, was struggling for survival.

When Susanne stood in her Mars coil holding her jasper, she felt, to her surprise, the anger flowing away. She saw in her mind an image of a warrior priestess she had seen in a book on Celtic myths in childhood, and of herself standing on rich red soil. Susanne felt excited at the possibility of a real challenge to her abilities and became determined that she would not only turn her sister's business around but also help Megan to continue to offer free treatment to all who needed it.

The Moon in the Sun The Moon mediates the outer competitive aspect of the Sun; it indicates that it might be time to withdraw, at least for a while. Susanne felt she had poured her energies outward for so long into the competitive and often harsh world of work, into her relationship with her husband, and into creating a lovely home. She had lost touch with the essential person she was inside.

Susanne hoped that she might have time to rediscover her essential self in the countryside where her sister lived and that she might explore her own healing abilities. She acknowledged that it was a risk and that she would have no guarantees her London job would still be available to her if the venture failed. Nevertheless, she also made the sudden decision to invest in a sanctuary in the countryside using the profits from the sale of her apartment and put all her efforts into the venture.

As Susanne stood in the sun coil holding her moonstone, she felt sunlight pouring into her body and filling her mind with light. She felt confident for the first time in years and saw in her mind a path of light leading into a grove of trees; she was aware of tingling in her fingers.

Susanne did go to Australia, and the center became a success. But, more significant, she herself found a real gift for healing, and now the center has a paid administrator so Susanne can concentrate on her crystal work. She has also created a special light-therapy room for children with emotional disabilities, built in the grove that stands at the edge of her sister's land.

Patrick's Archangel Reading

Patrick was ill with a chronic muscle disease in his legs that made it difficult to work or leave the house very often. Before the onset of his illness, he had traveled extensively around the world with his partner, Anna, and lived in a number of countries, making money using his extensive knowledge of languages as a foreign tourist guide.

Now he felt angry and frustrated. He found meditation and relaxation techniques unhelpful, and he was always tired because he rarely sleeps. Anna was very supportive but worked long hours to pay the bills.

With skepticism, Patrick tried the labyrinth technique at Anna's insistence. He downloaded and photocopied a classical labyrinth from the Internet and borrowed crystals from Anna. He decided to work with the archangel energies.

Patrick cast:

Cassiel, an obsidian, in coil two, Sachiel
Raphael, a citrine, in coil five, Anael
Anael, a jade, in coil two, Sachiel

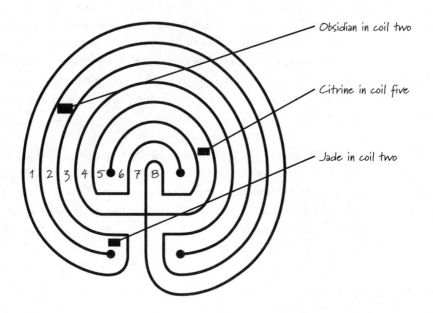

Obsidian in coil two

Citrine in coil five

Jade in coil two

Cassiel in Sachiel Patrick was not surprised to cast Cassiel, the archangel of solitude, stillness, and moderation, for he felt his own horizons had contracted so much since his illness. But Anna reminded him that Cassiel is also the angel of conservation and the keeper of wisdom.

However, Sachiel's coil spoke of expansion and increase in using what one has for the greater good. This suggested that

Patrick should use his recent limitations as a springboard for expansion, maybe into a new area.

As Sachiel is focused on preserving history and traditions, Patrick admitted that he had been considering writing a book about the need to prevent Westernization and modern technology from destroying the unique qualities of different cultures, but that he had felt too angry and depressed to focus thoughts.

As he held the obsidian crystal over the coil of Sachiel, he was, to his own surprise, aware of images of a huge book covered in gold with strange script on the front. He felt that he was being asked to carry it, though it was heavy, to save it from what appeared to be a tidal wave in the distance. Did he have the mental energy to save the knowledge of the old ways?

Raphael in Anael Raphael is the healing angel, but Patrick knew his health would slowly deteriorate and his condition would spread to other parts of his body over the coming decade. However, Patrick was aware that he had become very bitter and that this, as much as the condition, was sapping his energy.

The coil of Anael, the angel of love and the environment, seemed to be saying that he did have much to give to others. Patrick realized that, while traveling and constantly seeking new places and experiences, he had not recorded or shared his insights except with Anna. Suddenly the emphasis changed from his own helplessness to his ability to help and a new compassion for others born out of suffering.

As he held the sparkling yellow citrine crystal, Patrick was aware of light beams that seemed to be filtered through a dense rain forest, filled with the fragrances of wonderful flowers and the call of birds. He visibly relaxed as he realized the world was not lost to him but could be recalled as he spoke of his experiences and perhaps wrote them on his largely unused computer.

Anael in Sachiel A second crystal in Sachiel indicated that it was still possible for him to make a difference to others, by expanding his field of influence mentally, though he could not do so physically.

Anael was also a reminder to Patrick of how uncomplainingly Anna had supported him over the years and that he had been unappreciative of that love. Patrick had recently been asked to give a lecture to young people who had a more acute form of the illness, but he had declined. Patrick now knew he could not easily shed his own bitterness, but that he was surrounded by love and could in turn help others to reach acceptance and inner harmony.

As he held the jade crystal over Sachiel, Patrick felt as though he were being rocked on a very gentle blue sea, lulled by the sweetest singing of voices from another world.

After the reading, Patrick was his usual bluff, cynical self, but slowly he did make changes, researching the traditions of cultures he had visited. He has now started to record his own experiences of societies fast fading, though he has decided not to publish a book but to offer his insights to organizations that contribute aid to areas in need. He has joined an Internet group for people with his illness and is gathering research about ways of alleviating the condition's symptoms and slowing its progression. Anna has made a labyrinth in the garden, and, when he thinks no one is watching, Patrick sits in the middle.

More Complex Divination

When planning a major life change or for a life review, you can combine planetary and archangel energies. You will need to make yourself a set of dual-focus crystals with the planetary glyphs marked on one side; the other side will represent the corresponding archangel energy (draw or paint the outline of the angels on the crystals).

BLESSING THE STONES

As these are very special stones, you may wish to bless them before using them for the first time. You can also bless your separate planet and archangel stones this way.

To bless your planetary or archangel stones:

1. Place the crystals in a circle.

2. Scatter a ring of salt around the crystal circle to represent the ancient element of earth and say, "Mother earth, bless and sanctify this, my endeavor, and may your wisdom that went into forming these crystals take root and flourish in my daily endeavors."

3. Light a frankincense or sandalwood incense stick. Make a clockwise circle in the air just beyond the circle of salt, to represent the element of air, and say, "Father Sky, bless and sanctify this, my endeavor, and may your focused energies that went into the formation of these crystals cut through my illusions and remove all distractions from my true purpose."

4. Light an orange or red candle for the element of fire. Make a second clockwise circle in the air with the flame, just beyond the smoke circle, and say, "Brother fire, bless and sanctify this, my endeavor, and may your creativity that went into the formation of these crystals likewise inspire me to forge a new, more fruitful destiny." If you place your circle of crystals on a metal tray, you can also create a circle of candle wax around the circle of salt.

5. Finally, using water in which a clear crystal quartz or amethyst has been soaked for eight hours, sprinkle a few drops over the circle of salt to represent the ancient element of water, and say, "Sister water, bless and sanctify this, my endeavor, and may your tides that went into the formation of these crystals likewise help me to ebb and flow with what cannot be changed and to trust my inner as well as outer vision."

You have now created a mystical triple circle of protection, made up of the four elements, encircling your crystals. These four elements form, in their psychic fusion, a quintessence, or the fifth element, of pure spirit, the magical vibration that enables you to move in your divinatory work beyond the confines of the material world, time, and space. You can use this method of sanctifying your crystals before any major reading.

READING WITH YOUR DUAL-FOCUS CRYSTALS

Walk into the center of your full-size labyrinth gently and slowly, inhaling the rainbow colors and exhaling, in a smooth, continuous rhythm. In a miniature labyrinth, if you are using one, light a tiny candle of any color in each of the coils or visualize the color spreading inward and combining to create pure white or golden light in the center.

To read with your dual-focus crystals:

1. Put your hand in your crystal bag and remove three stones at once, taking as long as you need until the stones feel right.

2. Cast your three stones at the same time, this time allowing the unconscious forces to speak to you through the crystals rather than formulating a question. You can read the crystals in any order, but note which face is uppermost, since this will help you to identify the focus of the coil.

3. If you have cast more planet crystals than archangel crystals, the bias is toward action or decisions in the outer world, and toward the need to get yourself on track before diverting energies to help others. If you have cast more archangel crystals than planet crystals, this preponderance indicates that you need to make inner changes or decisions or focus your efforts toward helping others, thereby attracting positive energies into your own life. This change will only occur if you do have the inner resources available. There are times when, unless we build up our own strengths and sort out difficulties in our own lives, we cannot effectively tackle global issues.

4. Hold each crystal in turn from the innermost coil outward, allowing it to speak through your fingers and allowing impressions to enter your heart in the form of feelings and to enter your mind in the form of words and images.

5. Record your findings and any immediate insights, so you can refer to them later, since sometimes these more profound readings can take a while to unravel.

6. Finally, place the three crystals back into the bag, and, while holding it, ask either silently or aloud, "Who will be my guide?"

With your eyes closed, take a final crystal, again slowly, and clasp it in your power hand (the one you write with) but do not throw it on to the labyrinth. Open your hand and note which face is uppermost to see whether a planetary ruler or an archangel will guide you in the days ahead with all of his particular strengths and qualities.

You can carry out divinatory readings for yourself about once a month or when a need arises. Sometimes, you may wish to combine divination with a visit to a public labyrinth at a time when it is deserted, walking through the coils and meditating or chanting to open the channels for divination. Alternatively, add divination to rituals or meditation in your labyrinths at home, large or small, as a way of drawing together all the insights and channeled wisdom you have received.

Divination may seem to be an unusual activity for labyrinth work, but the labyrinth form is ideal for helping us understand our own deep unconscious wisdom and the wisdom of planets and archangels as well. Labyrinth pathways represent our walk through life; by linking the labyrinth coils with the different powers and qualities of planets and archangels, we can tap into information that we only realize on an unconscious level.

In the next chapter we will work with the labyrinth as a tool and channel for healing energies. We will remain on the higher planes that we explored in this chapter, but we will work on bringing the powers down to restore health and harmony to our lives.

Chapter 8

LABYRINTHS FOR HEALING

I N A SENSE, all labyrinth work involves healing, because the very act of creating and walking a labyrinth uplifts the spirit and creates a sea of harmony that extends to every level of being. Increasingly, modern physicians and psychologists are accepting that body and mind are two related parts of the human makeup, and that without their integration with the spirit or soul any healing is at best partial. Moreover, disease may recur if the root causes are not resolved, which may require a change in lifestyle and perspective.

The labyrinth is the symbol of wholeness and so can offer in its sacred space a chance to reintegrate the disparate parts of our selves. Labyrinths are increasingly being recognized as tools of healing. For example, a labyrinth at the California Pacific Medical Center in San Francisco (see chapter 12) is used not only by patients but also by their caregivers, especially friends and family members. They can often resolve—within the coils—their own anxieties and frustrations that arise from coping with a loved one's illness.

The labyrinth is a good tool to use to restore balance and counter obsessions, compulsions, and hyperactivity. Pupils with learning difficulties at St. Joseph's School, Cranleigh, in Surrey, England, will soon have their own permanent labyrinth, created from paving stones, shingles, and more than three thousand lavender plants. Deputy head teacher Mary Fawcett realized that children with severe autism or Down syndrome with communication difficulties could attain a state of tranquility while carrying out a walking meditation. The labyrinth will be based on the Chartres pattern, measuring more than sixty feet in diameter. Ms. Fawcett has discovered that labyrinth walking gives the children an enhanced sense of self-esteem and increased spiritual awareness of the environment and of God. In my own experience, children as well as adults are able to break spirals of anxiety by walking a labyrinth regularly.

The Labyrinth and Pain Relief

I have already written about the Hindu midwives who use a labyrinthine form to help women in labor. I myself use the small five-circuit stone labyrinth in my garden when the pain from my gallbladder condition becomes too intense. Until I built the labyrinth, I would frequently curl up in pain. Walking the coils rhythmically or tracing with my fingers the coils of a labyrinth drawn on paper seems to create a semihypnotic state that distances me from the pain but leaves my mind relaxed but aware. Sometimes, I draw four labyrinths around a center on paper, tracing the coils with my finger, and return to the center as I leave each one. Generally, by the time I reach the fourth I am in control of the pain, rather than the other way around.

Physiologically, labyrinth walking is helpful because meditative states induce the brain to produce slower alpha and theta waves, which release endorphins, natural painkillers. This same principle is used in hypnosis, a method increasingly used not only for pain relief but also during minor surgery, replacing anesthesia.

The reduction of physical tension also eases anxiety, which leads to increased pain. This is especially so with a condition like gallstones, where every time you anticipate the next bout you tense up, causing a sensation that is like squeezing a fistful of sharp stones. Full-size labyrinth walking also helps with headaches and migraines; however, working with miniature labyrinths is less helpful with these complaints, especially when the head pain is accompanied by flashing lights and visual disturbances.

A baby's teething pain or colic may be eased by being pushed in a stroller or carried in a baby carrier around a labyrinth (if the coils are wide enough for a stroller), bringing sleep to the infant—and relaxation to the exhausted parent, who may be so tired as to be beyond rest.

You may find, as many people have, that the act of walking the labyrinth and breathing gently and slowly in the center relieves pain quite spontaneously. But if you are worn down by pain, it can be hard to focus your mind on healing, and so a ritual may be needed in order to externalize the pain. The act of symbolically shedding pain, using your mind power, can actually move it from within you to beyond you.

Below is an exercise I have developed and used in the relief of a variety of pains with my family, especially among the women who suffer from hormone-related discomforts such as premenstrual to menopausal symptoms. The outdoor labyrinth works wonders for my own menopausal hot flushes, even on a hot day, seeming to steady my hormones.

This ritual is also especially helpful with chronic pain or an illness that has lasted many months and has depleted your energies. It can be repeated at regular intervals. The ritual action of shedding dead leaves or petals, which represent pain, galvanizes self-healing energies that are amplified by the power of the sacred form of the labyrinth.

In a miniature labyrinth use powdered dried herbs. Alternatively, use smudge smoke to represent the pain, asking the trails of smoke to carry it away and transform it, and afterward extinguishing and burying the smudge. Smudging is not advisable for pregnant women, people with chronic lung or breathing difficulties, and young children.

To use labyrinths to control pain or discomfort:

1. Depending on the nature of the pain you may decide to work a seven-coil labyrinth or a larger one. If a problem is complex then you may find that working with a labyrinth with more coils offers extra power for healing. Stand at the entrance to your labyrinth with a small basket of dead leaves, petals, or dried herbs that are powerful for healing, such as rosemary, sage, or thyme. You need not use very many.

2. Say, either aloud or in your mind, "I carry my pain to be transformed into healing light and so I enter in faith to lay my burden down." As with any prescribed labyrinth rituals you can substitute your own words.

3. Walk into the labyrinth. As you walk the coils, say rhythmically, aloud if possible, "Thus I cast away all pain and walk into the light of healing; light of healing, light of loveliness, enfold me." Visualize light flowing along the coils to meet you and filling your being with gentle warmth; this feeling is like being immersed in a warm sunlit swimming pool, melting away rigidity and pain.

4. When you reach the center, stand holding your basket, facing the way you will return. Picture any remaining pain, or the chronic disease, as a single dark, tight knot in your body or head, or as a knotted cord throughout your entire body, depending on the location of the pain or other symptoms.

5. Breathe in healing golden light flowing through the center of the labyrinth and absorb the warmth through every pore to melt the knot a little with each inhalation.

   As you breathe out through your mouth with a sigh, imagine that you are directing the dark knot in the form of a long black tendril of smoke, out of your body. Continue slow, deep, steady breathing, inhaling light and exhaling darkness, feeling the knot diminishing within and the light filling you with radiance.

6. When you feel completely light inside, begin your outward journey, scattering a few leaves or herbs on each coil, chanting, "Flow and go, pain, sorrow healing grow, peace to know." The leaves will either blow away or be absorbed and transformed by mother earth. Any leaves that remain in your basket you can bury near the labyrinth in your garden afterward or, if it is a windy day (or if the labyrinth you are using is one where you're not permitted to scatter leaves or petals), take to an open place where they may naturally disperse.

7. Facing the labyrinth center once more, visualize the golden rays still flowing toward you. Touch yourself in the spot where the pain was at its worst and say, "Whenever I feel pain here or in

any other part of my body, I will rub my hands three times gently counterclockwise on the spot; the discomfort or tension will disperse, replaced by the inflow of light and healing from this sacred center." If you have been working with a personally created labyrinth or a finger one, you can conclude the ritual by sweeping away the shed leaves or herbs in counterclockwise circles, so the labyrinth is quite empty once more.

8.   You may wish to recite one of the traditional folk chants our great-great-grandmothers used when they were cleansing their homes, not only of physical dirt but also of negative vibes: "Out with sorrow, out with pain, joyous things alone remain. Dust to dust, away you must, nine, eight, seven, six, five, four, three, two, one, sorrow begone."

Healing the Pain of the Modern World

Because so many of us live frantic lives and are assailed by constant noise, stimulation, and activity, it is all too easy to lose contact with the natural rhythms of life. Our ancestors were aware of the cycles of the moon and of the seasons and, before the invention of electricity and powered machinery, rested more during the long winter nights. Now we have twenty-four-hour-a-day heating and lighting, shift work, all-night supermarkets, and nonstop overstimulating entertainment. As a result, we can experience either burnout or an inability to relax.

Up to the Second World War, fresh, seasonal food was considered a prized commodity, with special meals mainly at feast times such as the harvest or Christmas. Now, in the Westernized world, we have a choice of foods out of season. Better transport and refrigeration have taken away the need to buy food daily as my family did when I was a child. Despite these advances, food-related disorders, either excessive dieting to conform to an impossible beauty ideal or overeating and drinking, have reached almost epidemic proportions.

The following is a labyrinth ritual to reconnect with the pleasure of food and the experience of genuine hunger. I have used food as a focus here, since dieting is a multi-million-dollar industry that too often leads people, women especially, into developing cravings. But you could instead use the ritual for breaking an addiction to cigarettes or cutting down on alcohol.

I have used oranges to symbolize all that is sweet and fragrant and pleasurable, but if you do not like oranges or are allergic to them, choose a food that gives you real pleasure. Try to avoid foods that are addictive—for example, chocolate—there are many other foods that can suggest sensuous pleasure and oral satisfaction.

If possible, work in a turf labyrinth. If you are creating your own labyrinth, strew the pathways with fragrant herbs, lavender, rose petals, or pine needles. You can use a labyrinth of any size, but I would recommend a maximum of nine circuits. The labyrinth could be a large table one; just make the center large enough to hold fruit or another food you enjoy.

To reconnect with the pleasures of food:

1. Avoid eating for a few hours ahead of time. Before you begin, place your symbol in the center. In this case I used a small cloth and five or six small sweet oranges for the focus. Also place a hairbrush in the center.

2. If your labyrinth is on a hard surface, set a rug in the center to sit on.

3. Stand facing the entrance and walk slowly into the labyrinth visualizing on either side rich orange groves, pine forests, or banks of fluffy clouds. Allow any thoughts or anxieties to float away by sending them upward in bubbles, so as you walk further inward the stillness increases. If you find it hard to relax, breathe slowly in and out, allowing one breath to follow another like waves in the sea.

4. When you reach the center, sit in a visualized grove of dark green orange trees below a brilliant blue sky with the sun caressing you. You are hungry and thirsty. Feel the sensation for a moment, breathing deeply and slowly so that it does not overwhelm you.

5. Stretch out your hand into the basket of fruit and feel a small, ripe orange. The fruit is warm, and the peel is pliant, rich with the flesh and juice pressing from within. There are many more, small and large, in the basket and on the visualized trees to be

taken at any time, so you can eat exactly as much or as little as you want. Check to determine whether you still feel hungry.

6. Hold the fruit in your hand, feeling its weight, the texture of the peel, the tangy smell. There is plenty of time. Pierce the rind with your fingernails, and taste the sudden spurt of sweet juice.

7. Peel the fruit, separate it into segments, and bite into one, very slowly savoring the taste and feeling the sensual warmth of the visualized sun on your face mingling with the growing sweetness within. The insects are humming, and colorful butterflies are all round. You are sleepy and content.

8. Close your eyes and slowly eat the orange, savoring every mouthful. You are warm, content. You can eat another orange if you wish or return to the grove at another time, whenever you feel the need.

9. If you do not want to eat any more, visualize yourself giving the rest of the oranges to golden-skinned children who are running barefoot through the grove. Hear their laughter and laugh yourself because you are happy to be alive. Be glad you are who you are, that you are what you are. Let any fears of inadequacy, ugliness, or loneliness float upward through the trees in sunlit bubbles to return to the sun; imagine these bubbles falling again as beautiful sunbeams, transforming you and allowing you to experience satisfaction with the person you are right now.

10. Look upward through the dark green leaves at the sky, and as you do so brush your hair just above your left ear and say, "Whenever I feel compelled to eat when I am not hungry, I will brush my hair and recall my total control over my body and awareness of its needs. If not hungry, I will make myself happy another way. If I am hungry, I will choose what to eat and enjoy it." You can change the empowerment if you want to overcome over-reliance on cigarettes, alcohol, pain killers, tranquilizers, or another substance that has become a prop in your life.

11. Open your eyes and eat more oranges if you want to. Leave the uneaten ones on the cloth in the center of the labyrinth as a gift for whoever follows you. Maybe birds or animals will eat them.

THE SHADOW IN THE LABYRINTH

We all have fears and anxieties, some of which are based in reality but can still hold us back from making positive change. Equally, some fears and guilty feelings can linger from the past, sometimes holding us back from taking opportunities or developing new relationships. The voices in our heads that remind us of past failures and childhood emotional wounds can linger throughout the years, so that even a successful business executive can suddenly feel like a clumsy child or unloved son or daughter when he or she makes a mistake or thinks about trying something new.

The labyrinth is very healing for emotional and spiritual pain, and this can be quite a moving experience. I would recommend that, if possible, you walk a sacred labyrinth in a church or a cathedral, even if you are not a Christian. Alternatively, create a labyrinth by the sea, where the tide will carry away what you leave in the center. You could draw a labyrinth in earth or sand so you can wash it away. The following ritual is an excellent one to try if you are carrying emotional or spiritual pain.

Spirits were believed to only move in straight lines; hence labyrinths were meant to trap trolls and other dark beings. The demons we create within us are equally as frightening as the dark external phantoms of our ancestors. Once we have externalized this negativity and trapped it in the coils, it can no longer return to haunt us. This method heals anger, pain left from broken relationships, or sorrow from betrayal and all forms of abuse.

Work in the early evening, if possible during the period of the waning moon, a very good time for taking away sorrow. Take nothing with you into the labyrinth. If you are creating one, spend the latter part of the afternoon creating a seven- or nine-coil labyrinth, endowing it with all the ebbing emotions. Say good-bye to all the words that ever made you sad or angry, the people who manipulated your feelings and then accused you of being jealous or possessive, the lost opportunities, the unfair criticism, the spite that wounded your sensitive heart, the guilt for that which you were too inexperienced to prevent.

To face the shadow in the labyrinth:

1. If you are walking a labyrinth in a church or cathedral, before beginning light a candle or sit looking at the altar, laying down in your heart all the burdens you can no longer carry. When daylight is fading, walk into the labyrinth, concentrating on your feet and the pathways.

2. When you reach the center, stand facing away from the entrance; slowly and gently breathe in the healing light of early evening. Exhale, in the form of a sigh through your mouth, the darkness within, establishing a very slow, natural rhythm that feels right. In front of you, you will see a shape forming from the dark exhaled mist. This is nothing malevolent, merely the darkness that was your pain and tension and that now has a definite, two-dimensional form.

3. Try to identify what the shape represents to you. Take your time. Once you have discovered the true source of your pain with the help of the labyrinth energies, you'll be able to remove that pain in the next steps in the ritual. What is it? Does the shape represent a person who has caused you pain, undigested anger, regrets, your job, a tangle of unfinished tasks, muddled finances, or an accumulation of hastily swallowed junk food during frantic weeks of stress-filled activity? Or does it represent past unkindness, betrayed love, inadequate parenting that has left you unsure of your worth, or a cruel or overcritical, insecure partner? It may even represent a combination of people and situations.

4. If you do not recognize the shape, ask it to tell you its name or what it represents. Understand and acknowledge the dark form as a part of you that you no longer need.

5. Now visualize the dark form with golden wings or enclosed in beautiful, swirling pink and lilac mists. The form is nothing to hate or fear or punish; it is merely misdirected energy that, once released from its prison within you, can be transformed into creative energies. Let the form rise upward, to be reabsorbed by the fading sun, join with the moon, or become a star. Dew was once believed to be mankind's discarded dreams and regrets,

transformed by the moonlight. Create your own concept of regeneration using this idea for inspiration.

6.   When the form has gone, slowly move back through the coils and out into the world, letting the sounds and sensations return.

7.   If you created the labyrinth, wash it away, either waiting for the tide to remove it or throwing buckets of water over it, saying, "Go in peace, darkness to light."

In your life, replace what has gone from you with positive action, such as a new activity, a reappraisal of finances and career, or a job-retraining course. If you have suffered a lot of sorrow or pain, you may need to repeat this ritual many times over a period of months. Each time the shadow will be smaller, until finally there is nothing left but peace in the center.

If walking a full-size labyrinth is not possible, you can use the labyrinth below, which can be created on a table, made from clay or drawn in pencil, and then rubbed out or dismantled. An ideal do-it-yourself labyrinth for the healing process, this five-coil design can be found in chapters 4 and 6, along with directions on how to make it. It takes you in to the center and out again before leading you back to the center once more.

After you have made this labyrinth, you can use it with the adapted ritual below, for releasing your emotional pain. Begin at the entrance with your burden of sorrow. Walk to the center in your mind or by tracing the path with a fingertip and carry out the breathing exercise in step two of the shadow ritual. Then begin your walk to the outer circle, symbolically shedding your burdens on each circuit. When you reach the outer circle, pause for a moment and feel your sorrows lifting. Now you are ready to continue back to the heart of the labyrinth—your inner self—where you can stop and feel yourself being reborn without that weight of guilt and pain. Stay there until you are ready to rejoin the world.

UNTANGLING THE PAIN

Sometimes personal pain can be caused by frustration over being held back—either by other people or by situations that keep you from fulfilling your potential. You can become entangled in destructive situations or feel knotted inside because of fear, guilt, anger, or confusion. You can feel lost in a maze of conflicting demands or opinions.

Because the labyrinth is unicursal, its gentle spirals can untangle the knots. This is an excellent ritual for stress-related conditions, allergies, chest conditions such as asthma, digestive disorders, skin problems, mobility problems caused by stiff limbs or joints, and panic attacks and phobias.

Work with a simple labyrinth form with nine coils or fewer. Choose a setting by the sea or one where you can sweep or wash away all traces afterward. You can also draw a table labyrinth with pencil on white paper and walk the coils with your index finger, afterward erasing the coils from the center outward.

To untangle the pain using a labyrinth:

1. Use a piece of dark cord or rope for each of the issues involved, not forgetting emotions such as anger, frustration, and confusion. Attach a silver letter opener or small penknife to your belt or to another cord tied around your waist.

2. As you walk toward the center, knot the cords together in intricate patterns, naming each and chanting the ancient knot

rhyme, "Tangle the anger, tangle the pain, by these knots make me free again."

3. When you reach the center, sit with your tangled web and again state the confusion or pain you feel.

4. Then cut the web with the knife, saying: "Tangle the anger, tangle the pain, I cut the knots and am free again." You may need to make many cuts. As you do so visualize the bonds that hold you melting away.

5. Wriggle and stretch and sway and dance in the center as you feel yourself able to move unconstrained. When you exit the center, leave the knots behind you, if you are working on sand, and let the sea carry them away with the labyrinth. If you are using a private labyrinth you can leave the cords in the center and sweep them away afterward, repeating the sweeping chant given in the pain-relief ritual earlier in this chapter. Use a small brush and pan to sweep clean a table labyrinth.

6. Scatter seeds on to the ground outside the labyrinth or at a more suitable spot close by, in order to bring new life. Indoors, intro-duce an herb or potted plant to the area in which you work.

Joint Labyrinth Work to Heal Relationships

In chapter 6, I mentioned how the labyrinth walk is like a dance in which people meet as they pass on the different coils, sometimes close enough to touch hands before parting again as the labyrinth pathways diverge. Here I come back to this theme, this time using it as a method of healing breaches in a relationship.

I first discovered this idea of meeting people on the paths when I went to the fifteen-coil turf labyrinth, complete with a world tree, in the private garden at Troy Farm at Somerton, near Bicester in Oxfordshire, England. No one really knows why it is there. It may be that the land once belonged to a monastery and that the labyrinth was constructed for use by the monks. Another theory suggests it was once part of an ornamental garden. It has been lovingly restored in recent years. (If you should visit it do ask permission at the farmhouse and offer a donation for the privilege of visiting this tranquil spot sur-

Troy Town at Somerton

rounded by trees. It is preserved by the owners at their own expense, who must haul water for the garden a good distance, across a road from the house.) One of my sons, Bill, was eventually persuaded to put down his portable video game to walk the coils with me and my husband. The three of us in the labyrinth were able to weave quite intricate patterns meeting and moving apart, which was very therapeutic.

When several people are walking the labyrinth at once, if each person begins a minute before the next, you may end up walking sometimes close to each other, at other times far apart, and at still others walking companionably on parallel coils.

You can use a labyrinth walk with a family member, partner, or lover to heal emotional wounds, doubts, and coldness or indifference. The ritual works well if you have had a misunderstanding with a friend or are engaged in intergenerational conflicts or partnership difficulties. If you choose to make a labyrinth, this can be a bonding experience as you collect and place stones or draw the coils with a stick. It is also a good way of bringing disparate family members together (see also "The Making of Relations" labyrinth on page 190). In this ritual avoid sexual contact or issues; when a relationship is right, sexual desire and fulfillment flow quite spontaneously.

To walk a labyrinth jointly:

1. First enter the labyrinth, each person beginning a minute after the other. You can add a third person to the walk, on the proviso that when two of the parties meet they can make only positive comments about the third person who is elsewhere in the labyrinth. If you invite a fourth, there may be times when you have two sets of two in the coils, and so it is essential to follow ground rules about positivity to prevent factions from forming. The ritual teaches an excellent lesson in the coordination of disparate interests as the four people harmonize in a pattern.

2. Notice how the pattern begins to emerge; pay attention to when you are close to another, and when you can touch. Each person should reflect on how the pattern mirrors or differs from your daily interactions. For example, perhaps on this first circuit you deliberately did not touch your partner even though you could have done so. Did you fear rejection if you reached out or did he or she seem to turn away?

3. When you have finished the first entry, sit in the center of the labyrinth together, holding hands only if you feel ready, and take turns describing how you felt walking the labyrinth and how it mirrored the relationship or seemed different. Allow the other person to speak uninterrupted and then add your interpretation, also without interruption. Avoid value judgments or point scoring.

4. Walk out of the labyrinth separately, reflecting as though you were the other person on how one might work to improve the relationship on the next walk.

5. On the second entry, reverse positions, so that the second person begins first. Walk even more slowly and anticipate points where you will come together and can touch (possibly risking rejection); at points where you touch exchange a few words of love, or at least kindness. These spontaneous words are the essence of the ritual and are an opportunity to build bridges. Then walk on alone, reflecting as you go.

6. The first one to reach the center should extend a hand to welcome the next person. This time speak only positive words, recalling happy memories, and joint dreams that may have become sidetracked or forgotten; offer healing and sympathy, and make plans for the future, if such plans are only to part in friendship and reconciliation.

7. When you are ready, walk out together as a unit. The paths in most labyrinths are quite tight, so you will need to be physically close, walking in step with each other, spiritually and emotionally.

Hopi Labyrinth Healing

At the end of every ceremony, many Native Americans use the phrase "We are all related," or a similar expression, to emphasize the link between all kinds of life, past and present.

THE MAKING OF RELATIONS

This ceremony can be used for healing wounds from family quarrels, welcoming new members not related by blood, or decreasing a sense of alienation of one individual in a family or group of friends. The Native American ceremony dates back many years to when children often became orphans as a result of disease or war and were adopted into other families. The ritual originally marked formal acceptance into another family, for to be alone without a bloodline and connections was inconceivable in the Native American world. This need for connection is equally relevant in the modern world, where due to increased divorce and remarriage, it is common for stepfamilies or foster families to acquire new members who are not linked by blood.

In earlier times the person to be adopted would sit on a carpet of sage and be covered with a blanket, or sit in the center of a medicine wheel. However, the labyrinth, either the classical seven-coil or the Hopi Mother Earth form, is equally potent for the making of relations rite (see chapter 2 for a description of how to draw the classical seven-coil labyrinth).

There are two forms of the Hopi Mother Earth labyrinth, the square and the round, found in Oraibi, Arizona. They recall the myth of the people's emergence from the First World beneath the earth. Examples of these Hopi Mother Earth symbols have been found carved on a rock and are called *Tápu'at* ('Mother and Child'). They represent spiritual rebirth from one world into the next. These labyrinths were never walked, since they were too small, but there is no reason you cannot adapt them to walkable size if you wish.

Hopi labyrinth

Square Hopi labyrinth

In a variation of the square version, one labyrinth is held within the other, depicting the unborn child within the womb of its mother and after birth held lovingly in her arms. The dotted line shows the path to the center.

Before the ceremony, the whole family including the person to be blessed can create the labyrinth in sand, on earth, or with stones, decorating it with feathers, crystals, and shells. The Hopi labyrinth is essentially a classical labyrinth placed within a square to represent the four directions and the pathway through life. You can carry out this ritual with the family members present or you can work alone using photographs or symbols of people who are far away. It is a ritual especially potent at noon on the day of the full moon and can be performed either indoors or in a garden or clearing. You will need quite a large center, because all participants will be in it together for part of the ceremony.

To perform the making of relations ritual:

1. Place a deep container containing a sage smudge stick or a sweetgrass braid in a bowl, and a book of matches, in the center of the labyrinth. If you wish, you can sprinkle the center with dried sage prior to the ceremony.

2. The new member who is entering an existing family, or a family member who feels alienated, should be led by the hand into the labyrinth center by the oldest member of the family or by a respected friend, who will lead the ceremony. The leader of the ritual places a colorful blanket in the center for the new member to sit on. The rest of the family members stand around the edges of the labyrinth.

3. The leader, still standing in the center of the labyrinth, lights the smudge. Beginning close to the ground, he or she smudges upward in spiral clockwise circles all the way around the body to the crown of the head of the new family member and then down again, chanting, "We embrace you in love." Other family members echo, thus creating a dual chant, "We are all one family."

4. The youngest member of the existing family enters the labyrinth and places a feather in the hair of the new member as the other members say, "So we grow together as one." Traditionally an eagle's feather was tied in the new member's hair, which, because of its constant growth, was considered a symbol of a person's life, wisdom, and connection to the past and future. The youngest person remains in the center.

5. One by one, in ascending age order, each member of the family enters the labyrinth, explaining simply why he or she welcomes

the person. Once in the center he or she offers the newcomer a small gift of personal significance.

6. The new member takes the sage and smudges a single clockwise circle waist high around those in the center, saying, "I welcome you my new kin and I ask Father Sky and Mother Earth, Brother Sun and Sister Moon, that we may live together in love and kindliness."

7. The leader places the blanket around the shoulders of the new member and repeats, "We embrace you thus in love."

8. All link hands and the new member leads the family out of the labyrinth, with the leader carrying the smudge at the end. The new member thereafter keeps the blanket on his or her bed as a reminder of the family's love.

If your family is absent or there has been a quarrel, you can carry out a private ceremony using a table labyrinth. Put a photograph or some personal possession of the estranged person in the center of the labyrinth and place beneath it a colorful scarf. Use the same ritual, smudging around the symbol and naming, as you walk each coil with your fingers, a virtue that you love about the absent person, saying, "We are all one family."

Let your love rise with the smoke. Place the feather on the scarf, and see your loved one smiling and moving closer. Weave the words suggested for the group ritual with your personal expressions of love or regret. Then walk out of the labyrinth.

Smudge a second time, and then release the feather at an open window or take it where it can blow away free after the ceremony. Keep the symbol wrapped in the scarf near your bed. If you can contact the person or family, by phone, in person, or even email, do so with a simple message of love or reconciliation. If this is not possible, wait in hope that your message of love has been accepted.

DRY AND SAND PAINTING HEALING IN THE LABYRINTH

Sand paintings are an integral part of the ceremonies for healing and regeneration throughout native North American cultures. Though we may not be able to follow the complex and often secret ceremonies of the Navajo healers, we can nevertheless try to capture their essence as a focus for our own healing energies. The center of the labyrinth is the perfect place to create healing sand pictures.

The paintings are started, finished, used, and destroyed within a twelve-hour period, their components being scattered to the six directions. They are traditionally made on cloth or buckskin, using sand, cornmeal, flower pollen, powdered roots, charcoal, and bark.

The actual pictures are credited with powerful healing powers. The patient sits on the picture, a representation of the Holy Ones and the powers of nature, and thereby absorbs their power, while chants, songs, and blessings are offered. In one version of the ritual, Father Sky and Mother Earth are depicted, so that they can recreate the Earth and humankind and restore the patient to health. Once the picture is completed, a line of corn pollen is drawn between the Father Sky and Mother Earth to show the path of harmony to be taken by the patient—his or her path through life that is sometimes called the Beauty Way.

You can use this method for healing yourself or someone close to you, because the link of love is a powerful channel for healing. A sand painting for healing purposes should have bold simple lines.

To make a dry or sand painting in a labyrinth:

1. Try to summon up from inside yourself images of Father Sky clad in moon, sun, cloud, and stars, and Mother Earth clothed in flowers, leaves, berries, and seeds. This ritual can be used for healing chronic or acute minor illnesses, for relieving stress, and for accepting unexpected or unwelcome change.

2. Prepare a very simple four-coil labyrinth, preferably drawn on sand or earth with a stick (see chapter 4 for instructions). Alternatively, use the square Hopi Mother Earth design.

3. Make the coils wide and the center large enough to create a sizable picture for the patient (possibly you) to sit on.

4. In the center (or in the inner part of the square Hopi design), place a piece of hessian, thick cotton, or calico on which to create your healing images.

5. Choose a quiet time, early morning or late afternoon, and create your picture either alone or with the person you are healing. Children are remarkably receptive to the old ways and will join in quietly and naturally, especially if they have a chronic illness or problem.

6. Before you begin, smudge the labyrinth and then your patient unless he or she is young, pregnant, or has a respiratory problem (if this is the case, smudge the labyrinth before he or she enters).

7. Ask the Great Spirit or your god or goddess that your healing may be for the greatest good and that only light and positive power may enter the labyrinth.

8. If the patient is someone other than yourself, ask him or her to help you create the picture and so build up a joint vision. Use natural symbols related to the patient's problem or create your own outlines of figures who seem to represent particular healing qualities. You could follow the tradition of drawing Mother Earth and Father Sky and placing a line of yellow seeds between them. Use a variety of natural materials kept in a special box, such as feathers, small dried beans and other pulses in a variety of colors (tinted with vegetable dyes, if you wish), stones of different colors, tiny crystals, bark, small sticks, and shells. You could make a rainbow-colored picture or concentrate on the four sacred colors of the earth, red, yellow, white and black, from which Spider Woman spun the First People.

Examples of images include:

Rain: colds and flu, throat and bronchial troubles, bladder problems

Sun: fevers or digestive disorders, illnesses of the blood

Moon: female problems, especially those connected with the reproductive system and childbirth; glands and the balance of fluids in the body; problems of the mind

Stars: visual disturbances; headaches; nightmares, insomnia, and other sleep disorders

Lightning: cuts, scratches, burns, unexpected and unwelcome change, surgery

Thunder: pain of all kinds, especially tooth- and earache, anger

Clouds: worry, depression, mouth and face disorders, absent-mindedness

Rocks: obstructions, kidney stones and gallstones, broken and bruised bones and limbs

Insects: infestations, irritability, an accumulation of minor illnesses

Snakes: inevitable change, skin disorders, problems related to aging

Snow: illnesses of the circulation system, loneliness, arthritis, and other illnesses that cause mobility problems.

There is no limit to the symbols you can use. The images are very personal; for you a whole scene of mountains, rivers, and trees blowing in the wind or only a single image may capture the sense of the disease or distress. You can use contrasting symbols as the curative element, for example, the sun or a rainbow next to the rain, or create a healing figure, a rain man, a corn woman or an eagle carrying light.

In time, you will find that about a dozen major symbols form the main components of your pictures and that these may feature in healing dreams. Solutions to problems will form as your hands work with the materials.

9. When the picture is finished, the person being healed should sit on it, facing either sunrise or sunset, according to the time of day.

10. You should both visualize or describe the golden healing energies rising from the earth through the body and also pouring down from the cosmos as sky and earth combine. Talk of the healing waters, the cleansing fire, the gentle winds of healing change, of sun and moon, rain and rainbows, mighty oceans, cascading waterfalls, and pine woods blowing in the breeze. If you allow words to flow, you may find you are speaking in verse or even singing some ancient song carried from the past on the wind. Ask for blessings, sing, sway, and chant, and you will find that you are connected to inspiration flowing down from the ages.

11. When you are finished, you or the patient should gather all the components of the picture in the cloth and carry them out of

the labyrinth, offering thanks in each coil either silently or aloud for the blessings of healing.

12. Once outside, facing away from the entrance, greet the six directions in turn—east, south, west, and north, and then hold the folded blanket up to the sky and down to the earth.

13. Scatter the materials to the four directions (first check the wind so the seeds do not blow back into the coils), or tip them into a large box or bag and dispose of them in a way that will allow them to return to the earth.

14. Erase the labyrinth once more offering thanks.

If your space or resources are limited, you can create a small picture on a silk square in the center of a table labyrinth and place your hand over that of the patient on top of the picture. Afterward, you can fold the components in the scarf, and if possible dispose of them in the open air. If time is of the essence, use a stick to create the picture in sand in the center of a sandbox labyrinth and afterward smooth it over.

Healing is one of the most creative uses of labyrinths. The power of the labyrinth shape does concentrate healing energies and for patient and healer offers a sacred and safe area in which to work.

In the next chapter I describe yet another dimension that can be accessed through the higher levels of awareness created in labyrinth work. Another doorway into the labyrinth leads into the past and enables us to explore past worlds and access information that can be applied to our present.

Chapter 9

LABYRINTHS
AND PAST LIVES

A

NY SACRED SPACE CREATES
a window through which it is possible to move into other dimensions.
Because of the energy packed within the spirals, as we walk a labyrinth
toward the center, we can attain a higher level of awareness, akin to
a waking dream. In this relaxed awareness, we are able to move into
the past, either in our minds or—as some people do—using our
etheric or spirit body, both to contact our wise ancestors and recall
our own past lives.

This spirit body is contained within the physical body. A number of peoples in regions around the world, from Siberia to sub-Saharan
Africa and from Greenland to New Guinea, believe the spirit body
goes walkabout, to use the Australian Aboriginal term, during sleep.
Research suggests that about a third of people even in the Westernized world experience the momentary sensation of floating or leaving
their physical bodies while waking. Is this an illusion, or could it be
the movement of the spirit body, which may be the part of us that
survives death?

You may not believe that you have had past lives. Even so, the collective past world experience may allow us to tap into earlier times and people, perhaps our ancestors with whom our present life has similarities, and resolve issues or dilemmas in our present world.

Labyrinths are especially important as gateways of time, because the center is like a vortex of power—not a black hole but a time tunnel. Through these gateways time follows a different path. For example, the Glastonbury Tor labyrinth center is said to lead into the Celtic otherworld; the entrance on Glastonbury Tor is guarded by Gwynn ap Nudd, "the White One," fairy king and lord of the otherworld. Sometimes associated with King Arthur, according to legends and accounts of those who claimed to have entered the mound, he lives in a palace within the Tor, sitting on a golden throne, surrounded by fairies wearing silks of all the colors of the rainbow.

Ancient Labyrinths

Some labyrinths date back to the Bronze Age. In England there are also a number of surviving ancient turf labyrinths. Many that did not survive were ploughed up for farming land, especially during the eighteenth century, probably with the blessing of local clergy who mistrusted their pagan fertility and seasonal associations.

One such labyrinth was the Shepherd's Ring, near Shrewsbury in Shropshire, an octagonal turf version of the medieval eleven-circuit labyrinth, which was destroyed to make way for a windmill on the same site in 1796. In the middle was a giant's head, a form of the ancient fertility symbol of the Green Man, the god of vegetation. Of those that remain, most are totally accessible to the public. Turf labyrinths are also becoming more popular in America, especially in rural areas, and are worth seeking out via the Internet and tourist information centers.

Probably the huge Saffron Walden town labyrinth, in Essex in East Anglia, a wealthy center for wool trading in the sixteenth century, is the oldest as well as one of the largest (120 feet across). It stands on the village green and so can be walked on any day of the year without restriction.

The Shepherd's Ring

In the center was an ash tree representing the World Tree. Now the large raised turf bank in the center is bare of any tree. The pathways are narrow but because the labyrinth uncoils over a mile in length to the center, you can have peace and privacy to work, even if other people are in the labyrinth. The path has been cut into the turf—over the centuries it has been recut several times—and bricks have been inlaid to provide a permanent track.

This was one of the labyrinths in which fertility rites were performed—rituals involving a young man running to the center and claiming his virgin bride (assuming he had any energy left for consummation after carrying her out of the labyrinth).

I visited it on a warm September afternoon when children coming home from school were playing in the outer coils as they would have done centuries earlier, and one or two people were meditating as they walked.

In the center I felt the most powerful earth vibrations, and I was reminded of legends of the home or sacred Native American *kiva* of the Earth Mother. As I lay down on the grass bank in the middle, the sun's rays like a wondrous kaleidoscope, rich red light and heat poured from the earth into my body. Never have I experienced such a positive surge of earth power.

Saffron Walden

The shape of Saffron Walden is quite special and one I would recommend that you photocopy and use for past and, indeed, future life work. The complexity fools the conscious mind into confusion, always a good thing in psychic work; as you walk it in your mind visualize a huge expanse of green surrounded by trees, a really stereotypical English setting (totally atypical of much of England now). Reinsert in your visualization the mighty ash tree, looming high, connecting earth with sky and the realms of mortals with those of heavenly beings.

Bouncing between the Bastions

Not all labyrinths are square or circular. One common feature that
sets some labyrinths apart from the classical design is the bastion.
This is the term for nodules on the labyrinth seen here on the
famous pattern on the green at Saffron Walden in Essex. The four
bastions face the towns of Newmarket, Chelmsford, Bishop's
Stortford, and Cambridge.

Saffron Walden bastions

I have numbered the bastions for convenience—there are no
numbers on the real labyrinth, although the Milton Keynes labyrinth,
a double-sized modern copy of this ancient maze, does have beautiful
ironwork faces in the center of each of its bastions (see chapter 12).

If you walk this mile-long circuit in actuality or with your fingers
as a table labyrinth, you will eventually pass round all the bastions

from one to four. At first glance it seems logical that you progress round the bastions first, working your way inward. However, with a labyrinth, nothing is certain; in fact, you have to walk most of the labyrinth before the winding track throws you out again into the bastions.

Finding Ancient Labyrinths in the City

You can connect with ancient energies even if the labyrinth you walk is relatively modern, for the land on which it is created is old. Indigenous peoples once had their hunting grounds where cities now stand; early settlers established their homes on the land and imprinted it with their hopes, fears, and dreams.

Lemuria, sometimes referred to as Mu, or the Motherland (of Mu), is said to be the source of much of the wisdom of indigenous peoples, for example, Native Americans and the Australian Aborigines. Some people believe that Lemuria was originally situated in the South Pacific between North America and Asia or Australia. Others say that Lemuria symbolizes the true universal core of wisdom that seems to have arisen quite independently in different lands. Thus Lemuria was, in a sense, the center of a labyrinth, and its wisdom was carried out along the labyrinthine pathways to many other lands and their peoples. Every labyrinth therefore taps into the root cultural heritage of all lands and ages. This basic knowledge or culture is then strengthened as it absorbs and reflects the cultural heritage of those who walk its coils. Even the most recent labyrinth in a twenty-first-century city contains the wisdom and past lives of the cultures of ancient Egypt, ancient Greece, Russia, Africa, and peoples who once lived as nomads.

A fanciful idea? Perhaps, but within a single, modern metropolis live and work the descendants of ancient Egyptians, Africans, Native Americans, Hebrews, Eastern Europeans, Celts, Mediterranean peoples, Scandinavians, Hindus, and those of countless other nations, who carry within them the roots of many cultures through their gene pool. Some people, through marriage and the migration of ancestors, may be affected by their genetic heritage despite the culture or climate in which they now live. Even in the height of summer in South Africa, Australia, or New Zealand, they may feel within them the deep snows of the frozen North and want to hibernate.

The labyrinth activates these dormant connections, and even if we do not believe we experience an actual past life, we can nevertheless, in and through the labyrinth, make connection with a past age of great spiritual resonance.

Walking the Path

It is possible to experience both spontaneous and induced past-life experiences in the labyrinth. By far the majority of past-life recollections within a labyrinth occur spontaneously, as the person walks rhythmically along the coils. However, you can induce a past-life experience by standing facing the entrance and asking the labyrinth mother, who oversees all labyrinth experiences, to show you an aspect of a past world that may be of help to you. Reserve past-life explorations for a time when you need guidance, since this is quite a powerful experience emotionally and spiritually.

It is important to clear the mind before seeking a past-life experience. One easy technique to clear the mind of clutter is to visualize a starry sky filling your mind; then, one by one, allow the stars to go out, leaving only velvety blackness. Or imagine a shady pool whose surface is covered with bubbles, and allow the bubbles to float away one at a time until only the dark water remains beneath. On this blank canvas your psyche can draw from the inner well of collective wisdom images, sounds, and fragrances of a past world with which you have a familial or psychic connection. Whatever the source, the life recalled from past worlds in the labyrinth will offer answers to current questions and dilemmas if you allow the ancient collective wisdom to flow.

The act of walking the coils, first clockwise and then as you turn into another coil counterclockwise, deactivates logic and allows the intuitive right brain to take the driving seat for once. The physical movements set the rhythm—all you have to do is follow the path, however complex. In this way your psyche can roam free while the feet take the strain. For this reason, larger labyrinths work especially well as a pathway.

In a large labyrinth, the earth energies tend to prevent even a sloth like me from becoming exhausted. As you walk, the images in your mind may increase in intensity and richness, so that you feel you are walking on a winding road through a different world, perhaps surrounded by trees or old buildings. A past-life labyrinth guardian, often a shadowy but entirely benign figure, may appear in front of you, showing you the way.

If you are using a miniature labyrinth, for example, a copy of the Saffron Walden or some other complex labyrinth, draw it in white or silver on black paper and shine lights on it in a darkened room to induce a sense of otherworldliness. Move your index finger along the coils very slowly, gazing through half-closed eyes.

When you reach the center of a large labyrinth, sit or lie and close your eyes, allowing layers of color to build up and scenes to form. In a miniature one, close your eyes, maintaining contact with the center with your finger. You may see in your mind's eye a group of people, one of whom resembles you and with whom you feel kinship. Some people become aware of the environment first, beginning with the temperature, then buildings, and finally a person who may lead them into a house or public place.

Allow the scene to unfold; usually such visions involve not a dramatic event but everyday interactions. Listen to the conversations and focus especially on your alter ego, the other you. Follow him or her, being aware that you are sharing that person's emotions but that you can come to no harm, because these are only pictures from the past. For though you can wander in and out of rooms or structures, the past is written and cannot be changed. The people present cannot see you—or, if you believe in parallel time scales, then you are no more than a shadow or a passing breeze.

You will become aware of your past-life guardian at your side, even if you did not see him or her earlier, and at this point you will be guided back into the physical center of the labyrinth and perhaps given a message explaining what you have seen.

Thank your wise guide and begin slowly to walk out of the labyrinth. The scenes around you, the fragrances, the sights and sounds will recede. As you exit, do not look back or attempt to analyze your experience. Let your feet do the walking and the talking; only when you reach the labyrinth entrance should you turn briefly for a final view of what you have experienced. Then mist will descend.

Do not be tempted to reenter the labyrinth. Another day you may return to that place in the center if you have unfinished business or lessons to learn, or you may enter a different life. Now you need time to allow the visions and the words to expand and form a pattern in your mind, for they may seem to be whirling round like the colors in a kaleidoscope.

Spend some time either alone or with a companion who will simply listen and not play guru. If you are away from home, find a park or a quiet coffee house where you can allow your visions to weave themselves into a meaningful tapestry.

At home, avoid being sucked back into the everyday world or satisfying the needs of others too quickly. Even spending fifteen minutes alone with your labyrinth journal will evoke images, perhaps expressed in drawings, poetry, or a story about the other world. Date these experiences in your journal so that you can refer to them later and see how they fit into the ongoing developing picture of your past world. You may also reenter your past life in your dreams.

Cindy's Labyrinth Past Life Experience

Cindy, a lawyer in her early forties who was in a permanent relationship, had come over from Australia on holiday and was visiting sacred sites in the United Kingdom. I met her when I walked the Saffron Walden labyrinth—labyrinths are very good places for making like-minded friends. She told me about an experience she had had some weeks earlier when she had visited the Miz Maze on top of the Winchester Downs, close to where several eight-thousand-year-old pathways once met. Such a meeting of ancient tracks can be thought of as another complex labyrinth form. The London-to-south-coast M3 motorway slashes its way through the adjoining Twyford Down, obliterating the intersection of the ancient traders' routes that once extended across England. However, the Miz Maze labyrinth is still unspoiled, as I described in chapter 3—a sky labyrinth, drawing power from Mother Earth beneath but exposed to the elements. It sits in a dip on top of the grassy hillside.

This is what Cindy told me:

I was disappointed at first when I reached the labyrinth. Hundreds
of years earlier, my family had lived in the town of Winchester,
so I had expected an immediate connection. It was a hot day,
and because of the foot-and-mouth agricultural crisis in England,
the labyrinth had only recently been reopened to the public.
For this reason the grass had grown into some of the narrow
grooves, and it took me a while to find the entrance.

I walked very slowly, and gradually the birdsong and the
distant mooing of the cows lulled me. It is so large and complicated I seemed forever in its coils. Gradually, however, I became
aware of a misty brown figure, very tall and thin, the color of the
soil walking slightly ahead of me on top of the grass, and I realized
he was guiding my path, which became increasingly effortless.

I realized that I was also part of a brown-clad procession
and that we were carrying panniers, filled with woven fabrics,
dyed in natural colors, green, brown, and cream. I was tired and
my pannier was heavy, but I was reluctant to accept the help of
the tall, clumsy boy next to me. This was the first time I had been
allowed to travel with the traders, but I was not going to let anyone know how tired I was. Besides, I was angry with the boy
because he had been chosen as my future husband and now he
followed me everywhere, acting as if he owned me and I was a
stupid child. Some of the women were singing softly as we walked,
and usually I joined in any singing. Now I felt apart, even from
my family. I knew how to weave and sew, but I wanted more.

Some Christian missionaries had come to our village
weeks before, and I was amazed at how strong and independent
the nuns were, equal to the men, physically and in their minds,
talking of far-off lands, wild seas, and pirate bands. One was
so calm, tall—the leader—and she had spent time talking to me
after dark when the others were asleep. Now they were gone,
leaving a priest in the church made of mud and reeds. With them
had gone my traditional way of life, which was the same as that
of my mother and grandmother, and would be the life of my

daughters: weaving, caring for the men even on the journeys to the market, talking about marriage, babies, and cloth.

I must have reached the grassy bank in the center of the labyrinth. I lay down in the hot sunshine on the prickly grass. I was suddenly in a market square, and, between the stalls, I saw her, the missionary, walking tall and straight, her gold cross hanging from her belt, followed by a group of women in white robes. She recognized me at once or I would have been too shy to speak and said, "You have come to join us, little one."

She spoke to my mother and my father, who were angry, but she gave them gold and promised them many orders of cloth from her abbey if they would allow me to stay—if I wished. I followed her, with scarcely a good-bye [to my parents], to the large wooden building on the hill, and she said, "You are free to go or to stay. I will help you if you do not wish to enter our order for I have not bought your soul, only your freedom. You should not have to marry a man you do not want or be tied like cattle to breeding his stock." I followed, and the herb-filled garden through which she led me became the labyrinth. I found myself outside, and the sun clouded over, followed by a sudden shower of cool rain.

As I stood in the copse of the tree on the other side of the hill, I thought how my partner was pressuring me to have a baby as time was running out. This tour was partly to give me time and space to think. I had an opportunity to take a lower-paid job working at a center to promote Australian Aboriginal welfare rights. However, since it involved extensive traveling, my partner was unwilling for me to change direction at a time when we were going to concentrate on having a baby. I don't know for sure what I will do. So I have decided to extend my holiday by a month, using up all my leave, and hope I may get more pictures in this new labyrinth.

I do not know if Cindy did have another past-life experience, since I had to leave to reach the next place on my own tour before dark.

Optimum Times for Contacting Other Dimensions

Though you can experience past worlds at any time in your labyrinth explorations, at certain times of the day, the month, and the year, transitions occur between one season and the next; at these times the veil between dimensions is especially thin.

TRANSITION TIMES

The sun is one of the main marker points, and as it sets, conceding to darkness in one hemisphere as it triumphs in the other, so the material world is at its weakest; the world of the night, dreams, and astral travel merge at the time of sunrise and sunset.

Dusk, or the hour before sunset in some magical traditions, is probably the best time of all for past-life work. Dusk is especially potent for past-life work in a labyrinth. You can begin before sunset so that you have reached the center at the moment of sunset. If you set your labyrinth entrance in the west, you can then walk out and see the sun's streaks across the sky in its nightly farewell. Since the time of sunset changes every day, you'll want to look up the precise time in either the weather section of a newspaper or a diary.

PAST LIVES AND TIMES OF THE MONTH

The very best days for past-life work are the two and one-half days from the new moon until the waxing crescent appears in the sky. The new moon is marked in a diary or newspaper by a black circle, indicating its invisibility to the human eye. Some practitioners call this period the "dark of the moon." Others consider the dark period to be the last three days before the new moon, when it does not rise until the early morning. Both periods are potent for past life work in the labyrinth, giving a total of five or six days for your past-life explorations. Check your local newspaper for the dates of these events, since the irregular orbit of the moon causes monthly variations.

MAGICAL DATES OF THE YEAR

The day on which past world energies are strongest is Hallowe'en itself. Hallowe'en, the last day of the Celtic year, called the period of Samhain, the time of the ancestors, began at sundown on October 31. This began a twenty-four–hour period of "no time," in which the barriers between the spirit worlds were said to open, lasting until sunset on November 1, when the Celtic New Year began. The festival continued until sunset on November 2. In Catholic lands from France to Mexico, these are regarded as the days of the dead when deceased family members and saints are remembered, and their lives are celebrated. Modern commercial celebrations of Hallowe'en have destroyed the spiritual significance of this most sacred festival.

In Celtic times, ghosts were believed to come shivering from the fields on Hallowe'en seeking food and shelter. The hearth was considered the central place of the home and also the meeting place of the upper and lower worlds. At festivals of the dead in both the Eastern and Western worlds, food and drink are left on the hearth so that deceased family members can return to the warmth of the family hearth.

Fires still burn brightly on Hallowe'en night in Ireland and parts of Northern Europe. In Ireland on this night in times past, all fires were extinguished and could be rekindled only from a ceremonial fire lit by the Druids at Samhain on Tlachtga (now the Hill of Ward). Bonfires were originally lit to guide the wandering ghosts of the good dead to their homes. Because it was a fairy festival, bonfires also kept mischievous fairies and malevolent witches away and prevented the fairies from stealing any souls before their winter departure to fairyland.

Druids would place a clove of garlic on their windowsills and ask that the good family dead might be welcomed within. With this idea in mind, you might like to put cloves of garlic at the four main compass points around your labyrinth.

Welcoming Wise Ancestors

An important part of past-life work is connecting with our own ancestors. We carry their genes and so can more readily connect with the lives of even our most distant ancestors.

HALLOWE'EN

You could make your special Hallowe'en labyrinth in time to enter
it before dusk, perhaps with candles surrounding it. Some people
work with the more modern New Year's Eve on December 31, around
which a whole new magical tradition has grown up. You can easily
adapt the following two rituals for New Year's Eve.

If you have children, they may want to walk the labyrinth
with you. You can then sit in a circle in the center (make the center
a big one, if necessary; it does not matter if this labyrinth is out of
proportion).

Inside the labyrinth center:

* Tell stories of beloved ancestors and family characters.

* Sing songs loved by deceased relations.

* Recall pets that have died and, using a well-protected candle on
  a broad base, burn tiny threads in the flame to banish sorrows
  and fears.

* On New Year's Eve you could follow the Scottish tradition of
  burning a calendar from the old year.

* In the center of an open-air labyrinth, light a small fire in a deep
  metal pot or a brazier and drop in dead leaves or petals, sending
  a message of love and thanks to the ancestors across the ages.

* If it is impractical to build a fire, set a huge orange candle in an
  iron pot, wedged in with sand. Surround it with seasonal nuts
  and berries. You may be rewarded by spontaneous glimpses of
  past worlds and lives in the flame. Children, too, may tell you of
  people whose faces they saw in the fire. Even a child who has
  never seen a photograph of her great-great-grandmother may
  describe with remarkable accuracy the kind lady who held her
  hand in the labyrinth. We should not fear this—children in their
  innocence have automatic access to spiritual planes and are
  guarded by their own special angels wherever they roam.

* Together, blow out the candle, if there is one, sending love and
  light to all in the present, past, and future who need it.

★ After you all leave the labyrinth, enjoy a special supper of favorite foods and drink once enjoyed by deceased relations, who live on within your memory.

★ Get out the old family photo albums and recall triumphs and disasters, courage and kindnesses from the lives of dead loved ones. This really brings history alive for children and can help us put our own deprivations into perspective.

★ End the children's evening with traditional Hallowe'en games such as apple bobbing, in Celtic times a form of marriage divination. The apple, floating in a bowl of water, was picked up with the teeth and placed beneath the pillow to bring prophetic dreams of a future lover. The first person to pick up an apple would be the first married.

This practice forms a wonderful counterinfluence to the images of evil that permeate Hallowe'en in its present commercial form. You can adapt the ceremony to include adult family members and friends. You can also use a table labyrinth and miniature candles on a circular table, seating the children around the outside. A circular seven-coil labyrinth is best for table work.

If you celebrated Hallowe'en with a labyrinth party like the one just described, you can return to the labyrinth alone later in the evening, relighting the candle or if necessary rekindling the central fire.

1. If you wish to make contact with a deceased relation, take a piece of jewelry that belonged to them, a tiny photograph, a favorite flower, or a scarf on which you have placed a few drops of that person's perfume or aftershave with you into the labyrinth.

2. As you enter the labyrinth, speak to the deceased relation or your ancestor, saying that you would welcome contact, if it is right to be.

3. For a glimpse of a more distant ancestor, as you walk visualize an archetypal figure from your root culture. It may be a Celtic warrior or bard, a Russian living on a steppe or lighting incense in one of the great gold-domed churches, or a colonist building

a log cabin in the New World or braving raging seas to bring family and friends safely to shore.

4. If none of your known ancestral roots feels right, allow yourself to form an image of a person from another age with whom you feel instant kinship. Do not force the picture if nothing comes during your walk—once you reach the center it will be much easier. Do not be surprised if this person does not belong to your known cultural heritage. This ancestor may be connected with one of your past lives—or an adventurer relation who crossed oceans to found a new dynasty long before family records. He or she may belong to a culture to which you have instinctively been drawn without realizing why.

5. When you reach the center, sit and wait. Say nothing and think nothing, and you may be rewarded by a glimpse of the family member, hear a few words of love and blessing on the breeze, experience an increase in fragrance, or detect another scent you associate with the person. A sudden memory may flash into your mind, perhaps a shared song. Or the encounter may be even subtler—you may feel a touch as light as gossamer on your shoulder or hair, or you may experience a sense of peace and being cared for, and the happiness or contentment that person evoked in life. Do not expect too much—the smallest sign is a blessing. Your awareness may increase in subsequent encounters, which are usually spontaneous or in dreams.

6. You will know when the time is right to leave the labyrinth. Perhaps there will be a sudden breeze, the sky will become dark, or night birds will begin calling overhead. Make a farewell as you would to a living family member or wise friend, and walk toward the outside world.

The gift of the labyrinth is the awareness that you are not alone, but part of a living family, past and future, even if you do not have children of your own. For what we are and what we do influences many people, known and unknown, and someday you may take your place as a wise labyrinth ancestor.

When you leave the labyrinth, do or plan something to make the world a better place for children. There are many organizations that will help you plant a tree, which may become part of a forest many years from now. You might campaign for better children's play facilities in your area, collect local folk wisdom and legends to deposit in an archive for future generations, or contact a family member (an older son or daughter) who is now alone or estranged.

I recommend that you do not, after this initial contact, try to make further contact with your deceased loved one without the guidance of a wise, reputable medium (although spontaneous contact from a deceased relation and words of love spoken by you on anniversaries are gifts of love that span dimensions). The deceased person may need to continue his or her journey through spiritual realms and will make you aware of his or her presence when you need reassurance in the future.

It is the same with a more distant ancestor. He or she may appear in your mind's eye quite spontaneously on other occasions after you have made the initial connection. This appearance may be in the form of a shadowy figure, a voice in your ear, or a series of impressions. The wise ancestor may offer words of counsel at times when you are worried or in need of help. Or you may more subtly be aware, in your daily life, of the sense of continuing deep kinship over the centuries or even millennia.

MAY EVE

The alter-ego of Samhain, May Eve, beginning at sunset on April 30, marked the beginning of the Celtic summer festival Beltaine. Sundown on this day, as winter is overcome by summer, is also a good entry point for past-life work. Surround your labyrinth with flowers for the protection of the earth.

Past Lives and Mirror Labyrinths

This is one of the most evocative ways of accessing past worlds. You can also use it in other psychic work, for example, out-of-body travel.

To work with mirror labyrinths:

1. Create or photocopy a seven-coil labyrinth. Transfer or draw it on black cardstock so that the coils are marked in white or fluorescent paint or ink.

2. Find a large square or rectangular mirror. Position and prop up the labyrinth so that you can quite clearly see it but not your own reflection in the mirror. You can do this by standing slightly to the side of the mirror, with it resting against a surface such as a table propped against a wall. Alternatively, paint a labyrinth with black glass paint on an old mirror, and lay that flat on the table or floor. You could also draw a labyrinth on the mirror with dark-colored lipstick.

3. Behind the labyrinth, light a horseshoe of white candles so that the light shines on the reflected labyrinth.

4. Work as dusk falls. Focusing on the entrance in the mirror, slowly inhale and exhale. As you inhale, visualize the mirror expanding all around you, so, like Alice, you enter the looking glass. You may experience a slight resistance as you pass through.

5. The mirror labyrinth of course reverses the actual directions and represents a journey into the inner psyche, so clockwise becomes counterclockwise. Slowly, in your mind, follow the pathway of light as you perceive it in the glass and walk toward the center of the reflected labyrinth, where there is a dark well filled with light. This is the well of the goddess of the labyrinth, the well of all knowledge, and a record of the experiences of all people and places, past and present.

6. Draw up water from the "well" and drink it from a glass filled with spring (still mineral) water left in moonlight of the night of the full moon. Say, "Hecate, Cerridwen, Isis, you mothers of the night and the mysteries, let me drink deep of your waters of remembrance that I may see in your dark waters what it is I need to learn from the past."

7. Focus hard on the dark center of the reflected labyrinth, close your eyes, open them, and blink. You will see a single scene,

a cameo of another time and place; the central character is you in a past world or a person with whom you have close kinship. This vision will be like a tarot card image, rich in detail and symbolism.

8. Close your eyes again, open them, blink, and look at the dark center. You will see a second cameo, related to the first.

9. Continue closing and opening your eyes until you have seen five or six scenes or you feel the psychic link weakening.

10. Now use your imagination or imaging powers to make the center spin until you are wrapped up in a skipping rope. Then suddenly uncoil it, so you are propelled out of the spirals at great speed, feeling exhilarated. As you spin you will see a final picture, larger and more vivid than the others, which will answer any questions or resolve any dilemma in your mind.

11. Remove the mirror and place the labyrinth flat on the table so you are looking down on it. Trace the pathways in and out by candlelight, seeing if any more symbols, words, or impressions add to the mirror wisdom. If you are working with a labyrinth drawn on the mirror, trace the actual paths with your finger.

12. When you have finished, light more candles if necessary and in your journal record the cameos and any additional impressions while they are fresh in your mind.

    Work fast without analyzing or allowing logic to intrude. If you prefer, draw or paint the images as though they were tarot cards. If does not matter if you are not a great artist; the colors and the feeling are what is important.

13. Now weave the cameos into a story about a hero or heroine who represents you. The resolution of the story will answer your question or shed light on future paths you may walk in your life. The different cameos will reflect different aspects of the situation, influences upon you, or perhaps obstacles. Spend time studying each, whether in word or picture form, and the overall picture will become even clearer.

14. Create cards of any cameos that seem particularly significant, for example one depicting the hero standing up to the dragon as it dissolves into smoke.

Each time you use this method—and I would recommend having no more than one past-life experience of any kind in a given month—make more cards so that over the months you build up a whole set of past-life situations. When you have a choice or dilemma you can shuffle the cards (keep the backs plain) and select one without looking. This will shed light and suggest ways to move forward, for they all depict aspects of your personality, past or present, and so can be turned to strengths.

Past Lives and Fragrances

Herb labyrinths are very special. In chapter 8, I described a labyrinth created with lavender bushes at a school in Cranleigh in Surrey to induce tranquility and prayerfulness in children with special needs. We know from old records that herbal labyrinths were fashionable in formal gardens during the fifteenth and sixteenth centuries and that the herbs in each coil represented specific planets.

Of course, it would take absolutely ages and many plants to create a full-size labyrinth of herbs, although the results of such a labor of love would be especially rewarding and powerful. Fragrance, especially of herbs, is a powerful pathway to the past that I have used in many contexts, not just labyrinth work. But it is also a gentle method that may be especially healing if you are new to past-life work or have suffered by visiting a bad regression therapist.

A MINIATURE LABYRINTH GARDEN

Even if you do not have the energy or resources to create a full-scale herbal labyrinth, you can use a large ceramic dish or circular flower container. It must be deep enough to contain soil and large enough to hold seven circles of small herb plants. For ease of reference I will again reproduce the seven-coil labyrinth and its seven planetary associations, for herbs have been associated with specific planetary rulers from the times of ancient Greece.

Here I name one main fragrance, which I have found especially potent, for each of the seven coils. However, later in this chapter I suggest other herbs and their ruling planets that you can use in the labyrinth.

Numbered labyrinth

From the inside out:

8 the earth, where you absorb all the fragrances

7 the moon, jasmine, the weaver of dreams

6 Mercury, lavender, the healer

5 Venus, rose, the gentle peacemaker

4 the sun, frankincense, bringer of nobility

3 Mars, fennel, endower of courage

2 Jupiter, sandalwood, the wise soul

1 Saturn, patchouli, preserver of tradition and the environment

At the end of this book I have listed some titles that give planetary associations for a variety of herbs around the world, so that you can substitute those that grow in your region. Alternatively, you can use any herbs that suggest to you the power of each planet (see chapter 7). You can plant the appropriate herbs around the perimeter of each coil, using seeds or small plants, and trim them back regularly.

HERBAL LABYRINTHS FOR PAST LIFE WORK

If you do not want to make an herbal labyrinth, you can use incense in the different planetary fragrances in jars or heatproof cans (see chapter 7), placing one in each coil of a small table labyrinth or more at regular intervals around a large labyrinth. Use tiny incense sticks in a miniature labyrinth and ventilate the room so you are not overwhelmed by the fragrances. The seven fragrances listed on page 219 are especially good for introducing this experience (but pregnant women should always avoid using incense).

To use a labyrinth for past-life work:

1. Light the incense from a taper as you enter each coil, either walking or tracing the pathways with your finger in a table labyrinth. By the time you reach the center, you will have absorbed the cumulative energies. If it is a table labyrinth, rest your hand in the center to make connection with the labyrinth energies.

2. As you sit in the center, close your eyes and allow the fragrances to weave their own images and carry you into past worlds where people experienced the same fragrances—lavender growing in hedgerows, frankincense in temples, and rose-filled gardens where lovers exchanged vows. The fragrances have been described as psychic prompts or reminders, evoking memories of times and places that lie beyond the grasp of the conscious mind.

3. Keep your eyes closed so that your outer senses are focused entirely through the sense of smell and your psychic senses can work unimpeded by external visual stimuli. Fragrance-induced past-life experiences have an almost dreamlike, muted quality, as if seen through a faint rainbow. Impressions are an important

tool for clairsentience. Psychic sensing is the higher form of the physical sense of smell and is activated by timeless fragrances.

4. You may lose track of time as you float back through the centuries on your magic carpet of fragrance. Allow yourself to flow with the emotions and the sense of deep overwhelming peace and connection with the world.

5. When you are ready to leave you may feel as though you are waking from a beautiful dream. Move slowly out from the center with your feet or fingers.

6. If possible, allow the incense to burn down as you sit outside the labyrinth, reconnecting with the fragrances.

This is one form of labyrinth work where it is better to sleep on your experiences and record them when you awake refreshed, for it is likely that they will continue in peaceful but vivid dreams of those other places and times.

PAST LIFE WORK WITH A SINGLE FRAGRANCE

You can also work with a single planetary herb, herbal incense, or herbal essential oil if you wish to direct your past-life experiences toward dreams or intuitions that you have already experienced or if you want to develop an avenue discovered in other past-life work. You may need to experiment, since some fragrances work better than others for different people. Note the images evoked by each in your journal. In the process of experimentation you may discover your own core of seven planetary fragrances that are potent for you.

Before using any oil or inhaling incense in a confined space, read the labels carefully, since some are not suitable for pregnant women or for people with certain medical conditions. If in doubt, check with an herbalist or pharmacist. The following is a list—by no means comprehensive—of the more common fragrances to avoid during pregnancy:

★   Aloe vera, angelica, autumn crocus, barberry, basil, bay, bitter almond, caraway, cayenne, cedarwood, clary sage, clove, copal, cypress, dill, dragon's blood, fennel, feverfew, goldenseal, hyssop, juniper, male fern, mandrake, marjoram, mugwort, myrrh, pennyroyal, peppermint, poke root, rosemary, rue, sage, southernwood, tansy, tarragon, thuja, thyme, wintergreen, wormwood, and yarrow.

★ Sweet fennel, hyssop, sage, and rosemary should be avoided by anyone suffering from epilepsy.

★ People with high blood pressure should not use hyssop, rosemary, sage, and thyme.

You can draw a large labyrinth, use an existing one, or work with a miniature form; carry the incense with you in a holder as you walk through the coils. Alternatively, place candles scented with the individual fragrance within the coils. In a table labyrinth you can position an essential oil diffuser in a safe place outside the labyrinth or in the center.

Each planetary fragrance is especially potent for past-life and other psychic work on the day ruled by that planet. For each planet I have listed the past-life experiences that it specially evokes, so that as you become more experienced you can direct your work to fill in gaps in previous more spontaneous past-life experiences. Alternatively, you can experiment with the fragrances and see which of the worlds seems most real and closest to your own feelings of connection to certain places or terrains. The coil references will not apply, since all of the coils will contain the same fragrance.

Sunday, Day of the Sun Bay, benzoin, cinnamon, copal, frankincense, juniper, orange, rosemary, saffron, and St. John's wort
Burn incenses of the sun for visions of golden, sunny days and exotic places, of deserts and nomads with rich tents, of blazing bonfires celebrating the sun rising golden on the summer solstice above ancient stone circles.

Monday, Day of the Moon Chamomile, eucalyptus, jasmine, lemon, lemon balm, lotus, mimosa, myrrh, poppy, and wintergreen
Burn incenses of the moon for visions of robed priestesses in willow glades; of moon goddesses and their shrines; of brilliant

moonlit nights casting a silver pathway across the sea; of fairy-
tale castles, unicorns, and magical beings.

Tuesday, Day of Mars Allspice, basil, cedarwood, coriander,
dragon's blood, garlic, ginger, mint, pepper, tarragon, and thyme
    Burn incenses of Mars for visions of forests, mountains, and
scenes of nature at its most turbulent and magnificent. There
may be tall trees blown by the wind or winter celebrations with
pines decorated with scarlet candles; banners waving and cries
of victory as old oppressors fall and young crusaders on white
chargers liberate besieged castles or slay dragons by the score.

Wednesday, Day of Mercury Dill, fennel, ferns, lavender, lemon-
grass, lily of the valley, mace, parsley, and valerian
    Burn incenses of Mercury for visions of messengers riding
through the night with secret scrolls; poets, sculptors, actors, and
painters; doctors and healing deities; tricksters, jugglers, and all
the brilliance of circuses, fairs, and marketplaces.

Thursday, Day of Jupiter Agrimony, borage, cinquefoil, coltsfoot, honeysuckle, oakmoss, hyssop, mistletoe, nutmeg, sandalwood,
sage, and star anise
    Burn incenses of Jupiter for scenes of pharaohs, ornamen-
tal temples, shrines, processions, and pageants; of gods and goddesses with golden circlets and purple robes, living on their sky
mountains shrouded from mortals in mist; of wise Druids and
Druidesses and Viking courts of justice.

Friday, Day of Venus Almond, apple blossom, echinacea, feverfew, geranium, lilac, magnolia, mugwort, pennyroyal, rose, strawberry, vanilla, vervain, yarrow, and ylang-ylang
    Burn incenses of Venus for visions of past lovers, of trysts in
flower-covered bowers, of troubadours singing love songs beneath
balconies rich with blossom, of beds of rose petals, of marriages
and the consummation of love, of nobles in marble palaces, and
simple country maidens and youths in woodland weddings.

Saturday, Day of Saturn Aconite, bistort, comfrey, cypress, horsetail, mimosa, patchouli, Solomon's seal, and vetivert

Burn incenses of Saturn for images of starlit skies; dark, mysterious places; caves and woods where old, veiled priestesses make wise prophecies; of hermits, alchemists, and magicians creating spells from vats of fragrant oils, gleaming metals, and gems in shuttered castles.

The past remains one of the most fascinating and elusive forms of psychic experience. Whether you accessed a specific past life, contacted one of your ancestors, or linked with past words in a less tangible way, the labyrinth amplifies your ability to span dimensions. You may also be interested in exploring some of the ideas in this chapter away from the labyrinth.

In the next chapter we will focus on our own personal energy system, often called the "chakra system," and work on tuning into and linking its different centers to the labyrinth coils.

Chapter 10

LABYRINTHS AND CHAKRAS

T HE LABYRINTH CAN be a very
valuable tool for balancing energies and for healing chakras, the body's
psychic energy centers. There are a number of ways of linking the
seven main chakras of the body to the classical seven-coil labyrinth.
The system I have described in this chapter is one that has worked
well in my personal work and one I have taught successfully. However,
there are alternative theories of both chakras and their relation to
the labyrinth. Since we are dealing with psychic rather than physical
energy centers and since no authenticated traditional material exists
on this subject, it is a question of discovering what actually works
for you.

What Are Chakras and Their Effects?

If you are unfamiliar with the concept of chakras, you may find it
useful to read this section describing the function of each of these
energy centers, how they affect us, and the coil of the labyrinth in
which the energy of each chakra is most powerful. If you already
work with chakras, you may still find it useful to understand my perspective, so that you can adapt the suggested labyrinth work to your
own beliefs if they are different.

225

A chakra (Sanskrit for wheel) is an energy vortex, sometimes called *padma* or lotus because of its image as a jewel surrounded by whirling lotus petals. These psychic centers have also been likened to whirling discs, spheres, or spinning colored discs. They are the channels through which the life force flows from the sky and earth, from animals, trees, plants, and crystals as well as from other people. This core energy is processed and filtered via the conelike seal in the center of each chakra, a seal forming the channel from the seven layers of the etheric or spirit body to the physical body. The etheric, or spirit, body is within the individual physical body and energizes it, extending beyond the physical body in the form of layers of color that are called the aura. I provide much more detail later in the chapter, but it may be helpful now to establish the link between the chakras and the labyrinth.

Let's again look at the classical labyrinth and be reminded of how the coils are numbered. I have listed the name of the chakra usually associated with each coil. In practice, it works best to link the ascending order of chakra points in the body with the order the coils are walked.

Here is how the labyrinth's coils are linked with the chakras:

Coil three, the first circuit to be walked, is ruled by the Root chakra and is colored red.

Coil two, the second circuit to be walked, is ruled by the Sacral chakra and is colored orange.

Coil one, the third circuit to be walked, is ruled by the Solar Plexus chakra and is colored yellow.

Coil four, the fourth circuit to be walked, is ruled by the Heart chakra and is colored green.

Coil seven, the fifth circuit to be walked, is ruled by the Throat chakra and is colored blue.

Coil six, the sixth circuit to be walked, is ruled by the Brow chakra and is colored purple.

Coil five, the seventh circuit to be walked, is ruled by the Crown chakra and is colored white or gold.

Understanding the Energies

These energy points are not static but instead are whirling vortices whose energies intermingle. Imagine you are standing at the entrance of the labyrinth and looking inward toward the center. The seven-coil labyrinth represents the layers of the spirit body that exist within the physical frame and the energies of the chakras, which fuel the individual layers and carry the life force into and around the physical form.

The chakras are positioned at regular intervals along the spine of the spirit body, which mirrors the organs and structure of the physical body, so they are close to the physical spine. However, they take their names from areas at the front of the body, such as the throat and the brow, and are depicted as spheres on a forward-facing body.

These seven main psychic centers extend vertically from the Root chakra, located at the base of the spine, up to the Crown chakra, on top of the head. Imagine that the labyrinth is standing on one of its ends, so that as you stand in the Root coil on the ground or earth, you are looking upward as if at a standing or sitting giant. You can see through all the mists of the rainbow colors that represent the chakra colors as they spiral upward, swirling around each energy center, right through from the red Root chakra at the perineum, the point of contact if the giant is sitting on the ground, to the white or gold Crown chakra, at the top of the giant's head.

As you look upward to the center of your vertical labyrinth you may see pure white or golden light from the cosmos pouring downward and in through the head of the giant, spiraling down countless energy channels to his Root.

Color has always been of great importance in labyrinth work. Medieval cathedral builders knew this, and so they created glorious stained-glass windows that shone on the labyrinths inside, suffusing them with rainbows, and also painted their religious statues in brilliant colors and decorated them with gold leaf, so the intermingling of colored energies within a labyrinth would not have seemed strange even to the children who played within the coils. Our ancestors felt and used these same colored powers, even though they did not give them chakra names.

In chakra work, as in labyrinth work, the center of the labyrinth represents the source of divinity. The chakra energies pour inward and outward through all the chakra points into the rainbow aura just as sunlight filters through those beautiful stained-glass windows on to the cathedral labyrinths. The chakra colors do not travel in a single channel but, like the light beams breaking into a thousand rainbows, spiral through thousands of *nadis,* or tiny energy channels in the body, amplified and mingling with the new energies at each chakra energy point.

Scientists know now that matter is not solid but composed of moving energies and that we live in a sea of these energies. The energies move with a constant ebb and flow via the auric, or rainbow energy field, energy that surrounds each person, animal, plant, and crystal. So our chakra energies are constantly affecting and being affected by those of other people, animals, plants, and crystals. In open-air labyrinths these energies are especially potent. The labyrinth takes these energies and increases the swirling power, like a psychic spa bath that can cleanse and energize an individual's most stagnant or blocked chakras.

If this concept seems strange, think of a chakra labyrinth walk in this way: Choose a star in the sky directly above you, and imagine a straight axis going through your spine and straight up to that star. Now whirl round and round as you did when you were a child and before long you will be spiraling and the stars dancing in the giant labyrinth of the Milky Way. Or sit on a carousel, one of those wonderful gold-painted, mirrored creations, and focus on the scenery swirling by, multicolored and never still. That is what your chakra labyrinth walk is like. Just follow the coil numbers.

Dancing the Rainbow

Before you read the following section, create or find a seven-coil labyrinth, large or small (even a table one will do). You have danced the labyrinth before and so are aware of the increased energies that come from dancing. Now you are going to focus primarily on the colors and their individual energies as you dance.

Dance each coil, waving a scarf or ribbon in the color of that coil; as you move into each coil, add the new ribbon, in the color of that coil, to the old by knotting them together. Tie the end of the second ribbon or scarf to the end of the first one, then one end of the third to the untied end of the second. This way you make one very long ribbon of different colors. This can be a lovely group exercise, with everyone waving scarves as they spiral through the labyrinth. Alternately, each person could wear the appropriately colored ribbon or scarf in each coil so that seven people are dancing in unison. If the day is sunny, you could blow rainbow-colored bubbles in the coils instead and perhaps wear a scarf with metallic threads to reflect the light as you move.

If you are working with a miniature labyrinth, scatter sequins in the relevant color in each coil, so that you add to the rainbow as you move further within the spiral. For example, when you enter coil three, the first coil to be walked, you will scatter red sequins; when you enter coil two, the second coil to be walked, you will scatter both red and orange; by the time you reach coil one, the third coil, you will scatter red, orange, and yellow sequins in the coil, and so on.

Hang rainbows or suncatchers near windows to make the colors dance. Now you can feel the colored energies. Through your movement you will clear any blockages in your personal system; if working with others you will create a very positive collective power.

Chakra Well-Being

The color of each chakra is reflected in one of the layers of the aura as a halo around the whole body. A person's most prominent colors seen in an aura reading indicate that person's chakras that are most active at the time of the reading.

When the seven main chakras are open, they receive energy and vitality from the universal life force in its many forms. When they are operating efficiently, chakras are also able to filter out impurity or negativity that enters the auric field and transform negative energy into positive power. States of disease and potential problems appear in the spirit body before they appear in the physical one.

Blockages in the chakras can be caused by pollution, stress, negativity emanating from others or destructive situations, too much junk food, lack of sleep or exercise, and negative attitudes. These blockages can cause the chakras to turn only slowly if at all, resulting in aches, pains, a lack of energy, and an inability to tackle problems.

Labyrinth chakra walks can help to clear these blockages and restore balance to the chakras, while also eliminating possible future problems. Unlike other methods of cleansing chakras, you will also gain insight into what you need to do in order to avoid future difficulties.

Imbalances can be caused not only by our own innate personality but also by external pressures that can divert our power though a particular chakra. In the short term, this may be a useful strategy. For example, operating primarily through the yellow Solar Plexus chakra, which controls willpower, memory, and logic, may be necessary for a while if you must work to meet important deadlines at work or need to use your head rather than your heart to avoid being overwhelmed by the problems of others.

However, sometimes we continue to operate through the same chakra long after the crisis has passed, either by habit or because of fear that a negative situation will recur. Therefore, you might continue to pour all your energies through your Solar Plexus; this might lead to your becoming a workaholic or cut off emotionally. In this case, your aura would change from pale yellow to a harsher shade.

Identifying the Chakras Using a Pendulum

Though chakras are common to us all, in each one of us their positions may vary slightly. You can use a pendulum (purchase one from a New Age store or make one yourself with twine or ribbon and a piece of metal or crystal for the weight) for identifying any blocked chakras so that you can give them special attention in your labyrinth walk. A blocked chakra will be indicated by the swinging pendulum stopping or seeming to be caught as though by a knotted cord. An overactive or unbalanced chakra can be identified by the pendulum moving first one way, then the other, and emitting a buzzing sensation, like a mild electric shock, felt through the fingers.

If you are not certain of the positive response of your pendulum, hold it in front of you and think of a happy event. The spontaneous swing of the pendulum will indicate a positive response; this will occur when chakras are functioning well.

Dwelling briefly on a sad time will allow your pendulum to indicate its negative response. A negative response is usually the reverse of the positive response. So if your pendulum circled clockwise for positive, it will likely circle counterclockwise for negative. You may also be aware of a feeling of restlessness or irritability if a chakra is overactive, or a feeling of exhaustion if it is blocked.

Stand and hold the pendulum about two inches from the body. Beginning with the sole of your right foot, pass a crystal pendulum slowly upward over the front of the right side of your body, including your right arm and up to the head, allowing the pendulum to guide you by its positive or clockwise swing as it connects with the spiraling channels of chakra energy. Return down the left side of your body, this time over the left arm, finally leaving the body via the left foot.

Your pendulum will become especially active around your body's chakra circles. It will swing much faster clockwise and you may feel a pull toward your body, akin to the sensation of holding your hand over bathwater swirling down a drain.

Look at the chart of chakra centers below, and draw a chart showing your own chakra points using the result of the pendulum exercise. Their position may vary slightly from those on my sample chart. You will see that the chakra energies overlap. Color them using the appropriate colors and indicate by jagged lines, harsh colors, or darkness the spheres where blockage has occurred.

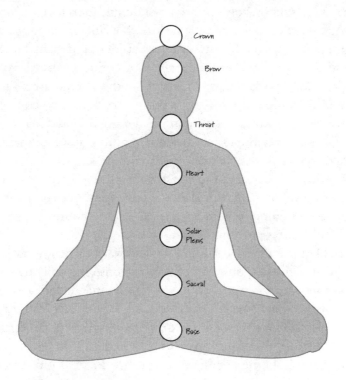

Chakra Energies and the Labyrinth

Draw a seven-coil labyrinth on white paper. After you read about the chakras below, color each coil in the appropriate shade, filling in every inch of white and not going over the edges. Color the coils in the order listed. Then, follow this procedure:

Focus on what the key word of each chakra means to you.
For example, the key word for the Root chakra is survival. Think about
the word and its related concepts. You might think, "I have survived;
I will survive. What is my baseline? What really matters to me? Am I at
home in my body? Am I in permanent fight or flight mode? Do I feel
angry right now? What makes me angry? Why? Is this a real or per-
ceived threat? How might I be able to channel my negative feelings?"

Using a dark pen, decorate each coil with an image or images
of the power creature or creatures who rule the chakra and the coil.
As you work, consider the qualities you admire in that creature and
how they could help you. What do you fear about the animal? How
can this fear be transformed into positive qualities or action?

You will build on this work as you walk the chakra labyrinth
over the coming months.

> **The Root or Base Chakra: Coil Three** The Root chakra, whose
> color is red, is the chakra of earth, drawing power as rich red
> light from the earth through the feet and through the perineum
> when we sit on the ground. The feet and the perineum are
> points at which the Root or Base chakra can be accessed and
> healed.
>
> Coil three is the most powerful of all, since it is the home
> of kundalini or serpent energy, which comes from our beautiful
> snake goddess we met in chapter 2.
>
> Kundalini is associated with the Shakti, the Hindu mother
> goddess whose force activates the creative powers that come
> from Shiva, the father god.
>
> In Eastern philosophy this primal kundalini power is visu-
> alized as being coiled at the base of the spine and as providing
> the driving power for the chakra system.
>
> The Root rules the large intestine, legs, feet, and skeleton,
> including the teeth.
>
> Its function is survival, physical identity, self-preservation,
> instinctive reproductive urges, happiness, and a sense of belonging
> in our immediate environment—of being at home in our bodies
> and at one with the earth and all its creatures.
>
> Blockages and imbalances can be manifested as pain or

tension in any of the bodily parts that the Root or Base chakra controls: symptoms might include constipation or irritable bowel symptoms, a general lack of energy, and an inability to relax even when exhausted. On a psychological level, unreasonable anger or paralyzing fear from trivial causes can occur when things are wrong in this chakra.

Its creatures are the serpent, bull, and dragon.

Its crystals are bloodstone, garnet, red jasper, lodestone, black tourmaline, obsidian, ruby, and smoky quartz.

Its key word is *survival*.

The Sacral Chakra: Coil Two This chakra's color is orange. It is the chakra of water. It is situated in the sacrum/lower abdomen, around the reproductive system, and focuses on all aspects of physical comfort or satisfaction. It controls the blood, all bodily fluids and hormones, the reproductive system, kidneys, circulation, and the bladder. This chakra is especially sensitive to the stress and imbalance that occur if our natural cycles fall out of harmony.

Its functions include dealing with unresolved childhood issues that may affect our adult lives for good or ill, the patterns of behavior we develop, and personal creativity and its expression. Some people believe personal past-life issues sit here.

Imbalances and blockages can show themselves as fluid retention, menstrual or menopausal problems, mood swings, men's impotence, and women's inability to relax during sex.

Disorders involving physical indulgence as a way of seeking emotional satisfaction, especially food and other oral-related obsessions, can also result from problems with this chakra.

Its creatures are fish, especially goldfish, dolphins, and whales.

Its crystals are banded orange agate, amber, carnelian, orange calcite, coral, fluorite, rutilated quartz, moonstone, and aquamarine.

Its key word is *desire*.

The Solar Plexus Chakra: Coil One Its color is yellow, and it is the chakra of fire. It is situated above the navel and around the stomach area or, according to some systems, near the central cavity of the lungs. You can locate this precisely in your own body by circling your palm or a pendulum over the area to identify the swirling sensation that indicates the presence of the chakra. When you hold your palm over a chakra you feel a pulling sensation in your hand, as if your hand is being tugged down over the chakra. This is the same sensation you feel when you hold your hand close to the bathtub drain as it is emptying.

The Solar Plexus chakra function is to galvanize personal power and individuality and to integrate experience, good and bad, absorbing what is useful and discarding what is destructive or redundant. It controls the liver, spleen, gall bladder, stomach, small intestine, digestion, and the metabolism.

Digestive disorders and hyperactivity can result from imbalances and blockages in this chakra. Obsessions, oversensitivity, a lack of self-confidence, a tendency to become overly emotional and find fault with others, and an inability to empathize can also result from the inefficient working of this chakra.

Its creatures are the ram, the salamander, the magical fire lizard, and the legendary phoenix, who burned himself every five hundred years on a funeral pyre and emerged golden and renewed from the ashes.

Its crystals are beryl, citrine, desert rose, yellow calcite, tiger's eye, and topaz.

Its key word is *power*.

The Heart Chakra: Coil Four Its color is green, and it is the chakra of air or the winds. It is situated in the center of the chest, radiating over the heart, lungs, breasts, and also hands and arms. There are minor chakras in the palm of each hand, the outlets for healing powers that stem from Heart chakra, which in turn draws power from the higher centers.

Compassion and connection with our still center of being are results of a clear Heart chakra. You may experience increased healing energies derived from natural sources such as herbs or crystals when this chakra is functioning well; you may also have the ability to see nature spirits and communicate with the wise ancestors. Gifted healers invariably have very open Heart chakras.

Constant coughs, breathing difficulties, and allergies can result from blockage or imbalance of this chakra, as can oversensitivity to other people's problems, which leave us anxious but unable to offer real help.

Its creatures are all birds, especially the white dove and the white peacock.

Its crystals are aventurine, green calcite, emerald, jade, moss agate, kunzite, rose quartz, and green tourmaline.

Its key word is *love*.

The Throat Chakra: Coil Seven Its color is blue, and it is the chakra of sound. Listen to a well-trained choir singing in a sacred setting with good acoustics and they will seem to be singing an octave higher than they really are, merging with the songs of the angels. That is the sound of the Throat chakra at its best.

The Throat chakra is situated close to the Adam's apple in the center of the neck. The Throat chakra controls in addition to the throat and speech organs, the mouth, the neck and shoulders, and the passages that connect to the ears.

Its clear functioning enables us to instigate meaningful communication with others and to express our creativity in a variety of ways. On a spiritual level, it brings communication with *devas,* higher nature essences, and personal spirit guides. Blockages and imbalances may be manifested as sore throats, swollen glands in the neck, mouth ulcers, and ear problems. Confusion, incoherence, and an inability to speak the truth in your heart may result if the chakra is not working efficiently.

Its creatures are the elephant and the owl.

Its crystals are blue beryl, blue lace agate, blue quartz, sapphire, lapis lazuli, and turquoise.

Its key word is *communication.*

The Brow, or Third Eye, Chakra: Coil Six Its color is purple, and it is the chakra of light. The Brow chakra is situated just above the bridge of the nose in the center of the brow. It controls the eyes, ears, and both hemispheres of the brain and radiates into the central cavity of the brain.

In this chakra, emotions are honed into global concerns and also tuned to the world of higher spiritual beings. At this level of functioning we are able to communicate personally with angelic beings and our higher self, a soul that may have evolved over a number of lifetimes but whose wisdom is inaccessible to us in daily life.

Blockages and imbalances in the Brow chakra can result in blurred vision without a physiological reason, headaches, migraines, blocked sinuses, and earaches. Insomnia or nightmares can also result from inefficient functioning.

Its creatures are cobras and turtles.

Its crystals are amethyst, azurite, lapis lazuli, sodalite, and sugilite.

Its key word is *clarity.*

The Crown Chakra: Coil Five Its color is white or gold as rays from the cosmos pour in. It is the chakra of spirit or pure ether and corresponds with the essence created by the union of Earth, Air, Fire, and Water. The Crown chakra is situated at the top of the head around the fontanel, where the three bones of the skull fuse and the spirit merges with the cosmos. Its energies extend about three finger-breadths above the top of the head. It rules the brain, body, and psyche. In this chakra resides our personal core of divinity, which connects us the source of divinity itself.

The Crown chakra's function is to allow the merging of the individual separate consciousness with the undifferentiated cosmic consciousness. It enables us to channel the wisdom of archangels and to momentarily glimpse the divine source through mystical or peak experiences.

Blockages and imbalances in the Crown chakra can result in headaches and migraines, inefficient functioning of the immune system, and a tendency toward forgetfulness and minor accidents. Psychological problems with this chakra are manifested as a sense of alienation from the world, unrealistic aims and unattainable standards, or the inability to settle into daily life.

Its creatures are the eagle and the magical golden phoenix.

Its crystals are white and purple-banded amethyst, clear crystal quartz, diamond, Herkimer diamond, pearl, and brilliant purple sugilite.

Its key word is *unity*.

The Harmonizing Labyrinth

It's all very well to identify problems, you may be thinking, but how can we use the energies of the different coils to offer healing to the blocked chakra? In addition, since each chakra rules an area of the physical body and also mental and spiritual functioning, how can labyrinth work improve our general well-being, as well as healing specific ills?

The secret lies in the interwoven, integrated energies of the labyrinth. By walking each coil of the labyrinth and focusing on the related chakra and its associations, you can energize your whole system and naturally restore the balance to any problem areas. By flowing with the powers and allowing the labyrinth to do its work, you cannot fail to attain a sense of well-being and harmony.

Because each coil works on a particular chakra and the chakras are innately self-regulating mechanisms, walking the whole labyrinth enables the system to slip back into healthy functioning. For example, if you need extra power from the Solar Plexus chakra, even if you are not consciously aware of this, when you walk in coil one you will spontaneously experience a great input of energy and feel the inrush of power physically around your stomach; in other coils you may feel a gentler inflow.

A LABYRINTH CHAKRA BALANCING RITUAL

You may wish to carry out this ritual once a month, or more often if you have been under stress or subject to external hostility. The best setting is a large labyrinth in a cathedral or church, walked at a time when the low winter sunshine casts colored light on the labyrinth through stained-glass windows. However, you can improvise with candles or fiber optic lamps around the perimeter of a labyrinth indoors or with garden torches outdoors. Alternatively, work in bright sunlight or moonlight so your labyrinth is suffused with light. If you are using a miniature labyrinth, you can set colored candles in their appropriate coils or a small rainbow fiber optic lamp in the center and turn off all the lights. You may also wish to create your own chakra empowerments for each coil.

To carry out the ritual:

1. Enter coil three (Root chakra), the first coil to be walked, and visualize rich red light rising from the earth and entering your feet, legs, and spine. As you walk your Root chakra coil, say, "I draw strength from my roots to survive and to thrive. I am filled with courage and the power to overcome all obstacles." Name an issue that is central to your survival or your feelings of security as you walk the coil.

2. Enter coil two (Sacral chakra), the second coil to be walked, and visualize warm orange light flowing into your womb or abdomen and genitals and mingling with the red Root energy. As you walk the Sacral chakra coil, say, "I am filled with inner radiance and love for myself, accepting without shame or blame who I am and what I am." Name an issue concerned with your self-esteem, your desire, or your needs that may be troubling you or that requires strengthening.

3. Enter coil one (Solar Plexus chakra), the third coil to be walked, and visualize clear lemon yellow light flowing into your stomach and digestive system, mingling with the orange and red light of the earlier coils. As you walk the Solar Plexus chakra coil say, "I am filled with power and focus, choosing my own path and my own destiny, for only by making myself happy can I fulfill the needs of others." Name an issue concerned with your self-confidence, your personal ambitions, and your independence and identity that may have become clouded or eroded by the judgments or pressures of others.

4. Enter coil four (Heart chakra), the fourth coil to be walked, and visualize rich green light flowing into your chest and heart, your arms, and your hands, mingling with red, orange, and yellow. As you walk the Heart chakra coil, say, "I am filled with love,

compassion, and connection with all creation, animals, plants, rocks, and crystals. I am dissolving the barriers between me and my fellow beings in the universe." Name an issue related to your relationships and your ability to ask for, receive, and give love.

5. Enter coil seven (Throat chakra), the fifth coil to be walked, and visualize deep blue light flowing into your throat, neck, and ears, mingling with the colored light from the earlier coils you walked. As you walk the Throat chakra coil say, "I am filled with creative light and inspiration and can speak the truth that is in my heart without fear, without cruelty, and without wounding or diminishing others." Name an issue concerning your unshakable ideals and principles, which may conflict with your desire to keep peace.

6. Enter coil six (Brow chakra), the sixth coil to be walked, and visualize dark purple light entering your brow, your eyes, and your sinuses, mingling with the light from the earlier coils. As you walk the Brow chakra coil say, "I fill myself with inner peace and harmony. I trust my inner voice and inner eye to show me the way to link my spiritual world with the world in which I live and work." Name an issue regarding your dreams and intuitive beliefs that seem at odds with the external material world.

7. Enter coil five (Crown chakra), the seventh coil to be walked, and visualize clear violet light mingling with white and gold and the colors from the other coils. As you approach the center of the labyrinth you will seem to be surrounded by a swirling rainbow. As you walk the Crown chakra coil say, "I am filled with light. I touch my own divine core, acknowledging the sanctity in the smallest blade of grass or the tiniest insect and thus offering myself as protector of the vulnerable and seemingly insignificant, who are a part of the divine source." Name an issue involving your struggle to reconcile mortality and immorality, suffering and evil.

8. Enter the center and see all the separate colors returning to a pure white and gold cone, a pyramid, or a prism as the rainbow colors join together. Sit here in silence, allowing the light from below, above, and all around to flow freely in and out of every

pore. See your own boundaries melting so that you are the part of the sea of energy.

9. When you feel cleansed and harmonized, walk outward slowly, pausing in each coil to allow an insight to form in your mind concerning the issue you raised on your inward path. These insights will come quite spontaneously in the form of words or images.

Afterward, you may wish to record any insights or strategies in your labyrinth journal.

George's Crystal Healing Ritual

If you feel overwhelmed, exhausted, or unable to relax, it may help to carry out a general healing labyrinth ritual, burying in the earth one or more of the crystals associated with each chakra (listed earlier in this chapter). This is an especially good ritual to use if you have been under a great deal of stress or have been ill.

Carry out this ritual on a large labyrinth drawn on sand or earth or on a small labyrinth in a small tray filled with sand or earth. You will need earth deep enough for you to bury your crystals. Alternatively, use your fingers to walk a table labyrinth while holding the chakra crystal for each coil, and taking your crystals out of a drawstring bag as you need them.

You do not necessarily need to use large crystals; if you cannot obtain any of these, use crystals of similar colors or even paint stones in the appropriate colors. Place your crystals in a small drawstring bag made of a natural fiber.

The idea behind burying crystals is that any blockages or harshness from the chakras will drain into Mother Earth, to be absorbed and re-formed; gentle new energies will then grow and flow through your chakras over the next few weeks.

If you are walking a full-size labyrinth you can carry seven chakra crystals, one for each coil, in a drawstring bag from your wrist. If any chakra seems to need special healing, you can add extra crystals to the bag beforehand and bury two of its related chakra crystals, either the same or different kinds. You can adapt George's ritual for any loss, illness, or crisis, focusing on how the issue has affected each of your chakras and how they can be healed.

George had been through a very traumatic relationship experience: his unemployed partner had suddenly emptied their joint bank account and disappeared with a former boyfriend. George had had no idea that there were problems with the relationship, but he felt that his partner's betrayal was somehow his fault.

The result was that George's chakras were scarcely functioning; a pendulum hardly moved when passed over his body. George was exhausted, had lost his appetite, and was missing deadlines in his freelance design business. Had there been problems in just one or two areas of the body and mind, then George could just have buried crystals in a couple of coils in order to receive relief, but his problems were much larger—he needed to heal all of his chakras.

George filled a large plant tub with soil. In it he drew his seven coils and made walls of earth between them. He traced coil three with the Root chakra crystal, a blood agate, focusing on all the anger and resentment flowing through the crystal into the earth. At the end of the coil he buried the blood agate, saying, "Thus I bury anger. May courage grow. Let it be so."

Next he took a piece of amber, a Sacral chakra crystal, that contained tiny plant matter, a reminder that life has continued for millions of years and so the present sorrow will pass. George focused on the loss of self-esteem and self-worth caused by the rejection, as he traced coil two with the crystal. At the end of the coil he buried the amber, saying, "Thus, I bury my own wounded feelings. May new trust grow, let it be so."

George selected a rich yellow jasper, a Solar Plexus chakra crystal, to trace coil one, concentrating on his loss of focus and personal power since the betrayal. At the end of the coil he buried the jasper, saying, "Thus I bury my lack of concentration and my current loss of direction. May new purpose grow, let it be so."

For coil four, George used a soft green jade, a Heart chakra crystal, to trace it. He focused on his sudden loneliness and introspection. At the end of the coil he buried the jade, saying, "Thus I bury my sense of loss and alienation from other people. May new love grow, let it be so."

In coil seven, George selected a blue lace agate, a Throat chakra crystal, to trace the circuit, focusing on all the words he had not spoken to his former partner. As he left the coil he buried the crystal saying, "Thus I bury the words that now will never be spoken, words of love and promise and betrayal. May new joys grow, let it be so."

For coil six, George used a deep purple amethyst, a Brow chakra crystal, to trace the coil, focusing on the dreams now broken and the lost spiritual bond he had shared with his partner. As he left the coil he buried the crystal, saying, "Thus I bury the discarded dreams. May new dreams grow, let it be so."

In the final coil, five, George traced the pathway to the center with a clear crystal quartz, focusing on his new cynicism and loss of faith in the innate goodness of the world. As he left the center he buried the crystal quartz, saying, "Thus I bury my disillusionment and lost innocence. May the wisdom of experience grow, let it be so."

When he reached the center, George clasped his hands and allowed the circuit of chakra energy to flow round his body, cleansing and healing him. On the way out, using his index finger to trace the coils, he named the salient quality and strength of each chakra coil that he would take with him. He stated them in the following chant:

Coil Five: wisdom
Coil Six: wisdom and dreams
Coil Seven: wisdom, dreams, and joy
Coil Four: wisdom, dreams, joy, and love
Coil One: wisdom, dreams, joy, love, and purpose
Coil Two: wisdom, dreams, joy, love, purpose, and trust
Coil Three: wisdom, dreams, joy, love, purpose, trust, and courage

George scattered lavender seeds in each coil so that as they grew, he would smell the fragrance and he would be reminded of the growth of new life.

If you wish, you can create your own outward journey chant according to the purpose of your customized ritual, perhaps listing the seven stages of recovery from illness or other problems.

Singing the Labyrinth

Each of the chakras resonates with a musical note on the scale. This means that in each chakra coil you can chant using its special note or, if you wish, you can carry on the previous note and add the new one, as described below.

To sing the seven-coil labyrinth:

1. In the Root chakra, coil three, sing, "I will survive," using middle C.
2. Then, in the Sacral chakra, coil two, sing, "I desire," using middle C and then rising to D.
3. Continue with each coil, singing your chant from middle C and continuing up the scale, going up one note with each coil.
4. By the time you reach the Crown chakra coil, you are using all seven notes.
5. In the center, finish the chant by continuing up one note to the C above middle C, perhaps weaving all the key words into a continuous chant.
6. On the way out, go down the scale one note at a time, completing your chant at middle C as you stand outside the labyrinth once more.

Singing is a very fast and effective way of harmonizing your chakras. You can also walk a tiny labyrinth with your fingers or in your mind as you sing your chakra mantra, either out loud or in your mind.

You can effectively lower work-related stress by using a rainbow seven-coil labyrinth, which you can place on your computer screen as a screen saver. Look at your labyrinth screen saver and walk it in your mind while you sing the seven color names (silently or out loud, depending on whether your office has a door), one in each of the seven coils, beginning with red, middle C in the Root, and then all eight in the center, again using the entire octave. Go down the scale again as you visualize walking out of the coils.

Sing your labyrinth on rainy days, while waiting for buses, when someone has spoken harshly to you, or whenever you need an infusion of color through your chakras.

The chakras of the human body can be empowered and purified by walking the labyrinth. And, in fact, many people who work with chakras and labyrinths regularly report seeing the rainbow colors in the labyrinth, even though they are not physically present.

In the next chapter we will examine the deity forms in more detail to fine-tune our labyrinth work and create our own rituals.

Part 3

DEITIES, LOCATIONS, AND RITUALS

Chapter 11

GODS and GODDesses OF THE LABYRINTH

Throughout the book I suggest working with various aspects of the goddess and god form. In this chapter I list some deities that I have used to great effect in labyrinth work. However, there are countless more; for example, if you do an Internet search for "god" or "goddess" plus the attribute you seek for example, "serpent goddess," you will find a number of entries referring you to different culture sites, often with downloadable images and small statues or artifacts that you can buy. You can also research deities in the many books listed in the appendix.

Though I have suggested using particular gods and goddesses in many specific rituals, you can use any of these deities in your labyrinth work whenever you need their particular strength. In this case you do not need to perform a complex labyrinth ritual. Instead, you might simply visualize their dwelling or country of origin as you enter a labyrinth. In the center you might talk to your chosen deity and ask for his or her particular strength. If you believe in a single god or goddess, then you can talk to him or her, focusing on the desired aspect or strength you seek.

You may find it helpful to collect small statues or images of your favorite deity (or his or her angelic forms), which you can find on the Web or in books on angels (see the appendix). You can keep these in your dedicated labyrinth place and at the appropriate time select one to set in the center of your labyrinth as you meditate on his or her individual qualities.

Mother and Serpent Goddesses for Finding Your Labyrinth Mother

I have organized the mother goddess forms below by culture, since their attributes are strongly influenced by the cultures in which they appear.

Ancient Egyptian—Isis Of all the goddesses of the ancient world, the Egyptian Isis is the one whose worship as a great mother has rivaled that of the Virgin Mary. Isis has been honored in many forms, as goddess of the moon; as Stella Maris, goddess of the sea; as Holy Virgin, the sacred bride; as Mother Nature; and as the Mistress of Enchantment, an important figure in the Westernized ceremonial magical system.

However, her widespread appeal over the millennia resides in the fact that she was a wife and mother as well as a great goddess. Like her consort, Osiris, she was regarded as mortal as well as deity, dwelling on earth and also as Queen of Heaven; as Osiris did, Isis promised ordinary people, not just great pharaohs and kings, hope of immortality.

Ancient Egyptian—Uadjet Uadjet, pictured as a winged and crowned cobra, and sometimes as a snake with a human face, was a goddess of the Underworld, justice, and truth. She guarded the infant Horus in the reeds while his mother, Isis, was looking for the body of her husband. She was called Lady of Heaven, being associated with the heat of the sun that daily traveled through the sky. Uadjet was both protector and destroyer, spitting poison at any who would do the pharaoh harm but also administering the

death sting when his appointed time on Earth was over. In her
role as a bone or death goddess, she guided souls past the snares
of the spirit serpents on their Underworld progression.

Ancient Greek—Demeter She was the Greek Earth and Corn
Goddess or Barley Mother, the archetypal symbol of the fertility
of the land. Demeter is often pictured as rosy cheeked, carrying
a hoe or sickle and surrounded by baskets of apples, sheaves of
corn, garlands of flowers, and grapes. She is mother of the mystery
religions.

Ancient Greek—Gaea, or Gaia She was the all-embracing
and nourishing Greek Goddess of the Earth. Latter-day envi-
ronmentalists have adopted her as Mother Earth, who, it is said,
supplies in her bounty all the necessary plants to cure any disease.
Even in the face of human pollution, she constantly heals and
renews the planet. She is also a goddess of marriage.

Ancient Roman—Ceres Ceres was the Roman form of Demeter,
goddess of the grain, of the growth of food plants, of all forms
of fertility and abundance, and of the natural cycles of the year.
Her daughter, Proserpina, was taken into the Underworld by
Pluto, Lord of the Underworld regions. Ceres mourned and so
the crops died, causing winter; when Proserpina was brought
back to her, she rejoiced, which brought spring. She is a focus
of rites concerning grief, mourning, and hope for women,
especially mothers.

Ancient Roman—Tellus Mater Tellus Mater, or Terra, was the
earth mother of the Romans, the alter ego of Ceres, the grain
mother, and, like Ceres, was a guardian of the fertility of people,
animals and crops. However, Terra was also the mother who
received the dead in her womb to comfort and re-form. Like Gaea,
she is associated with the environment, especially deforestation
and pollution of the earth's surface—the original green goddess.

Australian Aboriginal—Warramurrungundjui According to
Australian Aboriginal myth, the creator woman, Warramurrungundjui, emerged from the sea and gave birth to the first people.
She was an amazingly practical creator—rather like a mother
arranging a picnic for her children, she carried a digging stick
and a bag of food plants, medicinal plants, and flowers. Having
planted them, she went on to dig billabongs, or water holes, and
then, leaving her children to enjoy the fruits of her work, she
turned herself into a rock.

Celtic—Aine Goddess of the cycles of the solar and lunar year,
she was the daughter of Manananann, Sea God and ruler of the
Isle of Man. Even during the last century on the Hill of Aine
in Ireland she was invoked through torchlight processions and
burning straw at midsummer and also at the old corn harvest
Lughnassadh at the beginning of August. She was also linked
with love, fertility, and healing.

Celtic—Brighid or Brigid She was the Celtic Triple goddess
whose worship was transferred to the Celtic Christian saint
Bridget (Saint Bride in Wales). Once considered a sun goddess,
on Imbolc, the early spring pagan festival of light (February 1,
now Saint Bridget's day), the maiden goddess was believed to
bring fertility to the land and the people, melting the snows
with her white wand. She was the goddess of poetic inspiration
for the Bards. As a mother figure, she represented the goddess
of midwifery and healing while as crone she was patroness
of the hearth fire, smiths, and craft workers. In her Christianized
mother aspect, she was called Mary of the Gael, the Irish Mary
who was, according to legend the midwife and foster mother
of Christ.

The holy fire at the saint's shrine in Kildare, dedicated
originally to the goddess and later to Saint Bridget, is believed
to have burned unquenched for more than a thousand years.
It was tended first by nineteen virgin priestesses called the

Daughters of the Sacred Flame and later by the nuns of the Abbey at Kildare. The goddess and later the saint were said to care for the fire on the twentieth day of the cycle.

European—Black Madonna The alter ego of the Virgin Mary, the Black Madonna appears in many guises. She is the queen of the earth as Mary is queen of heaven, and she is fertile and sensual as Mary is chaste and virtuous. The Black Madonna is the virgin who belongs to no man or deity, since all life emanated from her as Mother Nature.

Black Madonnas are found all over Europe, especially in France, the most famous ones being at Chartres in France, Czestochowa in Poland, and Montserrat in Spain. Black Madonnas may also be found in the Americas, having traveled with European settlers or, in the case of the Virgin of Guadalupe, having evolved from the mingling of indigenous goddess worship with imported Christianity.

Some Black Madonna figures are pregnant rather than holding a baby, representing the fertile mother of the earth. Black Madonnas are most frequently associated with the Egyptian mother goddess Isis, usually depicted with the infant Horus in her lap, the original mother and child icon. Other sources of her identity may be Artemis, Cybele, or Diana of Ephesus, black goddesses who were still worshipped in France and along the Mediterranean coast from Antibes to Barcelona during the later centuries of the Roman Empire.

The majority of the Black Madonna statues were created in the Middle Ages, often modeled on older statues that had been lost or destroyed. At that time there was still a strong undercurrent of the old ways; Black Madonnas were frequently discovered hidden in trees in France and Spain as late as the seventeenth century. These may have been representations of the pagan goddesses, such as Artemis, the goddess of the hunt, who were still worshipped in groves. Black Madonnas were also associated with and found close to caves. In churches too the statues may have been kept in a crypt or subterranean part of a church or cathedral, usually near a sacred spring or well. In this sense, the

Black Madonna bears similarities to the winter aspect of the Greek corn goddess, Demeter, or the Roman Ceres, emerging from her cave, and who is sometimes depicted as dark skinned.

Hindu—Ananta In Hindu myth, Brahma, the Hindu creator god, and other gods slept on the coils of the world serpent goddess Shesha or Ananta, goddess of infinite time. She is identified with the goddess Kundalini, the psychic life force that according to Eastern philosophy resides coiled like a serpent at the base of the human spine. This area corresponds with the Root chakra, the lowest psychic energy point in the human body (see chapter 10).

Hindu—Anapura The Indian goddess Anapura, or Annapurna, whose name means "food bringer," rules over the production and distribution of food and is shown feeding a child from a full cooking pot using a ladle, as she nourishes all her children. At her autumn festival a food mountain is created at her shrines, to attract abundance, mirroring the harvest supper of the European autumn equinox celebrations. In the spring, she is associated with the sprouting rice.

Hindu—Mahadevi Mahadevi is the creator of the universe who oversees the main cosmic functions, creation, preservation, and destruction. The three supreme gods of modern Hinduism, Brahma the Creator, Vishnu the Preserver, and Shiva the Destroyer, assume these functions, it is said, by her will. According to one myth, Ammavaru (another name for Mahadevi), a goddess who existed before the beginning of time, laid an egg out of which hatched Brahma, Vishnu, and Shiva.

Minoan—Ariadne Ariadne is the first-named labyrinth goddess. Although many of the early Cretan goddesses were depicted with spiraling serpents coiled around their arms, the most notable was Ariadne, the goddess weaver of fate, who is best known for her downsized role in the classical labyrinth myth of Theseus and the Minotaur. Ariadne the goddess in this context is not the helpful virgin who assisted Theseus, but a powerful fertility mother whose oracular priestesses used snakes in their divination.

She was guardian of the sovereignty of the land. Because of her associations with sacred sex, by which she granted the king his power to rule in her name, Ariadne is also a good focus for labyrinth love and sex rituals.

Native American—Grandmother Spider Throughout the myths of many Native North American nations runs the symbol of Grandmother Spider, the female creative being who wove the web of the world, taught wisdom and various crafts to her people, and protected them from bad dreams with her Dreamcatchers.

In Hopi myth she shared the creating power with the sun, but she was the more powerful, mainly because she remained involved in the lives of the people and taught them practical skills, reflecting the importance of women as teachers and healers in the Native North American world.

According to myth, Spider Woman and Tawa, the sun deity, created the earth between them with magical songs from the thoughts and images in Tawa's mind. Spider Woman fashioned from clay wonderful animals and birds, and finally man and woman. Human beings were given life as Spider Woman cradled them in her arms, and Tawa blew his warm breath over them.

Gods of the Labyrinth
and Their Female Counterparts

In myths of many cultures, it was common for a sky god to be married to his sister, also his alter ego (for example, Hera was Zeus's long-lost sister). This was because it was believed that they formed two halves of a twin soul, and this type of union avoided interrupting the bloodline or allowing a foreign dynasty to gain power through marriage.

Labyrinths are a feature in some of the rituals in the cultures of the sky gods.

Apollo The Greek Sun God made the fruits of the earth ripen, and the first crops were offered to him. At Delos and Delphi,

Apollo rededicated the prophetic mother goddess Oracle of
Delphi to himself. He killed Python, the serpent son/consort
of the Delphic Mother. Apollo, therefore, was God of Prophecy
as well as Music, Poetry, Archery, Healing, and Divination.

His strong animus makes him a good focus for labyrinth
rituals for power, ambition, inspiration, and those areas under his
patronage. Men tend to work better with him than women.

Female counterpart: His twin is Artemis, the moon and
huntress goddess. She helped to deliver him and so stands as a
mother figure as well. Artemis herself dates from Neolithic times
and is a form of the ancient Mother of the Herds, who released
animals for the hunt, protected pregnant creatures and their young,
and watched over human mothers in childbirth. As a virgin
goddess, and although she had many liaisons, she was nevertheless regarded as belonging to no man or god.

Arthur The real-life, not mythical, Arthur was an ancient-British
King of Celtic origin who united large parts of Britain in the
fifth century against hostile forces after the collapse of the Roman
Empire. However, he is also linked with an earlier Welsh god of
the same name and was regarded as the Sun God or King, with
his Round Table representing the solar wheel. His name means
"bear," and this animal was his emblem.

Arthur can form a focus for labyrinth rituals for courage
and nobility, for quests for spiritual enlightenment, and for
physical voyages. He is especially potent in redemption and
cleansing rituals.

Female counterpart: Gwenhwyvar or Guinevere, Arthur's
golden-haired queen, represented, because of his marriage to
and superiority over her, the usurpation of the sovereignty of the
land; for this reason the union remained barren.

Morgan le Fay, his raven-haired half-sister or cousin, granted
Arthur the Sacred Marriage, the symbolic sacred sex rite with
the earth goddess, in the guise of a priestess. This resulted in
the birth of Mordred, who killed Arthur because of his disregard
for the mother goddess. Some traditions see her as a form of the

Celtic mother goddess Matrona or Morgen, a goddess associated with winter and death.

Arthurian male–female labyrinth rituals are, unlike the others I have named, best for rebalancing the power within a human relationship, especially if the male has problems accepting his gentler, less dominant side.

Cernunnos His name was a generic term meaning "horned one," representing the various horned gods of the Celtic tradition. His origin dates back to Paleolithic times when shamanic figures were portrayed on cave walls. Cernunnos was a lord of winter, the hunt, animals, death, male fertility, and the underworld and was sometimes portrayed as a Triple or Trefoil god, a concept associated with Saint Patrick, with his emblematic shamrock.

Other forms of the horned god include the old British god Herne the Hunter; the Greek Pan, god of the woodlands; and Dionysus, Greek god of vegetation and the vine, whose ecstatic mystery cult involved ritual dismemberment and resurrection.

Cernunnos can be invoked in the labyrinth for prosperity, fertility, instinctual power, protection against predators, and the hunt, for employment or a home, for example.

Female counterpart: He can be focused on alone or as a counterpart to the goddess of the labyrinth, however you visualize her.

Helios This Greek god, known to the Romans as Sol, was regarded as the Sun himself. He ascended the heavens in a chariot drawn by winged, snow-white horses to give light, and in the evening descended into the ocean. Homer wrote:

> Drawn in his swift chariot, he sheds light on gods and men alike; the formidable flash of his eyes pierces his golden helmet, sparkling rays glint from his breast and his brilliant helmet gives forth a dazzling splendour. His body is draped in shining gauze, whipped by the wind.

Helios is associated with the life force and so can be a focus in labyrinth rituals for renewing health and energy, for increasing optimism and self-confidence, and for spiritual illumination.

Female counterpart: Selene, his twin, was the Greek goddess specially associated with the full moon, rising from the sea in her chariot drawn by white horses at night. She was a fertility goddess and goddess of the witches.

Jupiter Known as the Sky Father, Jupiter was the supreme Roman god, ruler of the universe, offering a role model for the ideal emperor—a combination of general, statesman, and spiritual leader.

Like his Greek counterpart Zeus, Jupiter controlled the thunderbolts, which were carried by his eagle, the noblest of the birds. However, he ruled not despotically but as the chief of a triumvirate of gods, the others of whom were Juno, his consort, and Minerva, goddess of wisdom, who provided the feminine principle of deeper, more instinctual wisdom. The oak is the special tree of Jupiter and Zeus.

Use Jupiter as a focus for labyrinth rituals for achieving lofty ambitions, for altruism, for attaining justice, and for concerns relating to the planet and its creatures.

Female counterpart: Juno was the Roman queen of the gods, the wife/sister of Jupiter. Protectress of women, marriage, childbirth, she is invoked in sacred sex magic, as is her Greek alter ego, Hera.

Lug/Lugh Lugh was the Celtic "shining one," who gave his name to Lughnassadh, Celtic festival of the first harvest (August 1). He was the young solar deity who ultimately replaced the Dagda, the old Celtic father god, as supreme King, because of his versatility and his skills in battle. He was a sacrifice god, a sun king who was reborn each year either at the winter solstice or the spring equinox, depending on the legend.

You can work with the energies of Lugh in the labyrinth when you need to make a personal sacrifice or undertake extra work. Lugh is also helpful in rituals for abundance and for bringing versatility, innovation, and originality to a stagnant situation or mind-set.

Female counterpart: At Lughnassadh, Lugh ritually married Eriu, the Celtic earth and sovereign goddess, rededicated his vows to serve her, and transferred to her what was left of his solar strength that had been poured into the crops during the summer months.

He can also be twinned with the Triple goddess Brighid, especially her maiden aspect at Imbolc, the early festival of spring when she mated with the chosen chief to renew the sacred marriage (see chapter 3).

Odin The Viking Father God, known as the All-Father Odin (Woden in the Anglo-Saxon tradition) was a god of inspiration, wisdom, and poetry as well as war.

Odin was desperate to acquire the wisdom and knowledge of the older order of giants. He traded one of his eyes for wisdom and then obtained the knowledge of the runes, the ancient symbols of spiritual knowledge, by sacrificing himself on the World Tree, hanging for nine days without sustenance till enlightenment came. Odin then acquired the gift of divine utterance. The ash is his tree, the World Tree that held the nine worlds of existence, with Asgard, the realm of the gods, near the top.

Odin can be invoked in labyrinth rituals for magic and divinatory power, especially for casting the runes, for inspiration with words and oration, for expansion of horizons, and for male power magic.

Female counterpart: Frigg/Frigga (Frige in the Anglo-Saxon tradition) was his consort and a goddess of fate who, although she saw the future, would never reveal it, even to Odin. She invited devoted husbands and wives after death to her hall that they might never be parted again; for this reason she is known as a goddess of fidelity.

Osiris Osiris became one of the most important and popular gods in ancient Egypt, mainly because he promised nonroyal believers that resurrection and salvation from death were for everyone, poor as well as rich.

He was also a god of vegetation; the fertilizing, flooding Nile; and the corn, and so he represented the annual dying of the land and rebirth with the flood. Osiris had a complicated family life. He married his sister Isis and was destroyed by his brother Seth, who imprisoned him in a chest. A mighty tree grew round the chest containing the body of Osiris, empowered with his strength. Thus the tree in the labyrinth is especially symbolic of Osiris. He was resurrected by Isis, Lady of the Moon and Enchantment.

Consequently, Osiris is an important icon for rituals in the labyrinth concerning spiritual rebirth, regeneration of hope, and acceptance of the natural cycles of life with its ebbs and flows, endings followed by beginnings.

Female counterpart: Isis plays the roles of the faithful wife and also of the redeemer goddess who raised Osiris from the dead with her magical incantations and charms. As with the Hindu Shiva/Shakti union, it is the female power that generates the life force within the male.

Shiva, or Siva Shiva is the Hindu god of both creation and destruction, good and evil, fertility and abstinence. With Vishnu and Brahma, he forms the trinity of the modern Hindu gods. He is the Lord of the Dance, which, it is said, will one day bring about the destruction of the material world.

His symbol is the phallus, representing creative power, and many Hindus regard his benevolent creator aspect as predominant. Shiva has three eyes: the sun, the moon, and fire. The third eye allows him to see inward and also to destroy whatever it looks on.

Invoke Shiva in the labyrinth for animus power, potency, change involving transformation, and all male concerns.

Female counterpart: Shakti is the female energy or power that activates Shiva. Her name is also used for the wife of any Hindu god. She is the mother goddess and, like Shiva, both creator and destroyer in her different aspects.

260

One of her main forms is as Parvati, gentle mother and wife of Shiva. The marital unity of Shiva and Parvati is an example of the ideal couple; in sacred sex their sexual union may be momentarily channeled by human couples.

In Hindu spirituality, Shiva and Shakti may be represented united in a single figure known as Sakti Hakini or Ardhanarishvara, with the male part of the figure on the right and the female on the left.

Wild Mothers: Nature Forms in the Labyrinth

It may require some perseverance on your part to relate to the wild mothers whom you may encounter within the labyrinth as they lack the charm of some of the more glamorous goddesses. But they will fight for you fiercely, like a mother wolf. Contact one of these wild mothers in your labyrinth rituals if you feel you need some strong support to help you fight opposition or injustice. They are also wonderful for any open-air labyrinth work and for times when you need to reconnect with nature or your roots. (See chapter 13 for a ritual using this goddess form.)

Ardwinna The Celtic goddess of the wild wood, Ardwinna rode on a wild boar and demanded an offering for every animal she allowed to be hunted. Ardwinna offers a focus for labyrinth rituals for establishing and claiming what is rightfully yours and for strengthening your identity.

Bugady Musun This Siberian mother goddess of the animals was an old but very physically powerful huntress goddess who sometimes assumed the form of an elk. She can give you physical and emotional strength and the impetus to seek what you want.

Cailleach is the Celtic generic name for a number of hag goddesses, meaning "the veiled one." They are powerful crone goddesses, mistresses of wild things who have retained their early associations with the winter.

For example, the Scottish Cailleach Bhuer, "the Blue Hag," appeared as a rag-clad old woman with a crow on her left shoulder, carrying a holly staff that could kill a mortal with a touch. She roamed the highlands by night during winter, when her power was at its greatest. Cailleach Bhuer is credited with creating the mountains by flying through the sky dropping stones, said by some folklorists to be the megaliths and stone circles and the origin of the nursery rhyme "There Was an Old Woman Tossed Up in a Basket."

Celtic hags were expert shapeshifters who might assume the form of lovely maidens, hares, cats, stones and even trees. One of her most intriguing aspects is a crone form of the Irish Triple goddess. Garbh Ogh was a giantess who lived for many centuries and was said to hunt the mountain deer with a pack of seventy dogs, all of whom had the names of different birds. When she chose to die she piled stones around herself in a single cairn and, according to a Celtic poem, "set her chair in the womb of the hills at the season of the heather-bloom and breathed no more."

These crone goddesses can offer a powerful focus in labyrinth work for all issues related to aging, the natural cycles and seasons, and letting go of the past.

Hyldermoder According to Scandinavian and Western European legends, "elder mothers" are tree mothers who live in elder trees, the most magical of all fairy plants. They are a version of the ancient mother goddess.

Only in medieval times were these fairies demonized as wicked witches. The original legend of the Rollright Stones, ancient standing stones in Oxfordshire, England, told of a hag goddess or fairy who guarded the countryside; the stones were an invading king and his army who had been turned to stone by the hag. After she performed this deed, she transformed herself into an elder tree close to the stones to stand sentinel throughout the centuries in case the enchantment was broken. On Midsummer Eve, locals would go to the King-stone and, after a feast, ceremonially cut the elder tree, which then bled, to bring fertility to the land. Some psychics have identified tree mothers in other tree species, especially those with mother-goddess connections such as the willow.

Tree mothers are good for all protective rituals and especially for more proactive magic to prevent attack on your home and those you love.

Mama Cocha, or Mother Sea The oceans and the sea are associated with the earth goddess, and the word used to describe the sea itself is, in many languages, akin to *mother;* for example, in French, the word for "mother" is *mère* and the word for "sea" is *la mer.* Mama Cocha, the Peruvian whale goddess, was originally worshipped by the Incas and has been revered through the ages by the peoples living along the southern part of the coast of Peru.

Sedna This Intuit sea goddess of the North American Pacific Coast was considered a very ancient fertility mother, known as "the old woman who lived under the sea." Because of the importance of the sea as the main source of food in the Inuit culture, she is still the most powerful spirit in this people's cosmology. She is given different names throughout the Arctic region: *Nerivik* in Alaska and *Arnarquagssag* in Greenland.

There are different versions of her story but all describe her as the source of marine life. Below is a summary of the most common myth about her origin:

Sedna was a beautiful Inuit girl who refused all suitors, until she fell in love with a handsome hunter who let his kayak sway on the waves while he sang to her in her hut. He offered to give her necklaces of ivory and a tent covered with the finest furs if she went to live with him in the land of birds. He then lured her into his canoe and abducted her, revealing his true form as Kokksaut, the bird phantom. Her father, Angusta, searching the oceans for his lost daughter, found her weeping alone on an ice flow and put her in his canoe. But Kokksaut pursued them and demanded that Angusta return the young girl. When Angusta refused to hand back his daughter, Kokksaut changed into his evil bird form and created a terrible storm. The waves demanded the sacrifice of Sedna. Angusta become afraid for his life, because he had offended the sea and spirits of the air, so he cast Sedna into the waves. When Sedna tried to cling to the boat, her father seized an ivory axe and cut off her fingers. The girl sank into the water, and her fingers became seals. Three times she tried to reach the kayak, but her father hacked at her wounded hands until she was lost beneath the waters. Her knuckles became walruses and whales.

The Inuit believe that Sedna controls storms at sea and can either provide or withhold sea creatures for hunting. When the people have trouble catching sea creatures, the shaman, in astral or soul form, dives to the bottom of the sea to entreat Sedna to set the sea animals loose. He passes first through the kingdom of the dead and then crosses an abyss with a wheel of ice and a boiling cauldron of seals. The shaman finally enters a tent under the sea, furnished with the skins of the finest sea animals. There the dark, gigantic Sedna, no longer the beautiful maiden but the sea mother/crone, listens to the magical chants of the shaman and tells him either that the tribe must move to another place to seek the sea creatures or that she will send shoals to the current hunting grounds. The shaman will comb Sedna's tangled hair, since with her damaged hands she cannot do this herself. She is grateful for this service and rewards the people.

In this story, Sedna emerges as a fertile sea mother who has transformed her pain and suffering into food for the people, though she demands that the people and their shamans meet her high standards. You can use her story as a powerful labyrinth meditation or visualization to transform sorrow into fertility in your own life.

Yemaya-Olokun She is the sea mother of the Yoruba peoples in West Africa. Even centuries after the slave trade brought Africans to the Americas, she is also a primary deity of Santeria, the form of voodoo practiced in Cuba and Brazil.

Yemaya, the Womb of Creation, is the bringer of dreams and prosperity. In Brazil, on New Year's Eve, her worshippers create altars on the shore with candles and food that are accepted by Yamaya (also called Iemanja) in the morning tide—for she is an elemental force who not only lives in the sea but actually is the sea.

In a similar practice in the Western magical tradition, bonfires are created below the high tide mark and then surrounded by and eventually consumed by the sea. In this way the four ancient elements of Water, Air, Earth, and Fire are combined, but the primal waters reign supreme.

If you wish, you can carry out a powerful beach labyrinth ritual focused on this goddess to bring the tides of change into your life.

Zongei She was another Siberian mistress of the herds. She ruled all birds and animals, and the people who hunted them. Game animals would allow themselves to be trapped if she ordained it, and so the shamans made sure that she was given offerings and that the creatures were treated with reverence so their food supply would not be cut off. Zongei is quite a complex goddess, associated with free will and due respect, and she is a good ritual focus for any person who has been undermined or abused in any way. She also provides assistance with resisting emotional blackmail.

Having examined some of the deities whose powers can be used to strengthen and enrich your labyrinth work, I will now go on to describe labyrinths I have visited and places where you can discover them in your own region and around the world.

Chapter 12

LOCATING LABYRINTHS

VISITING LABYRINTHS should
always be an adventure, and the setting of the labyrinth may be as
rich as the labyrinth itself. But sometimes, however well planned your
visit, you may be disappointed. For example, the labyrinth may be
temporarily closed even on a day and time when it is listed as being
open. Calling ahead can often help you avoid this circumstance,
although sometimes the people you speak to may not have the necessary information or may not speak the same language as you do.
Or you may find that, even at times when the labyrinth is supposed
to be accessible, chairs used during a late service at one of the churches
or cathedrals may not have been cleared, so that the labyrinth coils
are partially obscured; the labyrinth may also be crowded or occupied
by noisy children. Or you may get lost and arrive late, as I did at
Bayeux Cathedral in northern France; only thanks to the kindness
of the warden was I able to walk the labyrinth by torchlight. However,
as a bonus I was given a tour of the cathedral's crypt, which features
splendid medieval frescoes depicting angels playing bagpipes, an accor-
dion, and even a bombard, a flute-like instrument popular in that region
of France. So, there are always compensations. If you can absorb the

atmosphere of the labyrinth and walk at least part of it, you can mentally recreate the full experience at home using a photograph from the site.

In order to make sure you'll get to experience the labyrinth you're visiting, make a day or even a weekend of your trip and visit the labyrinth early in your stay. If necessary, you can then make arrangements to return the next day, even if the labyrinth will be officially closed at that time—once you talk to them face to face, people are usually very willing to move mountains to accommodate you, especially if you have come a long way.

Find out as much as you can about the labyrinth beforehand so that you can plan your rituals accordingly. Whether you visit an outdoor turf labyrinth or a modern ecclesiastical one, you should, if possible, explore the whole area around the labyrinth so that you can absorb the energies of the place, which make every labyrinth unique.

Labyrinths to Walk and Use for Meditation and Ritual

In the pages that follow, you will find information about labyrinths in North America and Europe that are open to the public. Some of this information is stated earlier in the book, but in order to make your labyrinth search easier, I have collected and written here the details you'll need to know if you plan to visit any of these labyrinths. In some cases I give diagrams for labyrinths with which I have worked personally. For those labyrinths I have not visited, I give details sufficient to allow you to locate them. However, don't hesitate to write or telephone ahead to ask about the labyrinth and find out when individuals or groups can visit. A number of sites or organizations that house labyrinths offer evening or weekend events, consisting of music programs and guided walks.

There are hundreds of paved and turf labyrinths in the United States, both secular and religious, and more are being created every month. On the whole, these outdoor labyrinths are more accessible than indoor ones, and you can find many on the grounds of churches or cathedrals where you can walk after dusk or in the early morning.

I have listed a few of the major ones, but, since there are so many, I would suggest that you use the Internet to find labyrinths close to your home or vacation spot. Using your Internet provider's search engine, enter the word *labyrinth* and your state and you'll most likely be shown a list of websites that give times and dates when the labyrinth is open. You may be surprised to find that there is a labyrinth two or three blocks away or a nearby church where a huge portable labyrinth is displayed.

When you go on vacation, you may be able to find a number of labyrinths en route, and you can vary your labyrinth pilgrimage to include open air, secular, and religious settings. Also, when you visit new towns, ask about labyrinths at tourist information bureaus, where staff is invariably helpful and knowledgeable.

If you do come across any special labyrinths, contact me at www.cassandraeason.co.uk. I can then update this section in later editions and maybe even visit some of them myself.

North American Labyrinths

Most labyrinths in North America were built recently, beginning in the early 1990s. These labyrinths are used by churches, retreat centers, hospitals, spas, schools, and even prisons as meditative tools for healing. The forms these contemporary labyrinths take are as varied as their uses: there are portable labyrinths painted on canvases, indoor labyrinths inlaid in floors, and permanent outdoor labyrinths delineated by stones or bushes or painted on concrete or molded turf. Contemporary labyrinths are found in peaceful garden sanctuaries as well as busy urban environments. They are used for spiritual contemplation, relaxing walks, and play.

Thousands of labyrinths have been constructed as an outgrowth of a surging interest in this ancient archetypal form of walking. Unlike their European counterparts, contemporary North American labyrinths are not usually deeply embedded in the history of their specific setting. As a result, North American labyrinths are a dynamic, living part of their respective communities. Regardless of the belief system of the labyrinth's creators, most serve as sites for community ritual and worship as well as for workshops exploring the tradition and possible ways of walking a labyrinth.

Because so many new labyrinths are being constructed all the time, the best resource for finding your nearest labyrinth is the online World Wide Labyrinth Locator, a website jointly administered by the Labyrinth Society and Veriditas, www.veriditas.labyrinthsociety.org. Thousands of labyrinths are listed on the website, and each listing includes a brief description of the location, the type of labyrinth, and relevant contact information.

Other useful labyrinths websites include:

www.earthsymbols.com

www.geomancy.org/labyrinths

www.labyrinth-enterprises.com

www.labyrinthos.net

www.labyrinths.net

www.labyrinthsociety.org

www.lessons4living.org

www.maze-world.com

www.veriditas.net

The following section offers a selection of North American labyrinths. However, this list only touches upon the wide variety of labyrinths contained in the contemporary labyrinth movement.

Grace Cathedral, San Francisco, California

At the heart of the North American labyrinth movement is Grace Cathedral, located at the corner of California and Taylor streets in San Francisco, California. The cathedral's outdoor terrazzo labyrinth is open twenty-four hours daily and is located just north of the cathedral doors. There is also an indoor wool tapestry labyrinth inside the cathedral. Both labyrinths are replicas of the eleven-circuit labyrinth found at Chartres Cathedral in France. Grace Cathedral is open Monday through Friday 7:00 A.M. to 6:00 P.M., Saturday 8:00 A.M.

to 6:00 P.M., and Sunday 7:00 A.M. to 7:00 P.M. You should begin your indoor labyrinth walk at least a half hour before closing time. It is also recommended that you call ahead for indoor labyrinth walks, since special events and services are frequently held and might interfere with your plans. Call Grace Cathedral at (415) 749-6300 or check their website at www.gracecathedral.org.

The Reverend Dr. Lauren Artress built Grace Cathedral's outdoor labyrinth in 1991, arguably the first permanent modern labyrinth built in the United States. Dr. Artress went on to found the nonprofit organization Veriditas, which is a strong voice in the labyrinth movement, in 1994. Veriditas offers a range of workshops, lectures, and classes focusing on labyrinths, including pilgrimages to the Chartres Cathedral labyrinth, workshops to learn how to become a labyrinth facilitator, and yoga classes at the labyrinth. From the Veriditas website you can purchase hand-painted, portable canvas labyrinths as well as a labyrinth seed kit that describes how to create your own labyrinth using sacred geometry. Many churches that are part of the Veriditas labyrinth network use the Grace Cathedral labyrinths as models.

LABYRINTHS OF ALEX CHAMPION

Also worth mentioning are the labyrinths of Alex Champion. After he was trained as a biochemist, his interests shifted to sacred geometry, geomancy, and sculptured gardens. Since he founded his company, Earth Symbols, in 1987, Champion has built more than forty earthworks, mostly in Northern California, where he lives. He uses dowsing in the construction process to work more effectively with the energy lines of the site. His labyrinths are some of the most outstanding contemporary labyrinths in the United States. Five of his labyrinths are located on his property in Philo, California. If you are interested in visiting them, contact Alex Champion by calling (707) 895-3375 or by sending an email to earthsymbols@earthlink.net. More information about Alex Champion and his labyrinth designs can be found on his website, www.earthsymbols.com.

ST. LUKE'S EPISCOPAL CHURCH, BETHESDA, MARYLAND

St. Luke's Episcopal Church has a beautiful turf labyrinth that is easily accessible by car from Baltimore; Washington, D.C.; and Virginia. St. Luke's labyrinth is based on the labyrinth found at Breamore House in England. Built in 2001, the St. Luke's labyrinth is an eleven-circuit design, sixty feet in diameter, surrounded by a grass concourse and planting beds and located near a memorial garden. The St. Luke's labyrinth is open twenty-four hours a day and is used as a place of healing and comfort for everyone in the community. More information can be found on the St. Luke's website, www.stlukesbethesda.org.

PRAIRIE LABYRINTH, KANSAS CITY, MISSOURI

Located forty-five minutes outside of Kansas City, Missouri, the Prairie Labyrinth is a striking example of a living labyrinth. Set on five acres of land restored with a variety of prairie grasses, the Prairie Labyrinth is a left-handed, seven-circuit Minoan-style labyrinth more than 150 feet in diameter. At the center of the labyrinth are four benches set in an open area fourteen feet in diameter. The prairie grass "walls" of the labyrinth can reach up to eight feet tall in the fall. The paths were cut with a riding mower using construction flags, clotheslines, and dowsing rods as guides. Every two or three years a controlled burn is done to clear out the dead grasses and weeds and to spur new growth.

The Prairie Labyrinth experience changes with the seasons and is open throughout the year. To visit the Prairie Labyrinth, make an appointment with Toby Evans at toby@homeisp.com. A fee is charged for admission, which includes a guided introduction. For more information, including photographs, go to www.prairielabyrinth.com.

OLCOTT CENTER, THEOSOPHICAL SOCIETY, WHEATON, ILLINOIS

At the Olcott Center, on the grounds of the American headquarters of the Theosophical Society, Wheaton, Illinois, is another seven-circuit Minoan-style labyrinth. It is composed of a path of circular stepping stones on a field of pebbles and is located on the west side of the campus. The Olcott Center hosts a number of lectures, seminars, and workshops on theosophical studies, and the Quest Book Shop, also located on campus, contains an impressive array of metaphysical and spiritual books. The extensive grounds, which include many memorial gardens on the forty-two-acre estate, are open to the public during daylight hours. Groups of six or more are asked to contact the operations manager or the national secretary before visiting by calling (630) 668-1571, extension 321 or 328, or through the website, www.theosophical.org/society/national center/.

JOHNS HOPKINS BAYVIEW MEDICAL CENTER, BALTIMORE, MARYLAND, AND CALIFORNIA PACIFIC MEDICAL CENTER, SAN FRANCISCO, CALIFORNIA

Labyrinths are being installed on many hospital campuses because of their restorative healing potential. Hospital labyrinths offer relaxation and stress relief for patients, patients' families, and hospital staff. Two such examples are the labyrinths at Johns Hopkins Bayview Medical Center in Baltimore, Maryland, and the California Pacific Medical Center in San Francisco. The Johns Hopkins and California Pacific labyrinths are both eleven-circuit outdoor stone installations that are open to the public twenty-four hours a day and seven days a week. The labyrinth at Johns Hopkins was built as part of a collaboration with the Baltimore-based dance company, The Moving Project. The Labyrinth Garden at the California Pacific Medical Center is located near the corner of Clay and Buchanan streets just inside the main entrance to the hospital campus.

Not all labyrinths are meant for spiritual contemplation—some have been built purely for diversion's sake.

SNOOPY LABYRINTH, SANTA ROSA, CALIFORNIA

At the Charles M. Schulz Museum in Santa Rosa, California, is a small labyrinth in the shape of Snoopy's head. You begin at Snoopy's collar and wander through his head before reaching the center of the labyrinth in his ear. The path is a two-circuit classical design. Snoopy's nose is a two-ton granite boulder from the Mother Lode area, west of Yosemite. For photographs and more information, check out www.schulzmuseum.org.

PINWHEEL LABYRINTH, SAN FRANCISCO, CALIFORNIA

Alex Champion's PinWheel labyrinth is painted on a playground on Sacramento Street between Grant and Stockton streets in San Francisco's Chinatown. The design has four different entrances with paths to the center.

Many retreat centers and bed-and-breakfasts have labyrinths on their grounds.

ANGEL'S NEST LABYRINTH AND SANCTUARY, OXFORD, NORTH CAROLINA

The Angel's Nest Labyrinth and Sanctuary in Oxford, North Carolina, houses an outdoor living labyrinth along with chakra centers, meditation gardens, and a temple. The grounds and labyrinth are open to the public. The sanctuary offers classes, full-moon walks, energy work, and private retreats. Angel's Nest can be contacted by phone at (919) 693-3229 or by email at info@angelsnestlabyrinth.org. Learn more on their website, www.angelnestlabyrinth.org.

CORTEZ LABYRINTH, SOUTHWEST COLORADO

The Cortez Labyrinth is part of the Foxfire Institute of Experimental Shamanism in southwest Colorado. The labyrinth is a Hopi design made of native sandstone. The institute is less than an hour's drive from Chaco Canyon, Mesa Verde, and other sites with petroglyphs and pictographs, some of which depict labyrinth-like spirals. The Foxfire Institute can be reached by phone at (970) 565-7163 or through their website, www.foxfireinstitute.com.

DRAGONFLY RANCH, HAWAII

Dragonfly Ranch, an eco-spa bed and breakfast on the Big Island in Hawaii, has a rainbow-colored labyrinth inlaid on the floor of a tented illuminarium overlooking the ocean. Contact the ranch online at www.dragonflyranch.com.

SAGE HILLS NATURAL HEALTH CENTER, CEDAR CITY, UTAH

Sage Hills Natural Health Center has a beautiful outdoor labyrinth constructed of naturally magnetized 22-million-year-old rocks. For more information, check out www.sagehillcedarcity.com.

BORDERLANDS EDUCATION AND SPIRITUAL CENTER, BLACK HILLS, SOUTH DAKOTA

The Borderlands Education and Spiritual Center is grounded in Lakota and Celtic heritage and spirituality. The center, which has an on-site labyrinth, offers pilgrimages and retreats. For more information, call the center at (605) 574-4746 or check their website, www.borderlandsranch.org.

Labyrinths in the United Kingdom

Museums with Roman ruins may have examples of the mosaic labyrinths that were very popular in Roman villas.

HARPHAM LABYRINTH

Ancient Roman labyrinths tend to be square with four quadrants, each protecting the city with a triple meander or spiral that must be walked in order to reach the center. One of the most famous in the United Kingdom was originally located in Harpham in Yorkshire and dates from the year 304. It is now in the city hall in Kingston upon Hull in Humberside and can be seen during normal business hours.

CAERLEON LABYRINTH

Caerleon Museum in Gwent, Wales, contains another Roman labyrinth, dating from ancient Roman times. You can see it during the museum's open hours.

Harpham labyrinth

COMPTON WATTS CHAPEL

This labyrinth site is located in Compton Village near Guildford in Surrey. There is one labyrinth you can touch, a grouping of four angels holding golden labyrinths around the exterior chapel walls, and one engraved labyrinth in a small golden altar, also held by an angel. It is possible to trace this one with your finger.

The memorial chapel itself was built about 1896 to commemorate George Frederick Watts, the Victorian artist and sculptor, by his widow Mary, with assistance from local artisans. It dates from around 1896. The altar labyrinth design is a copy of the floor labyrinth in San Vitale basilica at Ravenna, Italy.

Look for the Celtic cross design of the chapel, the fine Celtic cross on the door, and the fabulous paintings around the wall incorporating the Tree of Life. Best of all are the wonderful gardens, much beloved by modern Druids, with many different species of trees, including the yew, the tree of immortality, and a well. It is a place where birds sing, and there is an overwhelming sense of peace and sanctity. This site is open during daylight hours.

ELY CATHEDRAL

One of my favorites, this square labyrinth in Cambridgeshire was created (or re-created) in Victorian times by Gilbert Scott and stands inside the cathedral beneath the West Tower. Its pathways are the same length as the height of the tower.

The labyrinth is accessible whenever the cathedral is open, during daylight (except during services), and is very peaceful to walk, though people heading for the main cathedral can walk across it, possibly disturbing your meditation as you follow the coils.

ROCKY VALLEY CARVED LABYRINTHS

The Rocky Valley, between Boscastle and Tintagel in Cornwall, is a local beauty spot with a lovely mill house tearoom on the main, but very winding, road between the two towns. You can park your car and get leaflets with precise directions to the labyrinths from the tourist information center in Boscastle, where there is a wonderful museum of witchcraft with a labyrinth exhibition. You can also get information from the tourist bureau in Tintagel, a place with Arthurian associations.

Walk across a stream on a wooden bridge and you are in fairyland, a rocky valley leading along the river to where the sea rushes in. The seven-coil wall carvings are not very far along the valley and are said by many to date from the Bronze Age. Others date them from the eighteenth century, but they feel very, very old. You can trace them with your fingers. Ribbons hang from nearby trees, giving a sense of a sacred site.

Afterward, continue either on the valley walk or drive to the St. Nectan's Glen parking area closer to Tintagel, near the signposted St. Piran's Well. There is a long walk up through the woods by the river to another lovely tearoom high up in the woods. From here you can climb down to St. Nectan's Glen and waterfall. At the foot of this are cavern shrines to the mother goddess, called locally the Lady of the Waterfall.

GLASTONBURY TOR

Buy a detailed map of the labyrinth in Somerset, as the seven coils are in fact huge terraces that are carved into the hillside. Take drinks and raingear, and wear good shoes. The projected path in the center (beneath the ruined church tower of St. Michael on the top of the Tor) goes downward into the fairy world. You will need to enter with your spirit as there is no visible physical tunnel. Inside the tower that is open on the sides to the elements and the grassy banks around, you cannot fail to connect with the heart of this most mystical labyrinth.

Walking the whole circuit takes about five hours and requires crossing over farmlands. But if you follow the paths from the town upward to the Tor, you will naturally walk some of the ancient terraces in the path of Druids and before them the Neolithic peoples who worshipped there. The whole town is truly mystical, from the red springs of the Chalice Well to the white springs that can be traced to a cave under a newly created waterfall (still under construction at the time of writing).

There are also the holy thorn trees, the original reportedly planted by Joseph of Arimathea in the year 64, when he is said to have brought the Holy Grail to the town. Also connected with this place are the legends of Merlin, King Arthur, and his queen, Guinevere; the royal couple are said to have been buried in the ruined abbey grounds.

The town is filled with great spiritual power. I would recommend staying at the fourteenth-century George and Pilgrim Hotel in High Street, where pilgrims rested in times past, still complete with old beams, four-poster beds, and leaden windows—and so many magical energies.

We do not really know how ancient turf labyrinths are, though there are records that show their existence in medieval times. They were probably cut and recut many times, some annually on May Day or the summer solstice, when they were used for fertility dances and games. Many in England were destroyed during the eighteenth century and were simply plowed up or fell victim to the enclosure of common land. I have written about only English ones here, but you can find turf mazes in Germany and the United States. I have listed one or two grass labyrinths that are found in healing sanctuaries or churches, but many more are being created, especially in areas of natural beauty, so check the Internet regularly.

BREAMORE LABYRINTH

Breamore, a village six miles south of Salisbury in Hampshire, replicates the eleven-circuit Chartres design and is eighty-seven feet in diameter. It does involve quite a long walk from the village, so ask for directions or buy a local map. The path to the site can get muddy, but the labyrinth is encircled by trees and so is a magical spot. Unfortunately the labyrinth is fenced off and so cannot be walked. Nearby Salisbury Cathedral is well worth a visit, as is the nearby Old Sarum, a site of very powerful earth energies. You can then drive onward toward Stonehenge.

HILTON COMMON

This grass version of the eleven-ring Chartres labyrinth is in Cambridgeshire. Only nine rings are now left. A stone pillar standing in the center makes a good sky god symbol. The site, located on the village green, is easily accessible. You can combine this visit with a trip to the nearby Ely Cathedral labyrinth (described earlier in this section).

MILTON KEYNES LABYRINTH

This magnificent labyrinth in Willens Park, Milton Keynes, Buckinghamshire, has seventeen coils and is the largest in Europe. Not for the fainthearted, it is two miles into the center, where there was until recently a lovely oak, which I hope will be replaced. This labyrinth sits in a peaceful setting, close to a Buddhist Peace Pagoda, a large wildfowl lake, and a recently added stone medicine wheel. It is a wonderful labyrinth for peace and meditation and one you can take a whole day to experience. It is open during daylight hours, and the way from the town, which boasts a huge shopping mall for an alternative to spiritual pursuits, is clearly marked with signposts.

MIZ MAZE

A true sky labyrinth, the Miz Maze is located in St. Catherine's Down, Winchester, Hampshire, on top of a hill in an area of outstanding beauty. The square Miz Maze is really a labyrinth and not a maze, despite its name. It is about ninety-six feet square; the narrow paths are gullies and the grass forms the banks, so it is not particularly easy to walk. However, it is on the site of an Iron Age fort and close to where the very ancient trader track or ley lines meet, so the whole hillside is buzzing with power. There is a grove of trees close by and a ruined chapel, so you will not be short of magic. The labyrinth is totally accessible. Combine this visit with a trip to the beautiful city of Winchester with its ancient cathedral.

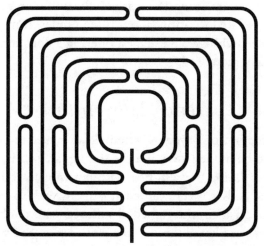

Miz Maze labyrinth

SAFFRON WALDEN

The most ancient turf labyrinth in England, this labyrinth in Essex is also one of the largest, with seventeen rings and a diameter of 132 feet (which means a walk of about a mile to the center). However, it is well worth the effort.

The paths are lined with bricks and are very wide, and there is a large grass mound in the center. The labyrinth is on the village green and was once used for fertility dances and games. There are four bastions, or projections, that carry the walker outward and in. The beautifully preserved sixteenth-century wool-merchant town is well worth a visit, as is the surrounding countryside. Being on the open village green, the site is totally accessible. East Anglia is full of magical associations and ghost legends.

TROY TOWN

This private labyrinth is in Somerton, near Ardley village, not far from Bicester in Oxfordshire. Because it is privately owned, permission should be sought from the owners of Troy Farm in advance in writing, since they are responsible for the upkeep of the labyrinth and its preservation. It is a fifteen-coil labyrinth, about fifty-seven feet in diameter, with trees and hedges around it. It is very beautiful and quite spiritual because of its isolated location, about fifteen miles from the magical Rollright stone circle. I would suggest offering a donation, although none is formally requested.

French Labyrinths

With the exception of Bayeux Cathedral, labyrinthine treasures in France tend to be hidden away, but the settings are so magnificent that it is well worth seeing them in situ; with persistence you can sometimes walk the coils. I was rewarded at Amiens with the sight of the most beautiful pillars in the cathedral suffused with rainbow lights as the low winter sun filtered through the stained glass. Sadly the labyrinths at the cathedrals at Rheims, Sens, Arras, and Auxerre were destroyed during the eighteenth century. A new labyrinth has been created in the cathedral at Evry, on the outskirts of Paris. It contains a smaller, but inaccessible, version of the Amiens labyrinth in the octagonal chapel off the main sanctuary.

AMIENS CATHEDRAL

This cathedral in Picardy has a large octagonal labyrinth, destroyed and later reconstructed (1894), across the center of which a shaft of sunlight shines on the midwinter and the summer solstices. The labyrinth is walkable on these and other special occasions. At other times the labyrinth may be covered with chairs. However, with determination you can move enough chairs to work your way to the center.

You step off the labyrinth down the nave into four quadrants representing Earth, Air, Fire, and Water, the ancient elements. The magnificent setting in the nave of the splendor-filled church is well worth seeing. The town is also very beautiful, with a system of canals and tiny islands just a ten-minute walk from the main waterfront. Don't believe the guidebooks that describe Amiens as unremarkable, but buy a map early in your stay, since it is easy to miss its beauty.

Amiens Cathedral labyrinth

BAYEUX CATHEDRAL

The labyrinth is in the chapter house and is quite compact—nine feet in diameter with ten rings. It is now marked on the floor tiles but was originally composed of painted tiles, some of which can still be seen around the side of the chapter house. The labyrinth can only be seen by daylight, as there is no electric light in the chapter house. The beautiful medieval cathedral has many original wall paintings and painted statues, and the crypt is adorned with painted angels and other scenes.

While there, you can also view the Bayeux tapestry woven by Queen Mathilda to celebrate the conquest of England by her husband William I in 1066.

Bayeux Cathedral labyrinth

CHARTRES CATHEDRAL

This huge eleven-coil labyrinth, forty feet in circumference, is situated in the nave of what is said to be the finest Gothic cathedral in Europe. It is walkable on most Fridays from March to the end of October (check before you visit), but at other times you can see and work with the inner coils and with ingenuity walk round the chairs.

However, the cathedral contains other treasures, such as the Druidic well and the replica of the Black Madonna statue, which was also a Druidic symbol of the virgin who would give birth to a great leader. You can at any time of the year follow the pilgrimage pathway through the crypt and through the center of the labyrinth, ending at the place in the east where on the summer solstice the sun strikes a nail in the paving, representing the birth into light.

The Chartres labyrinth is divided into four segments, representing either the four elements or the four Gospels of Matthew, Mark, Luke, and John, around a center rose that symbolizes the Holy Mother.

Veriditas, the U.S. labyrinth organization founded by the Reverend Dr. Lauren Artress, offers its "Walking a Sacred Path" events at Chartres one month out of each year in the spring.

Whether you visit labyrinths close to home or far away, may your experiences be full of joy and light.

Chapter 13

LABYRINTH RITUALS

T HE RITUALS IN THIS CHAPTER
reflect the ideas I have developed throughout the book. Start with my
suggestions, but feel free to further develop or change the rituals to
suit your own life. For protective rituals that are carried out in a labyrinth, and indeed for any of the rituals set out in this chapter, you
must first conduct a blessing ritual.

Blessing the Labyrinth

This is a ritual similar to blessing the divination stones (see chapter 7);
it can be used when you create a labyrinth of your own, large or small.
This is also a good way of cleansing a labyrinth if you have done a
lot of intense work in it. In a public labyrinth, which may contain
a lot of intense energies belonging to others, visualize the cleansing
elements as you walk. If you are working with other people, each
person can be responsible for blessing the labyrinth with a single
element both on the way in and on the way out. You can also bless
a miniature labyrinth in the same way.

For this ritual, you'll need a small dish of sea salt, frankincense
or sandalwood incense or a smudge stick, an orange or red candle

in a broad-based holder, and a dish of water in which a clear crystal quartz or amethyst has been soaked for eight hours. You can place the incense and water in the center before you begin the ritual.

To bless your labyrinth:

1. Beginning at the entrance, hold the dish of sea salt as you walk through the coils, scattering salt in each one to represent the ancient element of Earth. In each coil, say, "Mother Earth, bless and sanctify this my creation; bring wisdom, stability, and reverence for the sacred spiral to my labyrinth journeys."

2. In the center of the labyrinth, light the incense or smudge stick and walk back through the coils, making clockwise circles around you at waist height in each one, to represent the element of Air. In each coil, say, "Father Sky, bless and sanctify this my creation; bring focus, concentration, and freedom from illusion to my labyrinth journeys."

3. Standing once more outside the labyrinth, light the candle to represent the element of Fire and walk inward toward the center again. In each coil, say, "Brother Fire, bless and sanctify this my creation; bring creativity, illumination, and inspiration to my labyrinth journeys."

4. Finally, sprinkle the crystal water, representing the element of Water, in each coil as you walk outward. In each coil, say, "Sister Water, bless and sanctify this my creation; bring compassion, love, and acceptance of what cannot be changed to my labyrinth journeys."

Allow the candle and incense to burn down, the candle in the center and the incense standing sentinel at the entrance.

Invoking the Archangels: A Protective Nighttime Ritual

If you'd rather not carry out the full-fledged version of this ritual described in chapter 7, you can use this version in a miniature classical seven-coil labyrinth or in your mind as you lie in bed at night. This ritual will bring on sleep and peaceful dreams (see chapter 2 for instructions on drawing a seven-coil labyrinth).

This method is very effective with small children; draw and keep a special small labyrinth on flame-retardant card or in a sandbox to represent their nighttime sanctuary. This ritual can form a time of togetherness in the most frantic schedule. Such moments of family sanctity will remain with us and our children all our lives.

You can adapt this ritual to help a nervous elderly relation who fears the dark or being alone at night. You may want to try this ritual if you have been subject to hostility at work or feel under psychic threat. The light will protect your aura, your psychic energy field (see chapter 8), and keep you safe while you sleep.

To invoke the archangels in a night-time ritual:

1. Place two small, white candles in deep, nonflammable containers at the entrance to the labyrinth and one in the center.
   Place small, unlit candles in the colors listed below at each coil:

   Coil 3 (Samael or Uriel): red

   Coil 2 (Sachiel): blue

   Coil 1 (Cassiel): purple

   Coil 4 (Michael): gold

   Coil 7 (Gabriel): silver

   Coil 6 (Raphael): yellow

   Coil 5 (Anael): green or pink

2. Light the candles at the entrance and the center. Face the entrance to the labyrinth looking toward the center. Sit with the child, weaving stories about the angelic realms, using your imagination and a little angelic inspiration.

3. Touch the center of your brow with your power hand (the one you write with) and say, "Before me the pathway." Touch the center of your throat and say, "Before me the truth I speak." Touch the center of your chest between your breasts and say,

"Before me the love in my heart." Touch your navel and say, "With all my body, mind, and spirit. Amen." Young children can carry out the actions and later join in the words.

4.   Beginning at coil 3, as you enter the labyrinth with your finger, name and greet each archangel and light the colored candle in the designated coil. Continue through the coils, lighting the colored candles one at a time, in the order you would walk them in a large labyrinth.

5.   When all the candles are lit, focusing on the center candle, repeat the four invocations one after the other: "Before me the pathway," "Before me the truth I speak," "Before me the love in my heart," and "With all my body, mind, and spirit. Amen."

6.   Blow out each candle in turn, from the center outward, once more calling on each archangel in his coil, sending the light of each to protect the child and yourself.

The Rhythm of Life Walk

This can be a good way of centering yourself if you feel you are losing direction or being manipulated by others, or if you simply need to run a check on how well you are fulfilling your destiny. You can work in a labyrinth of any size, allowing the journey to unfold. This ritual can work well in an ecclesiastical labyrinth or in one in a place of great beauty, but it can also work in a miniature labyrinth walked with your fingers.

The purpose of the ritual is not to cast off the past, for even bad experiences have made us what we are, but to absorb the kernel of wisdom from each experience, leaving the sorrows and redundancies in the center for Mother Earth to absorb and re-form.

To perform the rhythm of life walk:

1.   As you begin to walk the labyrinth, focus on your earliest childhood memory and continue through elementary and high school, college, first job, first major relationship, and so on, right up to the present day. Let these memories roll past you like a reel of movie film. Pace yourself if you seem to be progressing

too fast. You may find that revisiting some memories takes longer than others and that the current phase in your life takes the longest of all. Treat all memories the same, not agonizing too long over past mistakes or dreaming of what might have been.

2. By the time you reach the center of the labyrinth you should be more or less up to date, but if you are still traveling through your memories, sit or kneel in the center and finish your life walk.

3. Think of the center of the labyrinth as a refueling and psychic pit stop rather than rebirth. Here, Mother Earth bandages our grazed knees and heart when we have fallen, washes our face, brushes our hair, and offers wise but maybe tough advice regarding what needs to be resolved. Then she sends us back again to get it right. Before you leave the center of the labyrinth, ask the mother to take anything you really do wish to leave behind. You will suddenly feel lighter.

4. The outward journey is very exciting. Walk really slowly to enjoy every minute as you run the film of your future destiny in which you are very definitely the hero or heroine. If any plot lines seem to be dead ends or you sense sorrow ahead, change the scene and maybe some of the supporting cast, for it really is your script. Fate of course can unexpectedly put obstacles in the best-planned path, but it is our actions and reactions that ultimately determine our destiny.

After your labyrinth walk, do some small activity that will make you happy—take a relaxing bubble bath, for example, or a walk on the beach.

Walking a Problem to Resolution

When you have a decision to make, sometimes after you have used all conventional methods, logic, and expertise, it can be helpful to toss the issue into the labyrinth. This allows its energies to work on your deep unconscious wisdom, which contains the answer to the problem or the correct choice hidden beneath the clutter of the conscious mind.

Each labyrinth coil represents a stage in this process. Follow the stages I have suggested, but allow the questions to emerge quite spontaneously and the answers to unfold as the labyrinth works its magic. Sometimes answers will come in the form of words, sometimes in the form of images. For this ritual you will need a labyrinth in which the coils are readily identifiable as you walk, so a seven-coil labyrinth, either a large or a miniature one, is ideal. We will use Alan's labyrinth walk as an example.

Alan was in his early fifties. He was divorced, with no family. His life was his work. Because of a takeover of the accountancy firm where he had worked for most of his life, however, he was offered early retirement. If he stayed he knew that the firm would change beyond recognition and that he would no longer work directly with people, which he loved. Yet how could he not work?

Alan carried out the ritual in a seven-coil labyrinth he had drawn in the soil of a large uncultivated flower bed in his garden. Doing everything with precision, his customary way of operating, he built earth walls between and around the coils.

To walk a problem to resolution, like Alan did:

1. At the entrance, face the center of the labyrinth and state your problem and the decision to be made. Alan stated the problem: Should he take early retirement?

2. In the first coil (coil three), outline the options without attempting to come to any decisions or weigh evidence: he could remain at work though it would no longer be what he enjoyed, or he could step into the unknown.

3. In the second coil (coil two), state the factors in favor of change (the most proactive option). An image of brilliant blue skies and Spanish olive groves came to Alan, and he recalled how much he enjoyed traveling in Spain. He wondered if he might even be able to move there.

4. In the third coil (coil one), state the factors in favor of the status quo (or taking the line of least resistance). Alan saw an image of a treadmill pulled by donkeys that disappeared into gray mist. He felt suddenly weary.

5. In the fourth coil (coil four), consider people who might influence or be affected by the decision that is to be made. Alan suddenly recalled the dusty English bookshop in the town in which he stayed in Spain and heard in his inner ear the throaty laugh of the woman with huge olive eyes who ran it. On his visits they had struck up a friendship, since they both collected old books and loved classical jazz, and had even been out for meals and to concerts. However, apart from the odd postcard, contact was now sporadic. He realized that this was due to his own caution and fear of being hurt again.

6. In the fifth coil (coil seven), consider the risks involved in any new venture. Alan saw himself sitting alone under an orange tree (more Spain) and yet he did not feel sad at being alone. He realized that his attachment to Spain was more than a romantic one.

7. In the sixth coil (coil six), consider the untapped potential, what might be achieved.

   This time Alan saw a music shop in the town square with brilliant flowers around the door and recalled his ambition to devote more time to the music he loved.

8. In the seventh coil (coil five), consider what lies over the horizon if the projected action is taken or a decision for change made. Alan saw images of more flowers, heard music playing late into the night, and experienced a feeling of warmth even though it was a cold autumn day.

9. In the center of the labyrinth is where all the images come into play. As pictures and thoughts unfolded in his mind, Alan found that his office played a relatively small part in his thoughts, although that was the focus of the original question.

In labyrinth work you often find that the initial question has changed subtly or even been transformed by the time you reach center. All you have to do on the outward journey is create a master plan, allowing the energies of the labyrinth to draw together all the strands.

10. Begin walking out toward the entrance. In coil five, consider what you really want. Allow the answer to come spontaneously and you may be totally surprised; in time you will realize that there was no other possible pathway. Wants, as opposed to thoughts, were quite an unfamiliar concept to Alan. A whole bundle of wants came tumbling out of the normally controlled, analytical Alan: love, music, sunshine, laughter, to encourage young musicians, to play in a jazz band as he had done in his youth.

11. In coil six, decide what, if anything, stands in the way of attaining the things you want. Alan recalled himself at age twenty being forced by his father to abandon his music studies and instead to join his father's accountancy firm. His father was now long dead, and early retirement would give Alan financial independence. The only real obstacles were the old voices in his head.

12. In coil seven, formulate your first steps toward happiness. Alan saw himself leaving the firm forever and not even bothering with a farewell party, for he had little in common with the other people with whom he worked. Having seen the image of Spain, the doors of understanding opened for Alan, and he realized that he did have an alternative to working with the firm he was beginning to hate. Of course, leaving his safe and familiar life was a risk, as these life decisions always are, but by the end Alan realized he could walk away quite happily.

13. In coil four, figure out what unexpected things may occur as a result of taking the first steps. Alan saw an image of himself bundling musical instruments into a large van, painted in bright colors, quite unlike the smart, discreet car he drove at present. He also saw himself surrounded by young musicians.

14. In coil one, make a decisive action or decision. Alan decided, quite spontaneously, that he would go on an extended holiday to Spain as soon as possible. He would see whether any shops were for lease in the small Spanish town he loved, so he could open a music store and perhaps help struggling young musicians.

15. In coil two, find allies. Alan decided that he would phone his friend in the bookshop and sound out his plans, risking ridicule and rejection but perhaps finding sound advice and enthusiasm.

16. In coil three, determine your new goal in life or redirection of energies. Alan made up his mind that at fifty-five he was still young enough to follow some of his earlier dreams—and maybe even to open himself to love.

You can adapt the steps above to find a form of labyrinthine decision making that is effective for you. I do not know if Alan followed his dream as I lost touch with him, but I know that he did accept early retirement and book his extended Spanish holiday.

Personal Development: Releasing the Inner Child

In chapter 6, you met your inner child in the labyrinth. As I have said, joyousness is a feature of the labyrinth experience. We know that in medieval times priests tossed a ball in the labyrinth to imitate the pathway of the sun and moon through the sky, and that right until the twentieth century (and even today in parts of Germany and Scandinavia) labyrinth games and dances are held annually.

The labyrinth, in addition to being a solemn and meditative device, is also a place of spontaneity where we can connect with the wonder of childhood and send our inner child out to play; this can give us a fresh perspective on the workaday world and enable us to tap our half-forgotten childhood psychic powers.

You can work either in a group or alone (although you will not really be alone but accompanied by your inner child, who is still your very best friend). The first ritual below is meant for a group, and the second is meant for a single person.

Use an outdoor public labyrinth at a quiet time or create a private one on the shore or in an open space, such as a large paved area. You will need a regular circular shape with the coils clearly defined. If you are working with others, each person should begin a few seconds after the preceding person, so that you are initially distributed around the first coil to be walked.

To find your inner child with a group:

1. The first person to enter the labyrinth holds a soft, large ball. The person holding the ball should call out a signal for everyone to chant, "Catch the sun." The first person should toss the ball to the nearest person, calling out a gift or blessing to the world, such as joy, laughter, or sunshine. The ball is thus passed around the coil, with each person calling out a blessing at each pass.

2. Everyone then moves to the next coil, and the person now holding the ball (the last to catch it in the previous coil) signals everyone to halt, tosses the ball to the nearest person, and everyone again calls out blessings as the sun is passed around the second coil to be walked. The blessings can be as profound or as trivial as you wish, as long as they represent joyous things—pink striped candy, hot tubs, sunrises, spring rain, newborn babies, and so on. Continue in this way until you reach the center.

3. Use the center of the labyrinth to toss the ball and call out blessings until finally you are all outside. Enjoy a picnic or a beach party to continue the mood of joy.

If you work alone, visualize your own inner child, perhaps yourself when you were a child or an invisible friend you played with as a child.

To find your inner child by yourself:

1. Move around the coils with a yo-yo, a bubble blower, or a ball, pausing two or three times in each coil to call out things that give you pleasure, no matter how simple or childish they seem. You may want to run or skip or dance.

2. In the center, turn to face your inner child. He or she may remind you of all those wonderful plans you made, perhaps for ending world hunger or for flying to the moon, which can still be achieved at least in part.

3. When you feel ready, leave the labyrinth joyfully in any way you like. As you leave, turn and look back to the center, smiling to where you connected with your real self.

A Power Animal Labyrinth

This is a very good ritual to bring power and energy into your life. Work with a seven-coil labyrinth, either miniature or of walkable size. Before undertaking this ritual, make a list of animals, birds, and other creatures you feel close to or whose strengths you admire. They need not be from your own land, but it may help you bring these creatures to life if you can visit them in a wildlife area or view them using your computer or VCR.

Consider which animal you would like in the center. Which animal do you consider to be the most noble or inspiring creature: a soaring eagle, a courageous lion, a fiercely protective bear? Perhaps, like some Native American peoples, you will choose the Mother Buffalo, protectress and bringer of abundance, whose skull is sometimes placed on a pole in the center of a sacred circle. You may also choose to work with mythological creatures that you have seen in dreams, during meditation, or in childhood tales. Below I have listed some of my favorite power creatures and their significance derived from various myths from different traditions.

Bear: protection and connection with the wise ancestors

Bird of paradise: radiance and splendor

Buffalo (bison): generosity of spirit and abundance

Bull: animus power and sexuality

Butterfly: transformation and renewal

Cat: sensuality and independence

Crane: health and dignity

Crow: wisdom and magical powers

Deer: sensitivity and swiftness of response

Dolphin: healing and spirituality

Dove: peace and love

Dragon: sovereignty, inspiration, and guardianship

Eagle: nobility, vision, and limitless potential

Elk: stamina and determination

Falcon or kestrel: focus and single-mindedness

Frog: empathy and fertility

Goose: domestic happiness, living according to natural cycles

Hawk: enlightenment, wide perspectives

Horse: stamina, harmony with others

Ibis: wisdom and tradition

Lion: courage and leadership

Otter: female wisdom and spirituality

Owl: knowledge of the power of the night and the shadow self

Pelican: devotion and worthwhile sacrifice

Phoenix: rebirth and perfection

Raven: hidden potential and challenging the status quo

Stag: male principle and the hunt

Stork: life-bringer, enduring love

Swan: creativity and shapeshifting

Tiger: courage and longevity

Turtle: strong foundations and stability

Thunderbird: instinctual power and fertility

Unicorn: purity and healing

Wolf: protectiveness and altruism

Below I use my favorite power creatures, but you can substitute the animals that are meaningful to you.

To perform a power animal labyrinth ritual:

1. At the entrance to a classical seven-coil labyrinth, stand and visualize each of your power creatures positioned in the coils

and the center so that you can see them quite clearly in your mind as you enter.

2. In coil three, greet the lion by saying, "I welcome you, mighty warrior, to this sacred labyrinth. I call on your courage, your strength, and your leadership to enable me to act nobly and boldly in my life and not to compromise my principles."

3. In coil two, greet the bear by saying, "I welcome you, fierce protectress, to this sacred labyrinth. I call on your devotion to your young, your foresight in preparing for the winter months, and your healing powers, to enable me to protect what is precious in my life and to guard against the mental and emotional predators that surround me."

4. In coil one, greet the wild goose by saying, "I welcome you, who flies far in the winter but always returns to build your nest safely in the reeds in the spring, to this sacred labyrinth. I call on you to enable me to flow with the natural seasons and to know when it is time to venture forth and when to prepare for the future."

5. In coil four, greet the turtle by saying, "I welcome you, who it is said held the world on your back and whose security can provide stability in changing times, to this sacred labyrinth. I call on you to give me the firm foundations to build on what I am and what I have and to not be deterred or distracted from my chosen course."

6. In coil seven, greet the bird of paradise by saying, "I welcome you, whose glittering plumage graced the trees of paradise and whose glory inspired poets and painters, to this sacred labyrinth. I call on you to fill my life with your rainbow beauty and brilliance, that I may reflect radiance in my daily life."

7. In coil six, greet the butterfly by saying, "I welcome you, whose transient joys broaden summer and offer a reminder to enjoy every golden day while it lasts, to this sacred labyrinth. I call on you to bring these pleasures and the promise that when I shed the chrysalis that is my life I too shall be reborn."

8. In coil five, greet the dolphin by saying, "I welcome you, whose acute sensitivity and healing powers bestow blessings on all who encounter your quicksilver flight through the waves, to this sacred labyrinth. I call upon you to bring me your intuitive awareness and ability to mend all sorrows, that I may walk the path of peace and understanding."

9. In the center, greet the eagle by saying, "I welcome you, creature that flies closest to the sun, lord of the skies, and servant of none, to this sacred labyrinth. I call upon you to help me likewise soar, unbound by fear or need of favor, to find my personal perpetual sun."

10. As you leave the labyrinth, in each coil thank the creature there for his or her gifts and state a way that you can apply that animal's strengths to your daily life as well as your spiritual growth.

Relationship Issues: Speaking the Truth That Is in Your Heart

This can be performed as a solitary ritual or with a person with whom you have had relationship difficulties. Create a small four-coil labyrinth on a table out of clay or dough (see chapter 4 for help with drawing one).

To perform a relationship ritual:

1. In the center of the labyrinth, set a small candle on a metal tray. If you are working alone, make a notch in the wax of the candle about an inch of the way down. If you are working with a partner, make a second notch about an inch below the first.

2. Trace the coils with your index finger (taking turns, if there are two of you) saying, "What is lost and what is gained are here in equal measure, what was said and what was done, what was not said and not spoken rest as one."

3. When you reach the center, using a taper light the central candle visualizing the other person with you, or light it simultaneously with your partner. Touch hands lightly and gaze at the candle.

4. If you are alone, say all the things that you have locked in your heart—sorrow, grief, anger, questions, your willingness to try again. Speak until the candle has burned down to the notch, and then write on paper a brief message to the absent person, which you may have formulated in your mind as you spoke aloud. Burn it in the flame and collect the ashes in the tray. If you are working with another person, allow him or her to speak uninterrupted until the candle has burned down to the first notch. Then, when it is your turn, speak until the candle has burned down to the second notch, trying to avoid sarcasm or cruelty, but letting the feelings flow. Alternatively, you could act as advocate for the other, expressing what you feel is the other person's point of view. This can be very illuminating and sometimes shows you have been reacting not to the actual person but to previous betrayals, or to the projection of your own fears. Each of you should then write your message and, without reading the other's, burn them in the flame, saying, "It is gone, it is done. Peace come."

5. Together or alone send a positive thought to the other through the flame, and together blow out the candle.

6. Go outside and scatter the ashes to the four winds.

Destroy the old labyrinth. Either alone or with the other person build a new one. Then, while scattering the coils with rose petals or lavender, talk quietly or think to yourself about what in your relationship can be rebuilt in a new, more solid form. If you realize the situation is irretrievable, plan how you can gently say good-bye.

Healing and Planetary Rituals: The Three Waters

This is an ancient Druidic ritual that ensures that we make or keep connection with the natural world, absorbing its energies to give us strength and purpose. The labyrinth spiral amplifies the potency of the ritual and is one I like to use whenever life and everyday worries overwhelm me. It also focuses energies on problems of drought and clean water in other parts of the world.

Use a private labyrinth or a public one when it is very quiet. Work with a labyrinth of any size, though probably it is easier with nine coils or less. You can also perform a very effective version in a miniature labyrinth with a small crystal dish or water feature in the center. To empower water, leave it in the open air or under the full moon from dawn till noon, or soak a clear crystal quartz or amethyst in it.

To perform a healing and planetary ritual:

1. Place a small jug of empowered water, a small cup or glass, and, if the light is dim, a beeswax candle and book of matches in the center of the labyrinth. Carry a small bowl of water into the center during your labyrinth walk.

2. As you enter the labyrinth, sprinkle a few drops of water from the bowl into each coil, saying, "Cleansing water, heal the earth, make it fertile, bring new life to desert places and clean water to all."

3. When you reach the center of the labyrinth, set down the bowl. Dipping your fingers lightly into it, splash water on your brow and say, "Healing waters, heal my life, make me whole and cleanse away all sorrow and stagnation."

4. Pour a little of the water from the jug into the cup and drink a few drops, saying, "Water of life, fill me with life, let hope and love and inspiration flow anew within me."

5. Finally, gaze into the bowl of water, adding to it from the jug if necessary. Watching through half-closed eyes, ripple the water with your fingers to create patterns that will catch the natural light. If it is dusk or before dawn, light the candle and allow the flickering beams to reflect in the water and the candle's honey-like fragrance flow through you. In your mind, let images or perhaps words form, telling of the way your life will flow and the opportunities that may be just over the horizon.

6. If you did light a candle, extinguish it, sending light to whoever needs it, not forgetting yourself. On the way out through the coils sprinkle any remaining drops of water from the bowl, imagining that you are planting them as seeds of new endeavors.

A Labyrinth for Peace

In my life as a Quaker and a Druidess, I have for a number of years realized the need for an individual or group to send out energies for peace on a regular basis. The following ritual can involve any number of people focusing on an aspect of peace, perhaps meeting together monthly to pray and work in the labyrinth. However, you can as I do and carry out the ritual alone, walking around each of the four compass positions in turn. You can also use a miniature labyrinth and tiny candles.

Work at the time of the crescent moon, the time of new beginnings. Focus on world peace, areas where there is great conflict and suffering for the people who live there, or any form of racial, industrial, or other unrest that is causing hardship and sorrow. Create a very simple four-coil labyrinth or another labyrinthine form with well-defined circular coils (see chapter 4 for help in drawing these). Alternatively, you can use a larger public labyrinth at a time when it is officially closed, gaining permission first, of course. If you use a church labyrinth, the minister may even agree to begin your ritual with a prayer.

To walk a labyrinth for peace:

1. Set four blue candles (blue is traditionally the color of peace) in floor holders at the four main compass points around the perimeter of the labyrinth. In the center of the labyrinth, set a larger blue candle in a floor holder or in a metal or ceramic pot filled with sand.

2. Those present can enter the labyrinth just before dusk and, standing around the coils, face the center. Each should carry a pure-white, unlit taper. One person should stand next to each of the blue candles around the perimeter of the labyrinth and face inward.

3. First, the person in the north faces outward and lights the candle, saying, "May there be peace in the North." He or she then turns to face the center again as everyone present says, "May there be peace throughout the whole world."

4. The person in the east faces outward and lights the blue candle, asking for peace in the East, turning once more to the center. Everyone joins in the response, asking for peace in the whole world.

5. The person in the south faces outward and lights the blue candle, asking for peace in the south, turning once more to the center. Everyone joins in the response, asking for peace in the whole world.

6. The person in the west faces outward and lights the blue candle, asking for peace in the west, turning once more to the center. Everyone joins in the response, asking for peace in the whole world.

7. The center candle is then lit by the person leading the ritual, who says, "May there be peace throughout the whole world." This is echoed by all present.

8. One at a time, each person, beginning with those standing at the four compass points, walks into the center in the order in which he or she lit the candle: north, east, south, and west. When each person reaches the center, he or she lights the taper from the central candle and makes a wish or blessing for peace, focusing on the chosen area of the world under threat.

9. Then, everyone involved in the ritual moves from the outermost coils into the center and repeats these actions. After each person has lit a taper from the central candle, he or she leaves the labyrinth to stand around the outside with the lighted taper. In this way you have a constant movement throughout the coils.

10. When two people pass in the coils, they join tapers briefly and say, "May there be peace throughout the whole world." The last person to leave the labyrinth is the leader of the ritual, who lights his or her taper and says, "May the labyrinth of peace remain unbroken and shed its light throughout the world."

11. The four perimeter and central candles are left burning, and the people around the perimeter may spontaneously begin to sing peace songs or remain in silence, sending private thoughts before extinguishing their tapers.

If you are carrying out the ritual alone, you can set the candles in advance and walk around the perimeter until you reach the north. Light that candle, and then proceed clockwise around the coil, lighting the west candle last. (If possible, set your labyrinth entrance in the west to avoid doubling back.) Utter all the blessings and responses in the order described above. If you decide to use a table labyrinth you can use a long-burning central candle and leave it to burn all night in a dish of sand.

Enhancing Psychic Powers: A Dream Walk

Often, when we have a significant dream, we wake before the resolution, and no matter how hard we try we cannot get back into it. Or, we may have a recurring dream in which we visit a particular place or meet a person who seems to have a special message for you. But whatever we do, we cannot identify the setting and the person disappears as we wake. Labyrinths are perfect places to unravel those dreams or even to weave a daydream that can help us to explore our own spirituality.

This is a ritual that benefits from a complex Chartres-type labyrinth, with its different quadrants, or even one of the really complex seventeen-coil labyrinths with bastions. These are very difficult to draw at any scale so unless you can visit one, simply photocopy the ones shown in chapter 9 and use them as a guide for creating your full-size labyrinth. Alternatively, trace, scan, or photocopy one to make a table labyrinth, and walk the coils in your mind.

In these complex labyrinths, you are constantly changing direction, turning clockwise and then counterclockwise and suddenly find yourself on the outside when you thought you were moving inward. You have to trust your feet. Complex labyrinths are very good for

dream work, since you lose all sense of earthly orientation and therefore can allow your unconscious mind to lead the way.

To perform a dream walk:

1. As you walk through the coils, begin to tell the story of your
   dream as though you were recounting it to a close friend. If you
   speak out loud, use a buttonhole microphone and mini tape
   recorder to record the dream journey. If the setting makes it difficult for you to talk as you walk, take a notebook and pen so
   you can scribble notes in the center before the outward journey.
   With a table labyrinth you may find that listening to gentle
   music helps to create the mood.

2. Once you reach the point in the narrative where the dream
   ended (or regularly ends), begin to count backward from thirty
   to zero. As you count, mentally step back into the dream and *see*
   the dreamscape on either side of the coil. Walk along a suddenly
   familiar street or through the enchanted forest of your dream;
   speak the words you cannot in waking life, or ask questions of
   the person you met during your dream encounter.

3. As you approach the center, visualize this as a halfway point,
   perhaps a star in the middle of the Milky Way, a tropical island in
   a blue ocean, a fluffy cloud in a wide sky, or a tree house high
   above the jungle.

4. By the time you reach the center, you will also be in the middle
   of the dream. But through the magical energies of the labyrinth,
   you will be aware that you are dreaming and so will be able to
   prolong the dream or change the ending: knowing that you are
   quite safe, confront mental or actual dragons, or become able to
   fly, float, or swim. Here you can rest and let gentle bubbles of
   color or beautiful creatures such as angels, nature spirits, or
   fairies float by.

5. If you are not tape recording the experience, scribble down
   some of the images, perhaps as pictures, from within your meditative state, before beginning your homeward journey. You may
   be surprised afterward at how your artistic abilities were temporarily much enhanced.

6. As you begin your outward journey through the coils, your creativity comes into full play. You can direct the actors, change the scenery, and discover in vivid detail the identity of people and places and their significance to you. As you near the entrance, decide whether you want a huge Technicolor finale or a gradual fading of the vivid colors, fragrances, and sounds. Either way, as you enter the final path toward the labyrinth entrance, begin to count again, this time from zero to thirty. Continue to count even if you leave the labyrinth before you reach thirty.

7. Sit quietly near the labyrinth and either complete the recording by adding some final thoughts or scribble down the images and words from the outward journey.

You may find that you continue the dream when you go to sleep that night or that it evolves further in subsequent labyrinth dream walks. Your dream walk may relate to past-life work (see chapter 9) or to another culture with which you have spiritual affinity.

The Labyrinth and the Tarot

Tarot cards are vividly illustrated cards that come in decks of seventy-eight, which date back to medieval France or Italy. Their subjects are universal: the Untested Innocent Youth whose journey brings enlightenment, the Mother, the Father, the Lovers, the Hero whom the youth becomes, the Trickster, the Virgin, the Priest, the Sun and the Moon, as well as virtues such as Patience, Endurance, Justice, and Moderation.

The first twenty-two picture cards especially, called the Major Arcana (Arcana means secret wisdom), are said to contain in symbolic and compact form all magical knowledge and wisdom.

If you choose a pack with an illustrated Minor Arcana (I would recommend the Rider Waite, the similar Universal Waite, or the Morgan Greer) then you can work with all of the cards in the labyrinth. Many of these illustrated minor cards also tell vivid stories. For example, the Eight of Wands in the Universal or Rider Waite tarot shows eight wands flying through the air and is a card that indicates travel, whether through physical movement or a change in lifestyle. The Ten of Cups, with its rainbow and happy family, speaks of finding fulfillment through relationships, and the solemn Six of Swords, which depicts a boatman steering his passenger into calmer waters, indicates that you are moving into calmer times after trouble or stress. This would suggest that you should give yourself some time before deciding to start a new venture or seek a new relationship after escaping from a bad one.

You do not need to know the conventional card meanings to use the tarot in labyrinth work or indeed in any form of meditation, though I have suggested books on this subject in the appendix if you do wish to learn more.

Each card is like a self-expanding zip file containing a whole storybook of concepts. If we allow our unconscious mind to have its way, we will spontaneously understand the meaning of each card. Indeed, when I have taught groups of adult students how to use the tarot cards, the very best reading they ever give is the first one, before they know the official card meanings. This is because they allow the pictures to tell the story and so relate to those self-expanding myriad layers of meaning.

If you are an experienced tarot reader, allow your mind to go blank in the labyrinth and let the chosen card speak to you directly, rather than using the interpretations you already know.

You can use absolutely any labyrinth, including a miniature one. If possible, work with a complex design so that your unconscious can come to the fore.

To walk the labyrinth with tarot cards:

1. Sit outside the labyrinth with your pack of cards. Shuffle the cards and ask your guardian angel or spirit guide or even your own wiser, higher self to help you choose the card that will be most relevant to your present situation.

2. Fan out the cards in a circle shape facedown, and move either the index finger of your power hand (the hand you write with) or a crystal pendulum slowly an inch or two above the pack. Your finger or pendulum should pause over one card and pull

downward as though responding to a powerful suction movement, akin to a very strong gravitational pull.

3. Turn the card over and look at it. Do not try to interpret it, but instead memorize every detail and color. Close your eyes and reproduce the card's image in the same rich detail in your mind. If you cannot do this on the first attempt, spend more time looking at the card until it is imprinted in your memory.

4. With your eyes still closed, identify the entrance to the labyrinth within the card's image. This may be an actual pathway marked on the physical card, or one that you mentally insert in the image; perhaps you will visualize yourself wading across a river, landing your boat on a bank, or walking through a forest or a field of sunflowers to the entrance. If nothing is obvious, expand the card in your mind so that there are additional features on all sides, a little beyond the edge. Maybe the field has a house in it or around the bend of the river is a bridge. Let your psyche lead you.

5. Open your eyes and, holding the card but not looking at it, begin your physical labyrinth walk. On the inward journey you are traveling from the present into the past; there you will pick up strands of experience that will help you to understand your present life using a broader perspective.

6. As you walk the coils, enter the card again, following the river even further. Or ride on one of those flying spears. If there are any characters in the card, enter into dialogue with them as you walk your labyrinth coils.

7. Allow the story to unfold as you continue to walk toward the center of the labyrinth. You may walk through a fairy story or shamanic land (see chapter 6). You may meet talking animals, wise guardians, trees with fabulous fruits, or spirits who can give you the keys to the past—and maybe even explain the interconnections between the present, past, and future.

8. When you reach the center of the labyrinth, settle down in the shade of one of your magical trees or buildings and study your imagined card once more. Focus this time on the small details,

such as splashes of color, a sun in a blue sky, flowers, or a design on a robe. Close your eyes and recall the colors. Then open them and scan the horizon of the imagined scene.

9. On your outward journey from the center of the labyrinth, walk in your mind toward one of the colors or patterns in the visualized card. Now you are facing the future, your future life outside the labyrinth, and so you will have a different perspective on the card. Now the figures or scenes may suggest potential routes you can take through the real outer world.

10. As you walk out of the labyrinth, you will understand how the past, present, and future are interwoven in the symbolism of the card. The sounds and colors will gradually fade until you are outside the labyrinth once more.

Allow the images to continue working as you spend a quiet day in the open air or engaged in physical activity, if possible. Gradually, the experience will make sense, and you'll be able to apply the relevance of your learning to the everyday world. Within a few days you may see a flower, a vivid bank of color, or a design that will link the labyrinth experience with your external life, and the final pieces of the jigsaw will fall into place.

Drawing Down the Moon

The phenomenon of drawing down wisdom from the moon or the moon goddess has ancient roots in the Dianic cults in ancient Greece that were first described around 500 B.C.E. However, these moon cults are probably much older, having worshipped Diana as goddess of the moon under different names. Some say this moon worship was part of the original nature religion that has evolved into modern witchcraft.

But no one, whatever their faith, who has stood on a shore or in a forest and gazed up at the full moon can fail to be moved by the moon's beauty and magic. At such times we can understand how early peoples must have regarded the moon as their beautiful mother, and we can see that moonlight is far more than reflected sunlight.

To draw down the power of the moon:

1. On a clear night of the full moon, create or find a simple labyrinth with seven coils or fewer, and walk into the center through the coils. A labyrinth on a shore, by a lake, close to the sea, or in your garden is totally magical. If your labyrinth is on a hard surface, place a soft, padded mat in the center.

2. Were you only to walk the coils and gaze up at the moon, it would be magical enough. However, if you want to take the experience further spiritually, stand in the center focusing on the full moon.

3. Swirl round and round, arms outstretched, faster and faster, as you did when you were a child, until you become dizzy (but just before you lose balance and fall over).

4. Stop and turn to face the moon again, and you will experience the physiological sensation of the moon rushing toward you (it beats any amusement park ride for exhilaration). Of course, this is a physiological reaction, but, as is so often true, we can use the physical as an entry point to the psychic realms. What we see approaching us is the essence of the moon, the spirit moon, or the moon goddess.

   You may hear a voice clear and low in your ear, talking to you of many things, both personal matters and more global concerns. Or the communication may be more subtle, coming to you in the form of knowledge that springs into your mind, clarity about certain puzzling issues, and an awareness of the interconnections between all of nature, life on earth, and the cosmos and the planets.

5. Gradually you will become aware of the physical moon once more. Write in the air a word of power or a secret phrase that summarizes your newfound awareness, and walk out through the coils of light.

6. If possible, bury a silver coin near the entrance or toss it into water as a tribute.

You can also work with a table labyrinth near an open window, placing in the center a silver bowl filled with water that will become suffused with silver light. Position the labyrinth so that you can see the moon through the window as you walk with your finger. When you reach the center with your finger, remove your hand, swirl it around the perimeter of the labyrinth while looking at the moon, and then place your clasped hands in the center of the labyrinth while you receive the channeled wisdom. Keep your moon water in a bottle, and add a few drops to your bath or drink it during the waning moon cycle to give you energy. You can also make moon water in the center of a large labyrinth.

Rites of Passage: A Naming Ceremony

There is no reason why the labyrinth should not be used for celebrations and ceremonies of all kinds. Weddings and blessing ceremonies in secular and ecclesiastical labyrinths will become increasingly popular over the coming years, as the labyrinth is recognized as a sacred space in its own right.

It can be especially meaningful, before an outdoor wedding or a child's naming ceremony, for guests to create a huge labyrinth from greenery or flowers following a design that has been drawn or marked in the ground beforehand. The design need not be complex, but the coils should be wide enough for people to stand in, and the center needs to be large to hold an altar and a number of key participants in the ceremony.

The following ritual is a baby's naming ceremony, but it can be adapted to suit the particular faith or desires of the participants. If you wish, before the ceremony begins, place a basket in the center of the labyrinth to collect symbolic blessings for the baby.

To perform a naming ceremony ritual:

1. The parents and any sponsors should enter the center of the labyrinth, walking slowly through the coils. A chosen person, the mother, father, one of the grandparents, or someone who wishes to assist in the spiritual (and practical) upbringing of the child,

should carry the baby. You may decide to ask a minister to conduct the ceremony or, following the ancient Celtic tradition, invite the midwife as well as the birthing partner to lead the ritual. The baby's godparent or the oldest relation might be other choices.

2. The person chosen to lead the ceremony should be waiting in the center to greet the infant on behalf of the community. He or she welcomes the child into the world and pledges the support of those present to help the child to grow up loved, secure, happy, healthy, and spiritually rich.

3. The parents then name their child formally and hold him or her first toward the four directions, and then upward to the sky and downward to the earth, repeating the child's name or names to be witnessed by those present. If you are holding a more conventional religious ceremony, blessings can be asked of the deity recognized by the parents in all six directions.

4. The minister, a chosen family member, or, in Celtic fashion, the midwife, can sprinkle sacred water (see chapter 1) in a circle around the child. You can also buy readily prepared holy water. Make a cross on the child's brow, asking for blessings from the cosmos and the earth or the deity recognized by the parents, to keep the child safe from harm and to bless his or her path through life.

5. The father or another chosen person then lights a pure-white candle and circles the infant, likening the life of the child to a newly lit flame and pledging the support of the community to tend the flame of love.

6. Another person scatters salt around the child and parents, asking for health and long life for the child.

7. The person nearest the outside of the labyrinth can light a sage smudge or incense well away from the baby and circle the perimeter of the labyrinth, stopping at each of the four major directions, beginning with the east and progressing to the south, and then the west and the North, to represent the beginning of the child's life in the community. Then, leaving the smudge in a safe place, he or she re-enters the labyrinth.

8. Each person moves slowly through the coils, naming blessings he or she would bestow on the newborn: health, happiness, a gentle nature, and so on. On reaching the center, the participants can place a token gift in the basket, a tiny gold coin for abundance, a silk flower for the free flow of the life force, a silver heart charm for love, or crystals for various qualities, for example, carnelian for courage or amber for wisdom. Afterward, these gifts can be wrapped in silk to be given to the child as he or she grows older. New gifts and attributes can be added at each birthday.

9. Finally, those present can scatter rose petals as the parents walk out of the labyrinth holding the infant.

You can adapt this ritual for any religion and may wish to add prayers, songs, or recitations of poetry at the point when the child is named.

The Labyrinth of Parting

Labyrinth rituals can help you to absorb the pain of parting from a particular person or a phase in your life; you can work with that person present or alone. The sacred form of the labyrinth will act as a container for the sorrow and allow you to leave it behind. For a major relationship change such as divorce, especially if you did not seek the parting, you may need to repeat the walk many times alone.

The ritual below is aimed at couples who are separating, but you can adapt it for use when a member of your family is leaving home for a happy reason, for example, when a child is leaving to go to college or to work in another state. Performing this ritual will help you to formally move away from your role as parent of a young child while reaffirming the love between you.

If possible, work in a labyrinth that can be destroyed after the ritual, whether a shore labyrinth that is absorbed by the rising tide, a yard labyrinth you can wash away with water, or even a paper or miniature clay one. You'll need only a few coils. Because the work is especially emotive you may wish to work in a private labyrinth.

Create the labyrinth with the other person involved if possible. As you work, endow the labyrinth with happy memories and good times so that it becomes a place of love and healing.

To perform a parting ceremony:

1. In the center of the labyrinth, place a white candle and two smaller ones on either side, together with tapers for each candle and matches or a lighter. Work at a time when there is some natural light.

2. If you are performing the ritual with another person, enter the labyrinth together, touching hands in silence, allowing only kindness to flow between you even if the parting is painful or relations between you have been bitter. If you are sending your child, another family member, or a friend into the world, then this will be a walk of unity.

3. In the center, a separating couple should light tapers and at the same moment ignite the central candle flame, saying, "So have we been joined as one in love, so are we still joined in friendship, so will compassion and kindness never die." Then, one at a time, each should light a separate candle from the joint candle and say, "Now we are two again, separating but not in animosity, not in blame, recalling the happy times and the loving days. Let us depart from this place with peace and goodwill." The couple should blow out the joint candle—unless they have young children or an ongoing business arrangement, in which case the central candle can be left burning to symbolize the continuing commitment.

4. The couple can softly speak any private words of regret and healing and then carry the separate candles from the labyrinth, this time each walking alone.

5. Outside the labyrinth, the couple can exchange small tokens, perhaps items the other cherished, and each can keep them in a special box.

6. If the joint candle is still burning, leave it to burn out, and then erase the labyrinth.

For a more joyous parting, you can adapt the words and the actions and perhaps give the child or family friend a special present. Afterward, if appropriate, enjoy a meal and music to bring back happy memories while you are waiting for the candle to burn.

If the other person is not present, you can speak all the words and carry out the actions, sending good wishes to the absent party. If there is hostility between you, you can ask that he or she might find peace and that any bitterness may be softened. In this case you will probably wish to extinguish the joint candle, sending light to the other person.

If the separating couple have young children, the ceremony can be adapted so that the children join their lights in a separate candle that represents the continuing family, including both parents.

Keeping Vigil

If someone close to you is very ill or has died or there are events in the world that are upsetting you, holding an overnight vigil in a labyrinth can be a very powerful way of aligning yourself with the prevailing energies and making a statement, whether of peace, faith, or mourning.

The ritual can be done by a solitary person sitting in front of a candlelit labyrinth on a table or in a garden labyrinth by the light of a small lamp or candle flame. Equally it might include a whole group illuminating a public or private labyrinth or, if the weather is bad, creating a labyrinth within a yurt or large tent. All of these approaches are equally potent and how you organize the event is up to you. You may wish to make building the labyrinth part of the ceremony, or gain permission to use one in a church and begin with a simple blessing ceremony led by the minister. Some vigils are conducted wholly in silence, and others are punctuated by music, poetry, and reminiscences.

To hold a vigil:

1. Begin at sunset. Each person enters the labyrinth in turn so that the participants are evenly spread around the labyrinth.

2. In the center of the labyrinth, perhaps on a table draped with dark cloth, set a photograph of the loved one, some flowers, or a collection of written messages about the person or situation. Tie ribbons to a large green plant or miniature tree. Surround the picture with candles. These can be lit one by one by the leader of the vigil, who can offer a prayer or thought for each candle as it is lit.

3. If you are working alone, sit in the center of the labyrinth with a picture of the loved one and a candle, naming the purpose of the vigil as you light the candle. In group work after the central candle is aflame, one by one each person, from the outer to the inmost coils (not in the order they are walked), lights his or her own candle and states the purpose of the vigil in his or her own words. Each person can add a blessing or tell of a fond memory of the deceased person or can utter healing wishes for someone who is sick or perhaps imprisoned unfairly in another land.

4. Sit evenly spaced around the coils on cushions or blankets to make your place and keep warm if necessary. Bring or make warm drinks that can be carried around at regular intervals.

5. Allow the vigil to evolve quite spontaneously. People may sing or chant, and other song cycles may start up. Others may recite favorite poems or recall memories and then there may be a period of silence. If you work alone, read inspiring passages by torchlight and sing, chant, and meditate the night away.

6. As dawn breaks, extinguish any remaining lights and greet the new day in whatever way seems appropriate. Spiral out of the labyrinth, perhaps leaving flowers or burying crystals near the entrance of an outdoor labyrinth.

conclusion

THE JOURNEY TO CREATE this book has been a long one. More than any other book I have written, this one has gone far beyond its original idea, which was to use the labyrinth as a focus for exploring one's inner power. I had not appreciated that every labyrinth—large, miniature, or imagined; set inside a church, built on an open village green, or etched on a wall—is in essence a living form.

The labyrinth draws us through its coils so we can explore our inner selves and enter into communion with mythology and history, wandering along its mysterious pathways to the past and future. Within the labyrinth we can dream, meditate, and plan, dance, pray, make love, and light a candle along pathways to a center that may change with every visit.

The self we encounter in the labyrinth center is filled with endless possibility. We can recall our dreams for the future and see quite clearly how to reach our goals. Sometimes Mother Earth will be waiting. Sometimes it will be the more challenging Father Sky or a wild goddess of nature summoning up storms and shaking life's kaleidoscope to create a picture that's very different from the one we thought we were creating. Once you have walked into the center of a labyrinth and have had the courage and strength to resist the urge to run back through the coils seeking light and noise, and have sat in the stillness and darkness acknowledging your true self, then loneliness will have lost its power to overwhelm you.

Tonight, on the beach near my trailer, which I use as a retreat from my home, I will draw a huge labyrinth in the sand and sit alone in the center watching the sunset, waiting for the sea to wash away the edges of the coils. Each time I draw the laybrinth I get a little braver, and tonight, empowered by all I have written, I will wait until the light has faded and the waves are lapping around the center. Then, I will splash to shore, no longer a middle-aged woman with a mortgage and family and work concerns that seem a mountain high.

In my labyrinth, I will be the child again, on vacation from my inner-city home, reveling in the sunset. Now, I am happy to go back to the trailer; I don't regret that no one is waiting with the lights on to tuck me into bed and tidy away my day. The labyrinth tells us that we carry our center with us and that the coils, or life paths, lead us to the knowledge that we make of ourselves what we will, no matter what life throws at us.

Although tonight's labyrinth will disappear under the waves, I can build more labyrinths and follow other constantly changing paths. I am secure in my knowledge that my center won't disappear, nor will the labyrinth mother and father that we carry within ourselves. Our constant access to their power makes us ever wiser about and in harmony with the world. That is the beauty and the secret of the labyrinth.

I wish you every joy in your labyrinth explorations and hope that your center may always be filled with abundant light and peace.

Appendix

USEFUL READING

LABYRINTHS

Artress, Lauren. *Sand Labyrinths: Meditation at Your Fingertips.* New York: Charles Tullis Co, 2000.

————. *Walking the Sacred Path: Rediscovering the Labyrinth as a Spiritual Tool.* New York: Riverhead Books, 1995.

Curry, Helen. *The Way of the Labyrinth: A Powerful Meditation for Everyday Life.* New York: Penguin, 2000.

Geoffrion, Jill Kimberly Hartwell, and Lauren Artress. *Praying the Labyrinth: A Journey of Spiritual Exploration.* Cleveland, OH: Pilgrim Press, 1999.

Kern, Hermann. *Through the Labyrinth: Design and Meanings over 5,000 Years.* New York: Prestel, 2000.

Lonegren, Sig. *Labyrinths, Ancient Myths and Modern Uses.* New York: Sterling, 2001.

Martineau, John. *Mazes and Labyrinths in Great Britain.* Norwich, U.K.: Wooden Books, 1996.

Schaper, Donna, and Carole Ann Camp. *Labyrinths from the Outside In: Walking into Spiritual Insight, a Beginner's Guide.* Woodstock, VT: SkyLight Paths Publishing, 2000.

West, Melissa Gayle. *Exploring the Labyrinth: A Guide to Spiritual Healing and Growth.* New York: Broadway Books, 2000.

ANGELS

Burnham, Sophie. *A Book of Angels.* New York: Ballantine Books, 1990.

Davidson, Gustav. *A Dictionary of Angels.* New York: Free Press, 1967.

RavenWolf, Silver. *Angels: Companions in Magick.* St. Paul, MN: Llewellyn, 2001.

CHAKRAS AND COLORS

Arewa, Shola Caroline, *Opening to Spirit.* London: Thorsons, 1999.

Davies, Brenda. *The Seven Healing Chakras.* Berkeley, CA: Ulysses Press, 2000.

Eason, Cassandra. *Chakra Power for Healing and Harmony.* Slough, U.K.: Quantum, 2001.

Wauters, Ambika. *Homeopathic Color Remedies.* Berkeley, CA: The Crossing Press, 1999.

CANDLES

Buckland, Ray. *Practical Candleburning Rituals.* St. Paul, MN: Llewellyn, 1992.

Conway, D.J. *A Little Book of Candle Magic.* Berkeley, CA: The Crossing Press, 2000.

Eason, Cassandra. *Candle Power: Using Candlelight for Ritual, Magic and Self-Discovery.* New York: Sterling, 2000.

CRYSTALS AND CRYSTAL HEALING

Bravo, Brett. *Crystal Healing Secrets.* New York: Warner Books Inc., 1988.

Eason, Cassandra. *The Illustrated Dictionary of Healing Crystals.* London: Vega; New York: Sterling, 2003.

Galde, Phyllis. *Crystal Healing: The Next Step.* St. Paul, MN: Llewellyn Books, 1991.

Devas and Fairies

Bloom, William. *Working with Angels, Fairies and Nature Spirits.* London: Piatkus, 1998.

Eason, Cassandra. *A Complete Guide to Fairies and Magical Beings.* York Beach, ME: Red Wheel/Weiser, 2003.

Dreams

Altman, Jack, and David Fontana. *1001 Dreams: An Illustrated Guide to Dreams and Their Meanings.* San Francisco: Chronicle Books, 2002.

Eason, Cassandra. *Night Magic.* New York: Kensington/Citadel, 2003.

Fornari, Hannah. *The Dreamers' Dictionary.* London: Hamlyn, 1989.

Parker, Russ. *Healing Dreams.* London: SPCK, 1988.

Earth Energies

Begg, Ean. *The Cult of the Black Madonna.* London: Arkana, 1995.

Lonegren, Sig. *Spiritual Dowsing.* Glastonbury, U.K.: Gothic Images, 1986.

Molyneaux, Brian Leigh. *The Sacred Earth.* London: Macmillan, 1991.

Wilson, Colin. *The Atlas of Holy Places and Sacred Sites.* London: DK Publishing, 1996.

Goddesses

Budapest, Z. *The Holy Book of Women's Mysteries.* New York: Harper Row, 1990.

Eason, Cassandra. *The Complete Guide to Women's Wisdom.* London: Piatkus, 2001.

Farrar, Janet, and Stewart Farrar. *The Witches Goddess: The Feminine Principle of Divinity.* New York: Phoenix Publishing Inc., 1987.

Gadon, Elinor. *The Once and Future Goddess.* London: Aquarian/Thorsons, 1990.

Healing

Brennan, Barbara Ann. *Hands of Light: A Guide to Healing through the Human Energy Field*. New York: Bantam Books, 1987.

Eden, Donna. *Energy Medicine*. London: Piatkus, 1999.

Verschure, Yasmin. *Way to the Light*. York Beach, ME: Red Wheel/Weiser, 1996.

Herbs, Smudge, Oils, and Incenses

Culpepper N. *Culpepper's Colour Herbal*. Slough, U.K.: Foulsham, 1983.

Cunningham, Scott. *Complete Book of Oils, Incenses and Brews*. St. Paul, MN: Llewellyn, 1991.

———. *Encyclopedia of Magical Herbs*. St. Paul, MN: Llewellyn, 1993.

Eason, Cassandra. *Fragrant Magic*. Slough, U.K.: Quantum, 2004.

———. *Smudging and Incense Burning*. Slough, U.K.: Quantum, 2001.

Kavasch, E. Barrie, and Karen Baar. *American Indian Healing Arts: Herbs, Rituals and Remedies for Every Season of Life*. London: Thorsons, 2000.

Magic and Ritual

Eason, Cassandra. *A Complete Guide to Magic and Ritual*. Berkeley, CA: The Crossing Press, 2001.

Fortune, Dion. *Applied Magick*. York Beach, ME: Red Wheel/Weiser, 2000.

Valiente, Doreen. *Natural Magic*. New York: Phoenix Publishing Inc., 1985.

Mythology

Gimbutas, Marija. *The Gods and Goddesses of Old Europe*. London: Thames and Hudson, 1986.

Green, Miranda. *Dictionary of Celtic Myth and Legend*. London: Thames and Hudson, 1992.

Walker, Barbara. *The Encyclopedia of Women's Myths and Secrets.* London: Pandora,1983.

PSYCHIC POWERS AND MEDITATION

Eason, Cassandra. *The Complete Guide to Psychic Development.* Berkeley, CA: The Crossing Press, 2003.

———. *Ten Steps to Psychic Power.* London: Piatkus, 2002.

Goldberg, Bruce. *Unleash Your Psychic Powers.* New York: Sterling, 1997.

Weiss, Brian L. *Meditation: Achieving Inner Peace and Tranquility in your Life.* New York and London: Hay House, 2002.

White, Ruth. *Karma and Reincarnation.* London: Piatkus, 2000.

SEXUALITY

Douglas, Nik. *Spiritual Sex.* New York: Pocket Books, 1997.

Eason, Cassandra. *A Magical Guide to Love and Sex.* Berkeley, CA: The Crossing Press, 2001.

Telasco, Patricia. *A Little Book of Love Magic.* Berkeley, CA: The Crossing Press, 1999.

SHAMANISM AND POWER ANIMALS

Johnson, Buffie. *Lady of the Beasts: Ancient Images of the Goddess and Her Sacred Animals.* San Francisco: Harper and Row, 1988.

Johnson, Kenneth. *North Star Road.* St. Paul, MN: Llewellyn, 1996.

Telasco, Patricia. *Shaman in a 9 to 5 World.* Berkeley, CA: The Crossing Press, 2001.

TAROT

Eason, Cassandra. *Complete Guide to the Tarot.* Berkeley, CA: The Crossing Press, 2000.

Nichols, Sallie. *Jung and the Tarot.* York Beach, ME: Red Wheel/ Weiser, 1988.

index